CHELSEA HOUSE PUBLISHERS
Modern Critical Views

HENRY ADAMS
EDWARD ALBEE
A. R. AMMONS
MATTHEW ARNOLD
JOHN ASHBERY
W. H. AUDEN
JANE AUSTEN
JAMES BALDWIN
CHARLES BAUDELAIRE
SAMUEL BECKETT
SAUL BELLOW
THE BIBLE
ELIZABETH BISHOP
WILLIAM BLAKE
JORGE LUIS BORGES
ELIZABETH BOWEN
BERTOLT BRECHT
THE BRONTËS
ROBERT BROWNING
ANTHONY BURGESS
GEORGE GORDON, LORD BYRON
THOMAS CARLYLE
LEWIS CARROLL
WILLA CATHER
CERVANTES
GEOFFREY CHAUCER
KATE CHOPIN
SAMUEL TAYLOR COLERIDGE
JOSEPH CONRAD
CONTEMPORARY POETS
HART CRANE
STEPHEN CRANE
DANTE
CHARLES DICKENS
EMILY DICKINSON
JOHN DONNE & THE
    17th-CENTURY POETS
ELIZABETHAN DRAMATISTS
THEODORE DREISER
JOHN DRYDEN
GEORGE ELIOT
T. S. ELIOT
RALPH ELLISON
RALPH WALDO EMERSON
WILLIAM FAULKNER
HENRY FIELDING
F. SCOTT FITZGERALD
GUSTAVE FLAUBERT
E. M. FORSTER
SIGMUND FREUD
ROBERT FROST

ROBERT GRAVES
GRAHAM GREENE
THOMAS HARDY
NATHANIEL HAWTHORNE
WILLIAM HAZLITT
SEAMUS HEANEY
ERNEST HEMINGWAY
GEOFFREY HILL
FRIEDRICH HÖLDERLIN
HOMER
GERARD MANLEY HOPKINS
WILLIAM DEAN HOWELLS
ZORA NEALE HURSTON
HENRY JAMES
SAMUEL JOHNSON
BEN JONSON
JAMES JOYCE
FRANZ KAFKA
JOHN KEATS
RUDYARD KIPLING
D. H. LAWRENCE
JOHN LE CARRÉ
URSULA K. LE GUIN
DORIS LESSING
SINCLAIR LEWIS
ROBERT LOWELL
NORMAN MAILER
BERNARD MALAMUD
THOMAS MANN
CHRISTOPHER MARLOWE
CARSON MCCULLERS
HERMAN MELVILLE
JAMES MERRILL
ARTHUR MILLER
JOHN MILTON
EUGENIO MONTALE
MARIANNE MOORE
IRIS MURDOCH
VLADIMIR NABOKOV
JOYCE CAROL OATES
SEAN O'CASEY
FLANNERY O'CONNOR
EUGENE O'NEILL
GEORGE ORWELL
CYNTHIA OZICK
WALTER PATER
WALKER PERCY
HAROLD PINTER
PLATO
EDGAR ALLAN POE

POETS OF SENSIBILITY &
    THE SUBLIME
ALEXANDER POPE
KATHERINE ANNE PORTER
EZRA POUND
PRE-RAPHAELITE POETS
MARCEL PROUST
THOMAS PYNCHON
ARTHUR RIMBAUD
THEODORE ROETHKE
PHILIP ROTH
JOHN RUSKIN
J. D. SALINGER
GERSHOM SCHOLEM
WILLIAM SHAKESPEARE (3 vols.)
    HISTORIES & POEMS
    COMEDIES
    TRAGEDIES
GEORGE BERNARD SHAW
MARY WOLLSTONECRAFT SHELLEY
PERCY BYSSHE SHELLEY
EDMUND SPENSER
GERTRUDE STEIN
JOHN STEINBECK
LAURENCE STERNE
WALLACE STEVENS
TOM STOPPARD
JONATHAN SWIFT
ALFRED LORD TENNYSON
WILLIAM MAKEPEACE THACKERAY
HENRY DAVID THOREAU
LEO TOLSTOI
ANTHONY TROLLOPE
MARK TWAIN
JOHN UPDIKE
GORE VIDAL
VIRGIL
ROBERT PENN WARREN
EVELYN WAUGH
EUDORA WELTY
NATHANAEL WEST
EDITH WHARTON
WALT WHITMAN
OSCAR WILDE
TENNESSEE WILLIAMS
WILLIAM CARLOS WILLIAMS
THOMAS WOLFE
VIRGINIA WOOLF
WILLIAM WORDSWORTH
RICHARD WRIGHT
WILLIAM BUTLER YEATS

Further titles in preparation.

Modern Critical Views

SAMUEL BECKETT

Modern Critical Views

SAMUEL BECKETT

Edited with an introduction by

Harold Bloom

Sterling Professor of the Humanities
Yale University

1985
CHELSEA HOUSE PUBLISHERS
New York

THE COVER:

The cover illustrates the final scene of Beckett's early novel, *Murphy*, where a child's kite is released into the atmosphere as an emblem of freedom and nostalgia not available to the book's characters.—H.B.

PROJECT EDITORS: Emily Bestler, James Uebbing
ASSOCIATE EDITOR: Maria Behan
EDITORIAL COORDINATOR: Karyn Gullen Browne
EDITORIAL STAFF: Linda Grossman, Peter Childers
DESIGN: Susan Lusk

Cover illustration by Cathy Saksa

Printed and bound in the United States of America

Library of Congress Cataloging in Publication Data

Samuel Beckett.
    (Modern critical views)
    Bibliography: p.
    Includes index.
    1. Beckett, Samuel, 1906–   —Criticism and
interpretation—Addresses, essays, lectures.
I. Bloom, Harold.   II. Series.
PR6003.E282Z7999   1985   848'.91409   85–9612
ISBN 0–87754–651–7

Chelsea House Publishers
Harold Steinberg, Chairman and Publisher
Susan Lusk, Vice President
A Division of Chelsea House Educational Communications, Inc.
133 Christopher Street, New York, NY 10014

Contents

Introduction..... *Harold Bloom* 1

Moran-Molloy: The Hero as Author..... *Edith Kern* 7

The Nightmare Life in Death..... *Northrop Frye* 17

Life in the Box..... *Hugh Kenner* 27

Trying to Understand *Endgame*...... *Theodor W. Adorno* 51

Comment c'est par le bout..... *Ruby Cohn* 83

Existence Onstage..... *Jacques Guicharnaud* 103

The Pattern of Negativity
    in Beckett's Prose...... *Wolfgang Iser* 125

Beckett as Poet..... *John Fletcher*.................... 137

Samuel Beckett: *Watt*..... *Fred Miller Robinson* 147

Samuel Beckett, Fritz Mauthner,
    and the Limits of Language..... *Linda Ben-Zvi* 193

Beckett's Late Works: An Appraisal..... *Martha Fehsenfeld* .. 219

The Intent of Undoing in
    Samuel Beckett's Art..... *S. E. Gontarski*............ 227

Beckett and Joyce..... *Aldo Tagliaferri* 247

Chronology 263

Contributors 265

Bibliography 267

Acknowledgments 269

Index 271

Editor's Note

This volume reprints a representative selection of the most helpful criticism devoted to Samuel Beckett in the last quarter-century, arranged in the chronological order of its composition. It begins with Edith Kern's examination of *Molloy* and with Northrop Frye's more general consideration of the trilogy in which *Molloy* is the first work. With Hugh Kenner and Theodor W. Adorno, the emphasis moves to Beckett's most popular works, *Waiting for Godot* and *Endgame*, later to be analyzed by Jacques Guicharnaud from a more theatrical perspective.

Ruby Cohn's reading of *How It Is* helps introduce the later intricacies of Beckett's prose, subsequently analyzed in Wolfgang Iser's sustained investigation. John Fletcher's overview of Beckett's verse helps to fill out the pattern of a more varied accomplishment than most readers tend to realize.

The remaining essays represent the current phase in literary studies. They range from Fred Miller Robinson's account of *Watt* through Linda Ben-Zvi's meditation on the philosophic backgrounds of Beckett's linguistic skepticism, and on to appraisals by Martha Fehsenfeld and S. E. Gontarski of the recent work and of Beckett's emptying out of tradition. The concluding essay is Aldo Tagliaferri's advanced treatment of the relation between Beckett and Joyce.

If there is a movement or progress in the quarter-century of Beckett criticism, it has not yet clearly manifested itself. This reflects the undoubted difficulty of Beckett's own development, which is a kind of *askesis* in which endless self-curtailment somehow never touches a limit. Criticism of Beckett tends to act out versions of Beckett's own aesthetics of failure. The Introduction in this volume expresses the editor's own nostalgia for the lost exuberance of *Murphy*, while acknowledging that Beckett is the living author who has done most to revivify an almost dying Sublime. Perhaps what Beckett implicitly teaches his critics and readers is a new Sublime of belatedness, in which easier pleasures have to be forsaken because only more difficult pleasures can strengthen us to bear the paradoxes of a cultural tradition made destitute by its own past strength. Aldo Tagliaferri's speculations on the influence relation between Joyce and Beckett thus form a fitting coda to this volume, since Beckett's heroic quest has been to go on despite his profound understanding of Joyce, Proust and Kafka, who between them can be judged to have culminated the tradition of Western prose fiction.

Introduction

I

Jonathan Swift, so much the strongest ironist in the language as to have no rivals, wrote the prose masterpiece of the language in *A Tale of a Tub*. Samuel Beckett, as much the legitimate descendant of Swift as he is of his friend, James Joyce, has written the prose masterpieces of the language in this century, sometimes as translations from his own French originals. Such an assertion does not discount the baroque splendors of *Ulysses* and *Finnegans Wake*, but prefers to them the purity of *Murphy* and *Watt*, and of Beckett's renderings into English of *Malone Dies*, *The Unnamable* and *How It Is*. Unlike Swift and Joyce, Beckett is only secondarily an ironist and, despite his brilliance at tragicomedy, is something other than a comic writer. His Cartesian dualism seems to me less fundamental than his profoundly Schopenhauerian vision. Perhaps Swift, had he read and tolerated Schopenhauer, might have turned into Beckett.

A remarkable number of the greatest novelists have found Schopenhauer more than congenial: one thinks of Turgenev, Tolstoi, Zola, Hardy, Conrad, Thomas Mann, even of Proust. As those seven novelists have in common only the activity of writing novels, we may suspect that Schopenhauer's really horrifying system helps a novelist to do his work. This is not to discount the intellectual and spiritual persuasiveness of Schopenhauer. A philosopher who so deeply affected Wagner, Nietzsche, Wittgenstein and (despite his denials) Freud, hardly can be regarded only as a convenient aid to story-tellers and story-telling. Nevertheless, Schopenhauer evidently stimulated the arts of fiction, but why? Certain it is that we cannot read *The World As Will and Representation* as a work of fiction. Who could bear it as fiction? Supplementing his book, Schopenhauer characterizes the Will to live:

> Here also life presents itself by no means as a gift for enjoyment, but as a task, a drudgery to be performed; and in accordance with this we see, in great and small, universal need, ceaseless cares, constant pressure, endless strife, compulsory activity, with extreme exertion of all the powers of body and mind . . . All strive, some planning, others acting; the tumult is indescribable. But the ultimate aim of it all, what is it? To sustain

ephemeral and tormented individuals through a short span of time in the most fortunate case with endurable want and comparative freedom from pain, which, however, is at once attended with ennui; then the reproduction of this race and its striving. In this evident disproportion between the trouble and the reward, the will to live appears to us from this point of view, if taken objectively, as a fool, or subjectively, as a delusion, seized by which everything living works with the utmost exertion of its strength for something that is of no value. But when we consider it more closely, we shall find here also that it is rather a blind pressure, a tendency entirely without ground or motive.

Hugh Kenner suggests that Beckett reads Descartes as fiction. Beckett's fiction suggests that Beckett reads Schopenhauer as truth. Descartes as a precursor is safely distant; Joyce was much too close, and *Murphy* and even *Watt* are Joycean books. Doubtless, Beckett turned to French in *Molloy* so as to exorcise Joyce, and certainly, from *Malone Dies* on, the prose when translated back into English has ceased to be Joycean. Joyce is to Beckett as Milton was to Wordsworth. *Finnegans Wake*, like *Paradise Lost*, is a triumph demanding study; Beckett's trilogy, like *The Prelude*, internalizes the triumph by way of the compensatory imagination, in which experience and loss become one. Study does little to unriddle Beckett or Wordsworth. The Old Cumberland Beggar, Michael, Margaret of *The Ruined Cottage*; these resist analysis as do Molloy, Malone, and the Unnamable. Place my namesake, the sublime Poldy, in *Murphy* and he might fit, though he would explode the book. Place him in *Watt*? It cannot be done, and Poldy (or even Earwicker) in the trilogy would be like Milton (or Satan) perambulating about in *The Prelude*.

The fashion (largely derived from French misreaders of German thought) of denying a fixed, stable ego is a shibboleth of current criticism. But such a denial is precisely like each literary generation's assertion that it truly writes the common language rather than a poetic diction. Both stances define modernism, and modernism is as old as Hellenistic Alexandria. Callimachus is as modernist as Joyce, and Aristarchus, like Hugh Kenner, is an antiquarian modernist or modernist antiquarian. Schopenhauer dismissed the ego as an illusion, life as torment, and the universe as nothing, and he rightly credited these insights to that great modernist, the Buddha. Beckett too is as modernist as the Buddha, or as Schopenhauer, who disputes with Hume the position of the best writer among philosophers since Plato. I laugh sometimes in reading Schopenhauer, but the laughter is defensive. Beckett provokes laughter, as Falstaff does, or in the mode of Shakespeare's clowns.

II

In his early monograph, *Proust*, Beckett cites Schopenhauer's definition of the artistic procedure as "the contemplation of the world independently of the principle of reason." Such more-than-rational contemplation gives Proust those Ruskinian or Paterian privileged moments that are "epiphanies" in Joyce but which Beckett mordantly calls "fetishes" in Proust. Transcendental bursts of radiance necessarily are no part of Beckett's cosmos, which resembles, if anything at all, the Demiurge's creation in ancient Gnosticism. Basilides or Valentinus, Alexandrian heresiarchs, would have recognized instantly the world of the trilogy and of the major plays: *Waiting for Godot, Endgame, Krapp's Last Tape*. It is the world ruled by the Archons, the *kenoma*, non-place of emptiness. Beckett's enigmatic spirituality quests, though sporadically, for a void that is a fulness, the Abyss or *pleroma* that the Gnostics called both forefather and foremother. Call this a natural rather than a revealed Gnosticism in Beckett's case, but Gnosticism it is nevertheless. Schopenhauer's quietism is at last not Beckett's, which is to say that for Beckett, as for Blake and for the Gnostics, the Creation and the Fall were the same event.

The young Beckett, bitterly reviewing a translation of Rilke into English, memorably rejected Rilke's transcendental self-deceptions, where the poet mistook his own tropes as spiritual evidences:

> Such a turmoil of self-deception and naif discontent gains nothing in dignity from that prime article of the Rilkean faith, which provides for the interchangeability of Rilke and God . . . He has the fidgets, a disorder which may very well give rise, as it did with Rilke on occasion, to poetry of a high order. But why call the fidgets God, Ego, Orpheus and the rest?

In 1938, the year that *Murphy* was belatedly published, Beckett declared his double impatience with the language of transcendence and with the transcendence of language, while intimating also the imminence of the swerve away from Joyce in the composition of *Watt* (1942–44):

> At first it can only be a matter of somehow finding a method by which we can represent this mocking attitude towards the word, through words. In this dissonance between the means and their use it will perhaps become possible to feel a whisper of that final music or that silence that underlies All.
>
> With such a program, in my opinion, the latest work of Joyce has nothing whatever to do. There it seems rather to be a matter of an apotheosis of the word. Unless perhaps Ascension to Heaven and Descent to Hell are somehow one and the same.

As a Gnostic imagination, Beckett's way is Descent, in what cannot be called a hope to liberate the sparks imprisoned in words. Hope is alien to Beckett's mature fiction, so that we can say its images are Gnostic but not its program, since it lacks all program. A Gnosticism without potential transcendence is the most negative of all possible negative stances, and doubtless accounts for the sympathetic reader's sense that every crucial work by Beckett necessarily must be his last. Yet the grand paradox is that lessness never ends in Beckett.

III

"Nothing is got for nothing." That is the later version of Emerson's law of Compensation, in the essay "Power" of *The Conduct of Life*. Nothing is got for nothing even in Beckett, this greatest master of nothing. In the progression from *Murphy* through *Watt* and the trilogy on to *How It Is* and the briefer fictions of recent years, there is loss for the reader as well as gain. The same is true of the movement from *Godot*, *Endgame* and *Krapp's Last Tape* down to the short plays of Beckett's current and perhaps final phase. A wild humor abandons Beckett, or is transformed into a comedy for which we seem not to be ready. Even an uncommon reader can long for those marvelous Pythagoreans, Wylie and Neary, who are the delight of *Murphy*, or for the sense of the picturesque that makes a last stand in *Molloy*. Though the mode was Joyce's, the music of Wylie and Neary is Beckett's alone:

"These are dark sayings," said Wylie.
Neary turned his cup upside down.
"Needle," he said, "as it is with the love of the body, so with the friendship of the mind, the full is only reached by admittance to the most retired places. Here are the pudenda of my psyche."
"Cathleen," cried Wylie.
"But betray me," said Neary, "and you go the way of Hippasos."
"The Adkousmatic, I presume," said Wylie. "His retribution slips my mind."
"Drowned in a puddle," said Neary, "for having divulged the incommensurability of side and diagonal."
"So perish all babblers," said Wylie. . . .
"Do not quibble," said Neary harshly. "You saved my life. Now palliate it."
"I greatly fear," said Wylie, "that the syndrome known as life is too diffuse to admit of palliation. For every symptom that is eased, another is made worse. The horse leech's daughter is a closed system. Her quantum of wantum cannot vary."
"Very prettily put," said Neary.

One can be forgiven for missing this, even as one surrenders these easier pleasures for the more difficult pleasures of *How It Is*:

> my life above what I did in my life above a little of everything tried everything then gave up no worse always a hole a ruin always a crust never any good at anything not made for that farrago too complicated crawl about in corners and sleep all I wanted I got it nothing left but go to heaven

The Sublime mode, according to a great theorist, Angus Fletcher, has "the direct and serious function of destroying the slavery of pleasure." Beckett is certainly the strongest Western author living in the year 1985, the last survivor of the sequence that includes Proust, Kafka and Joyce. It seems odd to name Beckett, most astonishing of minimalists, as a representative of the Sublime mode, but the isolation and terror of the High Sublime return in the catastrophe creations of Beckett, in that vision Fletcher calls "catastrophe as a gradual grinding down and slowing to a dead stop." A Sublime that moves towards silence necessarily relies upon a rhetoric of waning lyricism, in which the entire scale of effects is transformed, as John Hollander notes:

> Sentences, phrases, images even, are the veritable arias in the plays and the later fiction. The magnificent rising of the kite at the end of *Murphy* occurs in a guarded but positive surge of ceremonial song, to which he will never return.

Kafka's Hunter Gracchus, who had been glad to live and was glad to die, tells us that: "I slipped into my winding sheet like a girl into her marriage dress. I lay and waited. Then came the mishap." The mishap, a moment's error on the part of the death-ship's pilot, moves Gracchus from the heroic world of romance to the world of Kafka and of Beckett, where one is neither alive nor dead. It is Beckett's peculiar triumph that he disputes with Kafka the dark eminence of being the Dante of that world. Only Kafka, or Beckett, could have written the sentence in which Gracchus sums up the dreadfulness of his condition: "The thought of helping me is an illness that has to be cured by taking to one's bed." Murphy might have said that; Malone is beyond saying anything so merely expressionistic. The "beyond" is where Beckett's later fictions and plays reside. Call it the silence, or the abyss, or the reality beyond the pleasure principle, or the metaphysical or spiritual reality of our existence at last exposed, beyond further illusion. Beckett cannot or will not name it, but he has worked through to the art of representing it more persuasively than anyone else.

EDITH KERN

Moran-Molloy:
The Hero as Author

Molloy is not only the titular hero of
Beckett's novel. Nor is he merely a literary convenience, an invention on
the part of Beckett, to supply him with the appropriate "I" for his story.
As most perceptive readers have noted, Molloy is an author consciously
engaged in literary creation. To him writing is more than a pastime, more
than a concern to record for posterity the memory of his strange journey.
Writing is his only *raison d'etre*. For that purpose he was rescued from a
ditch, into which he had fallen more dead than alive, by those mysterious
forces that, in times of need, come to the aid of heroes. His trials served
but to lead him to his "mother's room," where writing is identical with
existence and existence means writing.

We first encounter Molloy after his arrival in this room. In its dim
vacuity, into which scarcely a sound penetrates, Molloy vegetates, "formulates his thoughts," and without "much will left," wants to finish
dying—though first he must write. The objects and human figures he
conjures up are, like himself, detached from time and place. Seen out of
all familiar context, they appear puzzling and purposeless. The men and
women he introduces are now old, now young. Some are completely
anonymous, referred to only as A or C. About the names of others Molloy
is uncertain. As for himself, he has long been aware of a dense anonymity
enfolding him, and barely remembers his name: ". . . even my sense of
identity was wrapped in a namelessness often hard to penetrate. . . ."

The symbolism of Molloy's arrival can be understood only in the

From *Perspective* 2, (Autumn 1959). Copyright © 1959 by Perspective Inc.

light of the entire journey and in the perspective of his departure. Yet we are not told by Molloy when and from where he set out. One day, he merely recalls, "having waked between eleven o'clock and midday (I heard the angelus, recalling the incarnation shortly after) I resolved to go and see my mother." He gives us vaguely to understand that there was an existence prior to the one he describes, when he used to be intelligent and quick; when he perhaps had a son to whom he tried to be helpful; and when only one of his legs was stiff (now they both are) so that he could move about on a bicycle, pedalling with his good leg while propping the other on the projecting front axle.

Not until we read the novel's second part, of which Moran is the protagonist, do we gain deeper insight into Molloy's journey and come to understand its point of origin.

There we discover first of all that Moran lays hesitant claim to authorship of Molloy: "Perhaps I had invented him. I mean found him ready made in my head." He even boasts of having invested his creature "with the air of a fabulous being, which something told me could not fail to help me later on." "For who could have spoken to me of Molloy," he reflects, "if not myself and to whom if not myself could I have spoken of him?" Moran thus insists on his authorial power to create characters, and see them in his mind's eye at places where neither he nor they can actually be, when he reflects: "For where Molloy could not be, nor Moran either for that matter, there Moran could bend over Molloy." To find Molloy—as he is asked to do by his distant employer Youdi—and thereby bring him into being artistically, that is Moran's mission and obsession as a creative artist. As Anthony Hartley so acutely observes, in his *Spectator* article on Samuel Beckett, "Beckett's characters create and are created. That is their singularity."

His reflections in anticipation of the Molloy mission, reveal Moran is the artist wrestling with the task of creation in the manner of the hero setting out on a superhuman quest:

It is lying down, in the warmth, in the gloom, that I best pierce the outer turmoil's veil, discern my quarry, sense what course to follow, find peace in another's ludicrous distress. Far from the world, its clamours, frenzies, bitterness and dingy light, I pass judgment on it and on those, like me, who are plunged in it beyond recall, and on him who has need of me to be delivered, who cannot deliver myself.

Moran is thus the hero as author who—in spite of his uneasiness and reluctance to set out on a mission which is a journey into the unknown, in spite of an awareness of his inadequacies and ignorance—

must achieve the task of delivering the one who needs him. His artistic vision becomes his obsession, and he is well aware of the fact that, like any other hero, he is harnessed to a task which transcends himself as well as the object of his endeavor:

> For what I was doing I was doing neither for Molloy, who mattered nothing to me, nor for myself, of whom I despaired, but on behalf of a cause which, while having need of us to be accomplished, was in its essence anonymous, and would subsist, haunting the minds of men, when its miserable artisans should be no more.

The world as Moran conceives it, can be redeemed only through art; in proclaiming this, he aligns himself with philosophers like Nietzsche and writers like Proust.

In the novel's second part, we discover, moreover, that Molloy originated not merely as Moran's artistic vision, clamoring to be realized, but that he was known to Moran long before Youdi's call was heard by the artist hero. Molloy's name had echoed frequently, though indistinctly, in Moran's soul, "a first syllable, Mol, very clear, followed almost at once by a second, very thick, as though gobbled by the first, and which might have been oy as it might have been ose, or one, or even oc." Indeed, Molloy had "come to" Moran at long intervals. What makes Molloy different from Moran's earlier "clients" Murphy and Watt (actually the titular heroes of Beckett's previous novels), is the fact that he is more than a mission, that he is a part of Moran and sporadically asserts himself. It thus becomes apparent that we cannot presume to grasp the symbolic significance of the Molloy journey without first giving due consideration to Moran and his artistic quest, that the two are in fact inseparable.

Before he receives Youdi's message to search for Molloy, that is, before Molloy becomes his artistic obsession, Moran lives smug and satisfied among his possessions. The world which he shares with his son and his housekeeper is arranged sensibly and by the clock. His entire life is governed by will and reason and falls into an easy pattern of discipline and habit wherein formalized religion finds its natural place. To turn his son into a worthy member of this small, well-ordered universe, he rears him according to the bourgeois precept of *"sollst entbehren,"* a precept which once incited the creative genius of Goethe's Faust to rebellion. The triviality of this existence, which reposes primly on convention and habit, is revealed in a masterpiece of satire: Moran's conversation with the parish priest. Turning to the priest in a moment of profound anguish, Moran is unable to express this anguish and converses instead about his hen's loss of appetite. For Moran has thus far excluded from his life all that is mysteri-

ous, incomprehensible, or irrational and admits that he finds it "painful
. . . not to understand."

To a man, "so meticulous and calm in the main, so patiently
turned towards the outer world as towards the lesser evil, creature of his
house, of his garden, of his few poor possessions . . . , reining back his
thoughts within the limits of the calculable so great is his horror of fancy"
(thus Moran describes himself) Molloy appears as a chimera that haunts
and possesses him. For Molloy is his very opposite. Molloy "comes to"
Moran and leaves an impression of utter absurdity. In his shapelessness
and restlessness, he is a frightening creature, lacking all discipline, will-
power and purposefulness. "He hastened incessantly on, as if in despair,
towards extremely close objectives," Moran tells us. "Now, a prisoner, he
hurled himself at I know not what narrow confines, and now, hunted, he
sought refuge near the centre. He panted. He had only to rise up within
me for me to be filled with panting." Molloy's existence is totally detached from all that is accidental or useful and knows neither pattern nor
reason. Whereas Moran is emphatically the individual living in time and
space, a man "wrapped in the veil of Maya," in Schopenhauer's phrase,
Molloy seems to be the unmolded, untamed essence of man: the stem *mol*
(whose Latin meaning is *soft* or *pliable*) not pinned down by any precise
suffix. Though mortal, he is timeless, ignoring the time-and-space-bound
language of *homo sapiens*.

Molloy's "visitations" represent, undoubtedly, the stirrings within
Moran of a subconscious, antithetical self. And each new assertion of that
other self threatens Moran's accustomed world. It has in store for him
change and suffering: "Then I was nothing but uproar, bulk, rage, suffoca-
tion, effort unceasing, frenzied and vain. Just the opposite of myself, in
fact." Thus Moran's quest for Molloy (who is a secret part of himself)
resembles the task which Yeats had set for each man, and the poet in
particular: to seek out the "other self, the antiself or the antithetical self"
and, indeed, to become—"of all things not impossible the most difficult"
—that other self. For as Moran advances upon his road into the Molloy
country, he slowly changes into that other self and comes to resemble
Molloy.

He becomes a restless wanderer detached from all that has been
habit and formula in his life. The accidental is swept away. His family ties
disintegrate. His son deserts him, and he no longer plays the part of the
stern but loving father. When he returns to his house, his reliable housekeeper has disappeared from his life and with her the pattern of well-
ordered existence. His certainties, his composure give way to doubt and
insecurity. Even physically, a change takes place. His body begins to

decay. One of his legs stiffens. He notices himself "a crumbling, a frenzied collapsing of all that has always protected me from all I was always condemned to be . . . it was like a kind of clawing towards a light and countenance I could not name, that I had once known and long denied." Moran's journey is, therefore, not merely a departure from the confines of the familiar, not merely a metamorphosis. It represents a descent into his own subconscious where dwells Molloy—a *via dolorosa* into Molloy's immense universe of uncertainty and absurdity.

Already in 1931, while discussing Proust's Marcel of *Le temps retrouvé*, Beckett had described the artist's *via dolorosa*, from the vantage point of the critic:

> The old ego dies hard. Such as it was, a minister of dullness, it was also an agent of security. When it ceases to perform that second function, when it is opposed by a phenomenon that it cannot reduce to a condition of a comfortable and familiar concept, when, in a word, it betrays its trust as a screen to spare its victim the spectacle of reality, it disappears . . . with wailing and gnashing of teeth. The mortal microcosm cannot forgive the relative immortality of the macrocosm.

Like Proust's protagonist, Beckett's author-hero discovers his world of art in the "inaccessible dungeon of our being to which Habit does not possess the key" but where "is stored the essence of ourselves, the best of our many selves." Unlike Marcel, however, Moran does not use involuntary memory as the occasional "diver" into that subconscious world of essences, but descends into it wholly to embrace there his antithesis and essence as man and as poet.

It is only appropriate that Beckett has cast the tale of this descent into the shape of ancient myths. For modern thinkers and writers, perhaps under the influence of Freud and Jung, have come to view the realm of myth as a reflection of the subconscious where is pooled the very essence of man. Thus the tale of Moran's journey is reminiscent of the myth of the "one hero in two aspects." Like this hero, Moran encounters innumerable obstacles on his way. His symbolic road towards Molloy is a series of trials. It is filled with mysterious encounters, with murder and deprivation. It occasions the rebellious departure of his son, on whom Moran had relied for companionship, filial devotion and ultimately guidance. Moran wanders in forlorn regions and dark forests, forever uncertain of his way, forever lonely. Joseph Campbell says of this "one hero in two aspects" that he ultimately "discovers and assimilates his opposite (his unsuspected self). . . . One by one the resistances are broken. He must put aside his pride, his virtue, beauty, and life, and bow or submit to the absolutely intolerable. Then he finds that he and his opposite are not different species but of one flesh." They are, in Joyce's words, "equals of opposites, evolved by a onesame power of nature or of spirit, iste, as the sole condition and means of its himundher manifestation and polarised for reunion by the symphesis of their antipathies."

Beckett's choice of "Molloy" as title for the entire novel reflects his insistence on the ultimate one-ness of Moran and Molloy in the manner of "the one hero in two aspects." Until we become aware of this underlying one-ness and the author-hero's development from Moran to Molloy, we remain puzzled by the fact that Moran, the apparent author-protagonist of the second part, is not accounted for in the title. In the light of their relationship, however, the novel's title brings to mind Beckett as the pseudo-philologist, the whimsical creator of such names as God-ot, Ma-g, Da-n, Ma-hood, and Mac-mann, who might well maintain that, stripped of their uncertain suffixes, the roots *mor* and *mol* are identical—r and l being interchangeable liquids to the etymologist. In analogy to Moran's assimilation by Molloy, the syllable *mol*, with its suggestion of soft and unshaped matter, was, of course, chosen to form the title in preference to the syllable *mor*.

In the light of this one-ness of Moran and Molloy resembling "the one hero in two aspects," we can begin to understand the significance of Molloy's journey. It must be seen as a continuation of the trek begun by Moran. As such, it represents an even further moving away from the realms of habit and will and a deeper penetration into that of essences, finding its symbolic culmination in the mother's room. There Molloy's artistic existence might be described in terms similar to those with which the critic Beckett evaluated that of Proust: "When the subject is exempt from will, the object is exempt from causality (Time and Space taken together). And this human vegetation is purified in the transcendental apperception that can capture the Model, the Idea, the Thing itself."

We must not be misled by the novel's structure which seems to belie this assumption of a Moran-Molloy continuity. Obviously we encounter Molloy, hero-author of the first part, before we even are aware of Moran's existence and without in the least suspecting his provenance or the complex one-in-two relationship of the two protagonists. Because of their apparent independence from each other, the two parts of the novel leave us with an impression of incoherence. We are bewildered. Yet this bewilderment is easily disposed of, if we reverse the order of the two parts. Disregard for chronology should not surprise us in an author as obsessed with the absurdity of logic as is Beckett. Indeed, Beckett is quite aware of the liberty he takes with the organization of the novel and justifies it on artistic grounds. He claims that it is the messenger (that mysterious voice which induced Moran to leave his life of security and comfort and which guided both Moran and Molloy through the wilderness to their existence as writers) who urges Molloy to rearrange his story so that what was once the beginning is now nearly the end: "It was he told me I'd begun all wrong, that I should have begun differently. He must be right. I began at the beginning." Thus is avoided that "vulgarity of a plausible concatenation," held in such contempt—so Beckett the critic had observed—by Proust and Dostoievski.

A reversal of the order in which the novel's parts are presented reveals, indeed, that the work would lose in artistic appeal what it would gain in clarity through such reorganization. If Moran's account of his adventures were to precede that of Molloy, the reader would be deprived of the element of suspense and the artistic challenge to pierce the mystery that shrouds their relationship, and with it the novel's meaning. The realization of the complex Moran-Molloy relationship—now the rich reward of the perceptive reader—would be reduced to something almost too obvious—that the author-hero Molloy continues the journey begun by the author-hero Moran. For Molloy's vague recollections of a past when he was sounder in mind and body and richer in human relationships coincide almost entirely with the facts we are told of Moran's life. Even the messenger, who urges Molloy to write, bears unmistakable resemblance to the messenger Gaber who played so vital a part in Moran's existence. Above all, Molloy's physical deterioration begins precisely at the stage where Moran's had ended. Deprived of the use of one leg, Moran dreamed of cleverly pedalling a bicycle with the help of his one good leg. Molloy, as we have seen, actually put into practice this manner of locomotion when he set out on his adventures. At least this is what he recalls at a time when he has lost the use of both legs and is, indeed, deprived almost entirely of the services of his body and his senses.

Once the novel's first part is seen, however, in chronological sequence to the second part, this process of physical and sensorial deterioration, beginning with Moran's departure and increasing rapidly during Molloy's trek until he is reduced almost to bodilessness, begins to stand out as the novel's *leitmotif*. It must be seen as Beckett's symbolic restatement of an artistic truth he had recognized earlier when, as a critic, he extolled the "invisible reality" of Vinteuil's "little phrase," that Proustian symbol of the essence of art, as damning "the life of the body on earth as a pensum" and revealing "the meaning of the word: 'defunctus.' " The destruction of the body and the senses is a further stripping away of all that is contingent in order to bare that which is essential. Thus Moran-become-Molloy, the antithetical self of his subconscious, proceeds even further on the road towards the core of artistic existence: his mother's room.

With its mythical overtones of rebirth and salvation, Molloy's quest is reminiscent of the traditional hero's road to the powerful "mother-destroyer" who is both mother and bride. His mother never calls him son. She calls him Dan instead, which, when the n is dropped, means father—so he tells us. He calls her Mag, which, without the g, means mother. The image of his mother which thus hovers between Ma and Mag is also strangely fused with that of another woman in his life. Although his mother is not presented as a symbol of beauty, youth, and virtue—quite the contrary in fact—Molloy says "Mother" in his hour of greatest need, as the medieval knight uttered the name of his beloved to guide him in distress. Molloy's particular manner of arrival, his realization that, after having crawled through slush and darkness, he is in his mother's room, suggests a return to the womb and reminds us of the various myths of rebirth, the Dionysian mysteries as well as the Christian rite of baptism, whose mythical origin Campbell recalls. Hence Beckett's evocation of the angelus at the beginning of Molloy's journey evoking the primary role of the Mother in the miracle of incarnation and as the instrument of salvation.

Yet Molloy, the hero as author in his quest of his mother, conjures up, above all, the poet's dreadful and difficult descent to the Mothers or Mothers of Being which Goethe presented in his *Faust*. Faust derives ultimate poetic knowledge from this descent to the very root and essence of things. Inspired by Goethe, the philosopher Nietzsche likewise considered arrival at the Mothers of Being as the ultimate to which the artist must aspire, though something to which he cannot attain without suffering. Nietzsche's conception of the manner of such attainment deserves, indeed, special mention because of its illuminating analogy with the Moran-Molloy dichotomy and fusion.

Nietzsche conceived of the world of art as the perpetual union and sundering of two elements: the Apollonian and the Dionysian. He saw the artistic world of Apollo as one of individual existence, a world concerned with reason and causality as well as measured beauty, but, by this very token, a superficial and sometimes empty world: the microcosm. He thought of the Dionysian world of art, on the other hand, as that of the macrocosm, where individual appearance is ephemeral, and birth and death are but brief manifestations in the endless ebb and flow of life. Such a world must appear absurd to the reasoning human being. However, in its very denial of the importance of individual existence and human rationality, it is nearer to the universal, the essence: ". . . by the mystical triumphant cry of Dionysus the spell of individuation is broken and the way lies open to the Mothers of Being (*Faust* II, Act 1), to the innermost heart of things."

Nietzsche's esthetic antithesis provides a striking backdrop to the Moran-Molloy relationship as Beckett presents it: microcosm versus macrocosm as artistic concern. The Dionysian destruction of individuation has its counterpart in the deterioration of Molloy's body and his advance towards anonymity. Both see the ultimate end of art in its arrival at that "invisible reality" that Beckett admired in the music of Vinteuil's phrase. "A purely musical impression," as Proust had called it, "non-extensive, entirely original, irreducible to any other order of impression." In Greek tragedy, so Nietzsche thought, the realm of Apollo was that of the *logos*, whereas the realm of Dionysus was that of music. Wherever the Dionysian predominates, art aspires to the universal, the immaterial. Beckett has, indeed, paid homage to the Dionysian element in art. For in *The Unnamable*, the last novel of the trilogy of which *Molloy* is the first, the realm of the immaterial is attained to such a degree that the nameless protagonist is "reduced to a disembodied voice, invaded and usurped upon by other voices," as Anthony Hartley put it so aptly.

This then is the Moran-Molloy journey as seen against the background of Nietzschean esthetics: a departure from the Apollonian and an arrival at the Dionysian element in art. It is not surprising, therefore, that Molloy, having virtually rid himself of his body and dwelling in his mother's room, lives in an immaterial world, a realm of essences, peopled with timeless creatures, detached from all that is tangible and accidental. His is a world without will, without causality, universal and nameless. From the pen of Moran there emerged a picture of people living within communities and, engaged in seemingly useful activity, communing with each other in everyday existence. His world was still filled with the individualized, tangible relationship of father and son, housekeeper and master, parish priest and parishioner, employer and agent. But the world of the writer-become-Molloy is the world of the macrocosm where individual existence shrinks into meaninglessness and human relations are reduced—or heightened—to the universal, the subconscious, the mythical.

In such a world Molloy has small belief in the power of language, the *logos*, to convey the essence of things:

> . . . there could be no things but nameless things, no names but thingless names. I say that now, but after all what do I know about then, now when the icy words hail down upon me, the icy meanings, and the world dies too, foully named. All I know is what the words know, and the dead

things, and that makes a handsome little sum, with a beginning, a middle, and an end as in the well-built phrase and the long sonata of the dead.

Yet, in his mother's room, Molloy achieves at times that mystic union with the universe which Nietzsche considered the prerogative of the Dionysian artist and which, for Proust, in the form of music, embodied the highest achievement of art:

> And there was another noise, that of my life become the life of this garden as it rode the earth of deeps and wildernesses. Yes, there were times when I forgot not only who I was, but what I was, forgot to be. Then I was no longer that sealed jar to which I owed my being so well preserved, but a wall gave way and I filled with roots and tame stems for example, stakes long since dead and ready for burning, the recess of night and the imminence of dawn, and then the labour of the planet rolling eager into winter, winter would rid it of these contemptible scabs. Or of that winter I was the precarious calm, the thaw of the snows which make no difference and all the horrors of it all all over again.

Moran's escape from time, habit, and intelligence and his surrender to the Molloyan, the Dionysian element within him are to a certain degree paralleled in Beckett's own artistic development. More and more Beckett has found artistic fulfillment in the creation of a world without causality and will, the new-old world of myth and the subconscious. It is interesting that Beckett has referred to himself in specifically Nietzschean terms as a "non-knower," a "non-can-er" and claimed that "the other type of artist, the Apollonian, is absolutely foreign to me." The author of the trilogy obviously sought and found himself an antithesis to the lucid Apollonian he proved himself in his essay on Proust. But Beckett recently confessed that *L'Innommable* landed him "in a situation that I can't extricate myself from." Perhaps we shall see, therefore, the Dionysian set out, in turn, in quest of the Apollonian.

NORTHROP FRYE

The Nightmare Life in Death

In every age the theory of society and the theory of personality have closely approached each other. In Plato the wise man's mind is a dictatorship of reason over appetite, with the will acting as a thought police hunting down and exterminating all lawless impulses. The ideal state, with its philosopher-king, guards and artisans, has the corresponding social form. Michael explains to Adam in *Paradise Lost* that tyranny must exist in society as long as passion dominates reason in individuals, as they are called. In our day Marxism finds its psychological counterpart in the behaviorism and conditioned reflexes of Pavlov, and the Freudian picture of man is also the picture of western Europe and America, hoping that its blocks and tensions and hysterical explosions will settle into some kind of precarious working agreement. In this alignment religion has regularly formed a third, its gods and their enemies deriving their characteristics from whatever is highest and lowest in the personal-social picture. A good deal of the best fiction of our time has employed a kind of myth that might be read as a psychological, a social, or a religious allegory, except that it cannot be reduced to an allegory, but remains a myth, moving in all three areas of life at once, and thereby interconnecting them as well. The powerful appeal of Kafka for our age is largely due to the way in which such stories as *The Trial* or *The Castle* manage to suggest at once the atmosphere of an anxiety dream, the theology of the Book of Job, and the police terrorism and bureaucratic anonymity of the society that inspired Freud's term "censor." It was the same appeal in the myth of *Waiting for Godot* that, so to speak, identified Samuel Beckett as a contemporary writer.

From *The Hudson Review* 3, vol. 13, (Autumn 1960). Copyright © 1960 by *The Hudson Review*.

As a fiction writer Samuel Beckett derives from Proust and Joyce, and his essay on Proust is a good place to start from in examining his own work. This essay puts Proust in a context that is curiously Oriental in its view of personality. "Normal" people, we learn, are driven along through time on a current of habit-energy, an energy which, because habitual, is mostly automatic. This energy relates itself to the present by the will, to the past by voluntary or selective memory, to the future by desire and expectation. It is a subjective energy, although it has no consistent or permanent subject, for the ego that desires now can at best only possess later, by which time it is a different ego and wants something else. But an illusion of continuity is kept up by the speed, like a motion picture, and it generates a corresponding objective illusion, where things run along in the expected and habitual form of causality. Some people try to get off this time machine, either because they have more sensitivity or, perhaps, some kind of physical weakness that makes it not an exhilarating joyride but a nightmare of frustration and despair. Among these are artists like Proust, who look behind the surface of the ego, behind voluntary to involuntary memory, behind will and desire to conscious perception. As soon as the subjective motion-picture disappears, the objective one disappears too, and we have recurring contacts between a particular moment and a particular object, as in the epiphanies of the madeleine and the phrase in Vinteuil's music. Here the object, stripped of the habitual and expected response, appears in all the enchanted glow of uniqueness, and the relation of the moment to such an object is a relation of identity. Such a relation, achieved between two human beings, would be love, in contrast to the ego's pursuit of the object of desire, like Odette or Albertine, which tantalizes precisely because it is never loved. In the relation of identity consciousness has triumphed over time, and destroys the prison of habit with its double illusion stretching forever into past and future. At that moment we may enter what Proust and Beckett agree is the only possible type of paradise, that which has been lost. For the ego only two forms of failure are possible, the failure to possess, which may be tragic, and the failure to communicate, which is normally comic.

In the early story *Murphy*, the hero is an Irishman with an Irish interest in the occult—several of Beckett's characters are readers of AE— and a profound disinclination to work. We first meet him naked, strapped to a chair, and practising trance. He has however no interest in any genuine mental discipline, and feels an affinity with the easy-going Belacqua of Dante's *Purgatorio*, also mentioned in *Molloy*, who was in no hurry to begin his climb up the mountain. What he is really looking for is a self-contained egocentric consciousness, "windowless, like a monad," that no outward events can injure or distort. He is prodded by the heroine Celia into looking for a job, and eventually finds one as a male nurse in a lunatic asylum. In the asylum he discovers a kinship with the psychotic patients, who are trying to find the same thing in their own way, and his sympathy with them not only gives him a job he can do but makes him something rather better than a "seedy solipsist." To take this job he turns his back on Celia and other people who are said to need him, but in the airless microcosm of his mental retreat there is the one weak spot that makes him human and not completely selfish, a need for communication. He looks for this in the eye of Endon, his best friend among the patients, but sees no recognition in the eye, only his own image reflected in the pupil. "The last Mr. Murphy saw of Mr. Endon was Mr. Murphy unseen by Mr. Endon." He then commits suicide. The same image of the unrecognizing eye occurs in the one-act play *Embers* and in *Krapp's Last Tape*, where Krapp, more completely bound to memory and desire than Murphy, and so a figure of less dignity if also of less absurdity, looks into his mistress's eyes and says "Let me in." Another echo in this phrase will meet us in a moment.

The figure of the pure ego in a closed auto-erotic circle meets us many times in Beckett's masturbating, carrot-chewing, stone-sucking characters. A more traditional image of the consciousness goaded by desire or memory (an actual goad appears in one of Beckett's pantomimes), is that of master and servant. Already in *Murphy* we have, in the characters Neary and Cooper, an adumbration of the Hamm and Clov of *Endgame*, a servant who cannot sit and a master who cannot stand, bound together in some way and yet longing to be rid of each other. *Watt* tells the story of a servant who drifts into a house owned by a Mr. Knott, one of a long procession of servants absorbed and expelled from it by some unseen force. Technically the book is a contrast to *Murphy*, which is written in an epigrammatic wisecracking style. In *Watt* there is a shaggy-dog type of deliberately misleading humor, expressing itself in a maddeningly prolix pseudo-logic. One notes the use of a device more recently popularized by Lawrence Durrell, of putting some of the debris of the material collected into an appendix. "Only fatigue and disgust prevented its incorporation," the author demurely informs us. The most trivial actions of Watt, most of which are very similar to those we perform ourselves every day, are exhaustively catalogued in an elaborate pretence of obsessive realism, and we can see how such "realism" in fiction, pushed to so logical a conclusion, soon gives the effect of living in a kind of casual and unpunishing hell. Watt finally decides that "if one of these things was worth doing, all were worth doing, but that none was worth doing, no, not one, but that all were unadvisable, without exception."

In *Waiting for Godot*, as everyone knows, two dreary men in bowler hats stand around waiting for the mysterious Godot, who never appears but only sends a messenger to say he will not come. It is a favorite device of ironic fiction, from Kafka to Menotti's opera *The Consul*, to make the central character someone who not only fails to manifest himself but whose very existence is called in question. The two men wonder whether in some way they are "tied" to Godot, but decide that they probably are not, though they are afraid he might punish them if they desert their post. They also feel tied to one another, though each feels he would do better on his own. They resemble criminals in that they feel that they have no rights: "we got rid of them," one says, and is exhorted by a stage direction to say it distinctly. They stand in front of a dead tree, speculating, like many of Beckett's characters, about hanging themselves from it, and one of them feels an uneasy kinship with the thieves crucified with Christ. Instead of Godot, there appears a diabolical figure named Pozzo (pool: the overtones extend from Satan to Narcissus), driving an animal in human shape named Lucky, with a whip and a rope. Lucky, we are told, thinks he is entangled in a net: the image of being fished for by some omnipotent and malignant angler recurs in *The Unnamable*. In the second act the two turn up again, but this time Pozzo is blind and helpless, like Hamm in *Endgame*.

When the double illusion of a continuous ego and a continuous causality is abolished, what appears in its place? First of all, the ego is stripped of all individuality and is seen merely as representative of all of its kind. When asked for their names, one of the two men waiting for Godot answers, "Adam," and the other one says: "At this place, at this moment of time, all mankind is us." Similar echoes are awakened by the Biblical title of the play *All that Fall*, with its discussion of the falling sparrow in the Gospels and its final image of the child falling from the train, its death unheeded by the only character who was on the train. Other characters have such names as Watt, Knott and Krapp, suggestive of infantile jokes and of what in *Molloy* are called "decaying circus clowns." The dramatic convention parodied in *Waiting for Godot* is clearly the act that killed vaudeville, the weary dialogue of two faceless figures who will say anything to put off leaving the stage. In the "gallery of moribunds" we are about to examine there is a series of speakers whose names begin with M, one of whom, Macmann, has the most obvious everyman associations. In this trilogy, however, there is a more thoroughgoing examination of the unreality of the ego, and one which seems to owe something to the sequence of three chapters in *Finnegans Wake* in which Shaun is studied under the names Shaun, Jaun and Yawn, until he disappears into the larger form of HCE. It is the "Yawn" chapter that Beckett most frequently refers to. In reading the trilogy we should keep in mind the remark in the essay on Proust that "the heart of the cauliflower or the ideal core of the onion would represent a more appropriate tribute to the labours of poetical excavation than the crown of bay."

Molloy is divided into two parts: the first is Molloy's own narrative; the second is the narrative of Jacques Moran, who receives a message through one Gaber from an undefined Youdi to go and find Molloy. The echoes of Gabriel and Yahweh make it obvious by analogy that the name "Godot" is intended to sound like "God." Youdi, or someone similar to him, is once referred to as "the Obidil," which is an anagram of libido. The associations of Molloy are Irish, pagan, and a Caliban-like intelligence rooted in a disillusioned sensitivity. Moran is French, nominally Christian, and a harsher and more aggressive type of sterility. Molloy, like many of Beckett's characters, is so crippled as to resemble the experiments on mutilated and beheaded animals that try to establish how much life is consistent with death. He is also under a wandering curse, like the Wandering Jew, and is trying to find his mother. There are echoes of the wandering figure in Chaucer's *Pardoner's Tale*, who keeps knocking on the ground with his staff and begging his mother to let him in. But Molloy does not exactly long for death, because for him the universe is also a vast auto-erotic ring, a serpent with its tail in its mouth, and it knows no real difference between life and death. Overtones of Ulysses appear in his sojourn with Lousse (Circe), and the mention of "moly" suggests an association with his name. He is also, more Biblically, "in an Egypt without bounds, without infant, without mother," and a dim memory of Faust appears in his account of various sciences studied and abandoned, of which magic alone remained. Like the contemporary beats (in *Murphy*, incidentally, the padded cells are called "pads"), he finds around him a world of confident and adjusted squares, who sometimes take the form of police and bully him. "They wake up, hale and hearty, their tongues hanging out for order, beauty and justice, baying for their due." The landscape around him, described in terms similar to Dante's *Inferno*, changes, but he is unable to go out of his "region," and realizes that he is not moving at all. The only real change is a progressive physical deterioration and a growing loss of such social contact as he has. The landscape finally changes to a forest and Molloy, too exhausted to walk and unable, like Beckett's other servants, to sit, crawls on his belly like a serpent until he finally stops. He arrives at his mother's house, but characteristically we learn this not from the last sentence but from the first one, as the narrative goes around in a Viconian circle.

Just before the end of his account, Molloy, who hears voices of "prompters" in his mind, is told that help is coming. Moran sets off to find Molloy, aware that his real quest is to find Molloy inside himself, as a kind of Hyde to his Jekyll. He starts out with his son, whom he is trying to nag into becoming a faithful replica of himself, and he ties his son to him with a rope, as Pozzo does Lucky. The son breaks away, Moran sees Molloy but does not realize who he is, and gets another order to go back home. He confesses: "I was not made for the great light that devours, a dim lamp was all I had been given, and patience without end, to shine it on the empty shadows." This ignominious quest for self-knowledge does not find Molloy as a separate entity, but it does turn Moran into a double of Molloy, in ironic contrast to his attitude to his son. Various details in the imagery, the bicycle that they both start with, the stiffening leg, and others, emphasize the growing identity. Moran's narrative, which starts out in clear prose, soon breaks down into the same associative paragraphless monologue that Molloy uses. The quest is a dismal failure as far as Moran and Molloy are concerned, but how far are they concerned? Moran can still say: "What I was doing I was doing neither for Molloy, who mattered nothing to me, nor for myself, of whom I despaired, but on behalf of a cause which, while having need of us to be accomplished, was in its essence anonymous, and would subsist, haunting the minds of men, when its miserable artisans should be no more."

The forest vanishes and we find ourselves in an asylum cell with a figure named Malone, who is waiting to die. Here there is a more definite expectation of the event of death, and an awareness of a specific quantity of time before it occurs. Malone decides to fill in the interval by telling himself stories, and the stories gradually converge on a figure named Macmann, to whom Malone seems related somewhat as Proust is to the "Marcel" of his book, or Joyce to Stephen and Shem. Here an ego is projecting himself into a more typical figure (I suppose Malone and Macmann have echoes of "man alone" and "son of man," respectively, as most of the echoes in Beckett's names appear to be English), and Macmann gradually moves into the cell and takes over the identity of Malone. Malone dreams of his own death, which is simultaneously occurring, in a vision of a group of madmen going for a picnic in a boat on the Saturday morning between Good Friday and Easter, a ghastly parody of the beginning of the *Purgatorio*. Dante's angelic pilot is replaced by a brutal attendant named Lemuel, a destroying angel who murders most of the passengers.

In *The Unnamable* we come as near to the core of the onion as it is possible to come, and discover of course that there is no core, no undividable unit of continuous personality. It is difficult to say just where or what the Unnamable is, because, as in the brothel scene of *Ulysses*, his fluctuating moods create their own surroundings. One hypothesis is that he is sitting in a crouched posture with tears pouring out of his eyes, like some of the damned in Dante, or like the Heraclitus who became the weeping philosopher by contemplating the flowing of all things. Another is that he is in a jar outside a Paris restaurant opposite a horsemeat shop, suspended between life and death like the sibyl in Petronius who presides over *The Waste Land*.

Ordinarily we are aware of a duality between mind and body, of the necessity of keeping the body still to let the mind work. If we sit quietly we become aware of bodily processes, notably the heartbeat and pulse, carrying on automatically and involuntarily. Some religious disciplines, such as yoga, go another stage, and try to keep the mind still to set some higher principle free. When this happens, the mind can be seen from the outside as a rushing current of thoughts and associations and memories and worries and images suggested by desire, pulsating automatically and with all the habit-energy of the ego behind it. Each monologue in the trilogy suggests a mind half-freed from its own automatism. It is detached enough to feel imprisoned and enslaved, and to have no confidence in any of its assertions, but immediately to deny or contradict or qualify or put forward another hypothesis to whatever it says. But it is particularly the monologue of *The Unnamable*, an endless, querulous, compulsive, impersonal babble, much the same in effect whether read in French or in English, and with no purpose except to keep going, that most clearly suggests a "stream of consciousness" from which real consciousness is somehow absent. *The Unnamable* could readily be called a tedious book, but its use of tedium is exuberant, and in this respect it resembles *Watt*.

The Unnamable, who vaguely remembers having been Malone and Molloy, decides that he will be someone called Mahood, then that he will be something called Worm, then wonders whether all his meditations really are put into his mind by "them," that is, by Youdi and the rest, for his sense of compulsion easily externalizes itself. If he knows anything, it is that he is not necessarily himself, and that it was nonsense for Descartes to infer that he was himself because he was doubting it. All Beckett's speakers are like the parrot in *Malone Dies*, who could be taught to say "Nihil in intellectu," but refused to learn the rest of the sentence. All of them, again, especially Malone, are oppressed by the pervasive lying of the imagination, by the way in which one unconsciously falsifies the facts to make a fiction more symmetrical. But even Malone begins to realize that there is no escape from fiction. There are no facts to be accurately described, only hypotheses to be set up: no choice of words will express the truth, for one has only a choice of rhetorical masks. Malone says of his own continuum: "I slip into him, I suppose in the hope of learning something. But it is a stratum, strata, without debris or vestiges. But before I am done I shall find traces of what was."

In *The Unnamable*, as we make our way through "this sound that will never stop, monotonous beyond words and yet not altogether devoid of a certain variety," the Unnamable's own desire to escape, to the extent that he ever formulates it as such, communicates itself to us. The tired, tireless, hypnotic voice, muttering like a disembodied spirit at a seance, or like our own subconscious if we acquire the trick of listening to it, makes us feel that we would be ready to try anything to get away from it, even if we are also its prisoner. There is little use going to "them," to Youdi or Godot, because they are illusions of personality too. Conventional religion promises only resurrection, which both in *Murphy* and in the Proust essay is described as an impertinence. But "beyond them is that other who will not give me quittance until they have abandoned me as inutilizable and restored me to myself." That other must exist, if only because it is not here. And so, in the interminable last sentence, we reach the core of the onion, the resolve to find in art the secret of identity, the paradise that has been lost, the one genuine act of consciousness in the interlocking gyres (the Dante-Yeats image is explicitly referred to) of automatism:

> . . . the attempt must be made, in the old stories incomprehensibly mine, to find his, it must be there somewhere, it must have been mine, before being his, I'll recognize it, in the end I'll recognize it, the story of the silence that he never left, that I should never have left, that I may never find again, that I may find again, then it will be he, it will be I, it will be the place, the silence, the end, the beginning, the beginning again . . .

Many curiously significant remarks are made about silence in the trilogy. Molloy, for example, says: "about me all goes really silent, from time to time, whereas for the righteous the tumult of the world never stops." The Unnamable says: "This voice that speaks, knowing that it lies, indifferent to what it says, too old perhaps and too abased ever to succeed in saying the words that would be its last, knowing itself useless and its uselessness in vain, not listening to itself but to the silence that it breaks." Only when one is sufficiently detached from this compulsive babble to realize that one is uttering it can one achieve any genuine serenity, or the silence which is its habitat. "To restore silence is the role of objects," says Molloy, but this is not Beckett's final paradox. His final paradox is the conception of the imaginative process which underlies and informs his remarkable achievement. In a world given over to obsessive utterance, a world of television and radio and shouting dictators and tape recorders and beeping space ships, to restore silence is the role of serious writing.

HUGH KENNER

Life in the Box

*"Once a certain degree of insight has been reached," said Wylie,
"all men talk, when talk they must, the same tripe."*

— *Murphy*

The drama is a ritual enacted in an enclosed space into which fifty or more people are staring. They are all more or less patiently waiting for something: the Reversal, the Discovery, the *Deus ex Machina*, or even the final curtain. Settled numbly for the evening, they accept whatever interim diversions the stage can provide: tramps in bowler hats, for instance.

The space into which they are staring is characterized in some way: for instance, A *country road. A tree. Evening.* "Evening" means that the illumination on stage is not much brighter than in the auditorium. "A country road" means that there is no set to look at. As for the tree, an apologetic thing tentatively identified as a leafless weeping willow, it serves chiefly to denote the spot, like the intersection (coordinates O,O) of the Cartesian axes. "You're sure it was here?" "What?" "That we were to wait." "He said by the tree." If it accretes meaning of an anomalous sort in the course of the evening, reminding us, when the two tramps stand beneath it with a rope, of ampler beams which once suspended the Savior and two thieves, or again of the fatal tree in Eden (and the garden has, sure enough, vanished), or even of the flowering staff in *Tannhäuser*, it does this not by being explicated but simply by its insistent continual

---

presence, during which, as adjacent events diffract the bleak light, we begin to entertain mild hallucinations about it. Only in a theater can we be made to look at a mock tree for that length of time. Drama is distinguished from all other forms of art by its control over the *time* spent by the spectator in the presence of its significant elements.

These events, these elements, assert only their own nagging existence. "The theatrical character," remarked Alain Robbe-Grillet in this connection, "*is on stage*, this is his primary quality—he is there." Hence, "the essential function of the theatrical performance: to show what this fact of *being there* consists of." Or as Beckett was later to write of a later play, "Hamm as stated, and Clov as stated, together as stated, *nec tecum nec sine te*, in such a place, and in such a world, that's all I can manage, more than I could."

In *Waiting for Godot*, the place with its tree is stated, together with a single actor engaged in a mime with his boot. His inability to get it off is the referent of his first words, "Nothing to be done," a sentence generally reserved for more portentous matters. To him enter the second actor, as in the medial phase of Greek Theater, and their talk commences. What they talk about first is the fact that they are both there, the one fact that is demonstrably true not only in art's agreed world but before our eyes. It is even the one certainty that survives an evening's waiting:

> BOY: What am I to tell Mr. Godot, sir?
> VLADIMIR: Tell him . . . (*he hesitates*) . . . tell him you saw us. (*Pause*)
>   You did see us, didn't you?
> BOY: Yes Sir.

The realities stated with such insistence are disquietingly provisional. The tree is plainly a sham, and the two tramps are simply filling up time until a proper dramatic entertainment can get under way. They are helping the management fulfill, in a minimal way, its contract with the ticket holders. The resources of vaudeville are at their somewhat incompetent disposal: bashed hats, dropped pants, tight boots, the kick, the pratfall, the improper story. It will suffice if they can stave off a mass exodus until Godot comes, in whom we are all so interested. Beckett, it is clear, has cunningly doubled his play with that absence of a play which every confirmed theatergoer has at some time or other experienced, the advertised cynosure having missed a train or overslept or indulged in temperament. The tramps have plainly not learned parts; they repeatedly discuss what to do next ("What about hanging ourselves?") and observe from time to time that tedium is accumulating:

> Charming evening we're having.
> Unforgettable.
> And it's not over.
> Apparently not.
> It's only beginning.
> It's awful.
> Worse than the pantomime.
> The circus.
> The music-hall.
> The circus.

Thus a non-play comments on itself. Or the audience of the non-play is reminded that others the previous night sat in these seats witnessing the identical futility ("What did we do yesterday?" "In my opinion we were here.") and that others in turn will sit there watching on successive nights for an indeterminate period.

> We'll come back to-morrow [says tramp No. 1].
> And then the day after to-morrow.
> Possibly.
> And so on.

And so on, until the run of the production ends. It will end, presumably, when there are no longer spectators interested, though it is difficult to explain on Shakespearean premises what it is that they can be expected to be interested in. Or perhaps not so difficult. What brings the groundlings to *Macbeth*? Why, they are waiting for the severed head. And to *Hamlet*? They are waiting for Garrick (or Irving, or Olivier). And here?

> Let's go.
> We can't.
> Why not?
> We're waiting for Godot.
> (*despairingly*) Ah!

The French text manages an inclusiveness denied to English idiom: "Pourquoi?" "On attend Godot." Not "*nous*" but "*on*": Didi, Gogo, and audience alike.

If the seeming improvisation of the tramps denies theatricality, it affirms at the same time quintessential theater, postulating nothing but what we can see on stage: a place, and men present in it, doing what they are doing. And into this quintessential theater there irrupts before long the strident unreality we crave:

> POZZO: (*terrifying voice*). I am Pozzo! (*Silence.*) Pozzo! (*Silence.*) Does that
>   name mean nothing to you? (*Silence.*) I say does that name mean
>   nothing to you?

This is at last the veritable stuff, that for which we paid our admissions: an actor, patently, with gestures and grimaces, who has furthermore memorized and rehearsed his part and knows how they talk in plays. He makes his entrance like Tamburlaine driving the pampered jades of Asia (represented, in this low-budget production, by one extra); he takes pains with his elocution, assisted by a vaporizer, like an effete *Heldentenor*; he recites a well-conned set speech on the twilight, with "vibrant," "lyrical," and "prosaic" phases, and contrapuntal assistance from well-schooled hands (two hands lapsing; two hands flung amply apart; one hand raised in admonition; fingers snapped at the climax, to reinforce the word "pop!"). This is theater; the evening is saved. Surely he is Godot?

But he says not; and we are disconcerted to find him fishing for applause, and from the tramps. They are his audience as we are his and theirs. The play, in familiar Beckett fashion, has gotten inside the play. So too when Lucky (who has also memorized his part) recites his set speech on the descent of human certainty into "the great cold the great dark" ("for reasons unknown but time will tell"), it is for the amusement of his master, and of the tramps, and incidentally of ourselves. The same is true of his symbolic dance, a thing of constrained gestures, as in Noh drama. So the perspective continues to diminish, box within box. In this theater, the tramps. Within their futile world, the finished theatricality of Pozzo. At Pozzo's command, Lucky's speech; within this speech, scholarship, man *in posse* and *in esse*, all that which, officially endorsed, we think we know, notably the labors of the Acacacacademy of Anthropopopometry; within these in turn, caca (Fr. colloq., excrement) and popo, a chamberpot: a diminution, a delirium.

Such metaphysics as the Beckett theater will permit is entailed in this hierarchy of watchers and watched. Throughout, and notably during Lucky's holocaust of phrases, we clutch at straws of meaning, persuaded at bottom only of one thing, that all four men exist, embodied, gravid, speaking; moving before us, their shadows cast on the wall, their voices echoing in the auditorium, their feet heavy on the boards.

The second act opens with the song about the dog's epitaph, another infinitely converging series of acts and agents. The Unnamable also meditates on this jingle, and discovers its principle: "third verse, as the first, fourth, as the second, fifth, as the third, give us time, give us time and we'll be a multitude"; for it generates an infinite series of unreal beings, epitaph within epitaph within epitaph. Correspondingly, near the end of the act Didi muses over the sleeping Gogo:

> At me too someone is looking, of me too someone is saying, He is sleeping, he knows nothing, let him sleep on.

So we watch Didi move through his part, as he watches Gogo, and meanwhile Lucky's God with the white beard, outside time, without extension, is loving us dearly "with some exceptions for reasons unknown but time will tell."

It remains to recall that the Beckett universe, wherever we encounter it, consists of a shambles of phenomena within which certain symmetries and recurrences are observable, like the physical world as interpreted by early man. So this stage world has its structure and landmarks. We observe, for example, that bowler hats are apparently *de rigueur*, and that they are removed for thinking but replaced for speaking. We observe that moonrise and sunset occur in conjunction two nights running, for this is an ideal cosmology, unless we are to suppose the two acts to be separated by an interval of twenty nine days. The tree by the same token has budded overnight, like an early miracle. All this is arbitrary because theatrical. Our play draws on Greek theater with its limited number of actors, its crises always offstage, and its absent divinity; on Noh theater with its symbolic tree, its nuances and its ritual dance; on *commedia dell'arte*, improvised before our eyes; on twentieth-century experimental theater; and on vaudeville with its castoff clowns, stumblings, shamblings, delicate bawdry, acrobatics, and astringent pointlessness. The final action partakes of the circus repertoire

(They each take an end of the cord and pull. It breaks. They almost fall),

synchronized with a burlesque house misadventure with trousers

. . . *which, much too big for him, fall about his ankles.*

The student of *Finnegans Wake* will identify this mishap as the play's epiphany, the least learned will note that something hitherto invisible has at last been disclosed, and everyone can agree that the final gesture is to a static propriety:

> VLADIMIR: Pull ON your trousers.
> ESTRAGON: *(realizing his trousers are down)*. True.
>   *He pulls up his trousers.*
> VLADIMIR: Well? Shall we go?
> ESTRAGON: Yes, let's go.
>   *They do not move.*
> *Curtain.*

II

This superimposition of dramatic economies was not achieved at once. About 1947, just after writing the *Nouvelles*, Beckett occupied himself with a radically misconceived dramatic enterprise, a play called *Eleutheria* in three acts, which entailed a large stage, two sets simultaneously on view, a place (Paris) and a time (three consecutive winter afternoons) uncharacteristically specified, and seventeen speaking parts, including a Chinese torturer, an officious member of the audience, and the prompter. "Eleutheria" means "freedom." The theme, clearly related to that of the first *Nouvelle*, "L'Expulsé," concerns a young man's act of secession from his intensely bourgeois family. This theme preoccupied Beckett a good deal at one time; it also underlies the remarkable fragment, "From an Abandoned Work":

> Up bright and early that day, I was young then, feeling awful, and out, mother hanging out of the window in her nightdress weeping and waving. Nice fresh morning, bright too early as so often. Feeling really awful, very violent. . . .

In the play, the family (surnamed Krap) entertains guests (named Piouk and Meck) and the conversation goes like this:

> MR KRAP: Have a cigar.
> DR PIOUK: Thank you.
> MR KRAP: Yes thank you or no thank you?
> DR PIOUK: I don't smoke.
>
> *(Silence)*
>
> MRS MECK
> MRS PIOUK   *(Together)*: I . . .
>
> MRS MECK: Oh, I beg your pardon. You were going to say?
> MRS PIOUK: Oh, nothing. Go on.
>
> *(Silence)*

Or ailments are discussed:

> MRS PIOUK: How is Henry?
> MRS KRAP: Ill.
> MRS PIOUK: What's wrong with him?
> MRS KRAP: I don't know. He's stopped urinating.
> MRS PIOUK: It's the prostate.

Such details, however, lack the fine formal emptiness of *Godot*, partly because they occur in the interstices of an elaborate exposition of familial relationships. Beckett drags the audience, with considerable distaste, up and down all the airshafts of a well-made play. It is from this that Krap *fils*, the young Victor, has absented himself. He scrounges in trash cans, speaks to no one, and is generally found in bed, in a garret flat.

All the rest of the play—two mortal acts—is devoted to punching and poking Victor, in his garret, and beseeching him to explain his conduct. This he will not do, one aspect of his freedom, we may suppose, being freedom from the necessity to devise explanations, even for his own enlightenment. The busybodies include not only Victor's parents, their relatives, and his fiancée (a certain Mlle. Skunk), but also an officious artisan who is on the premises to repair a broken window, and who constitutes himself spokesman of detached practicality. By the third act an exasperated member of the audience has taken up his seat on the stage, determined to see things resolved before midnight; the services of an Oriental torturer have been requisitioned; Victor has made a statement, later retracted as fiction; and alone at last on the bare stage he has lain down "with his back turned to humanity."

Since the figure of interest (and on the stage, not of much interest) has by definition withdrawn from communication, Beckett's problem is, as never before, to fill up the work. To this end he employs, with little conviction, the convention of formal dramatic structure, which is that when someone speaks someone else answers, more or less to the point. And this convention closes round Victor like water round a stone, incapable of assimilating him.

Though it doesn't work in this play, the strategy is not new. All Beckett's writings bring some sustained formal element to the service of some irreducible situation round which the lucid sentences defile in baffled aplomb. If we never understand the world of Watt, that is not because the presentation conceals it; as the presence of irrational terms does not prevent us from following every line of a computation. So in Molloy the twin circular journeys, and in Malone Dies the parallel narratives, supply the words with something formal to disclose, and circumscribe the implacable mysteries. Godot for the same reason is full of small rituals and transparent local rhythms. They are not the mystery, they do not clarify the mystery, or seek to clarify the mystery, they clarify the place where the mystery is, and the fact that, in the presence of the irreducible, people contrive to kill time by rehearsing their grasp of detail.

Let us be clear about this. Victor is not a new moral phenomenon. Beckett has been concerned with the withdrawn man from Belacqua onward. Nor is he structurally a new component. He is this play's version of the familiar surd, the irreducible element which no style, no clarity, no ceremony will dissolve or explain: the thing which makes itself felt, in Beckett's cosmos, as a prevailing and penetrating mystery, seeping through the walls of stage or book. This mystery, this irreducible, is generally of two sorts: (1) in the domain of existence, the implacable "d'être là": as we find ourselves situated on earth ("There's no cure for that") or as Malone finds himself placed in his mysterious room, surrounded by procedures that appear to take no account of his arrival or presence. Or (2) in the domain of will, the arbitrary decision, Molloy's determination to visit his mother, or Victor's to leave home. There is no looking into these sudden precipitations. In large, they make contact with the ambient terror and oppressiveness (what compels us to wait for Godot?). In small, they supply a repertory of comic effects. Part of the trouble with Victor in *Eleutheria* is that his presence confuses these perspectives; his sulkiness verges on being funny at the same time that his intransigence is growing unnerving; he can round on his inquisitors by asking them why it is that they find him of such consuming interest, when cripples, fools, nuns, and other outcasts barely detain them.

In the *Nouvelles*, three of which Beckett published though he had the sense not to publish *Eleutheria*, such problems of tact do not arise. "L'Expulsé," a sort of Victor, has generally preferred to keep to his room, and by preference the end of the room where the bed is, so much so that he barely knows the streets of his native town. At the beginning of the story he is recalling how his family finally threw him out.

> Even as I fell I heard the door slam, which brought me a little comfort, in the midst of my fall. For that meant they were not pursuing me down into the street, with a stick, to beat me in full view of the passers-by. For if that had been their intention they would not have closed the door, but left it open, so that the persons assembled in the vestibule might enjoy my chastisement and be edified. So, for once, they had confined them-selves to throwing me out, and no more about it. I had time, before coming to rest in the gutter, to conclude this piece of reasoning.
>
> Under these circumstances nothing compelled me to get up immedi-ately. I rested my elbow on the sidewalk, funny the things you remem-ber, settled my ear in the cup of my hand and began to reflect on my situation, notwithstanding its familiarity. But the sound, fainter but unmistakable, of the door slammed again, roused me from my reverie, where already a whole landscape was taking form, charming with haw-thorn and wild roses, most dreamlike, and made me look up in alarm, my hands flat on the sidewalk and my legs braced for flight. But it was merely my hat, sailing towards me through the air, rotating as it came. I caught it and put it on. They were most correct, according to their god. They could have kept this hat, but it was not theirs, it was mine, so they gave it back to me. But the spell was broken.

And the life from which he has been expelled is adequately summed up by the hat:

> How describe this hat? And why? When my head had attained I shall not say its definitive but its maximum dimensions, my father said to me, Come, son, we are going to buy your hat, as though it had pre-existed from time immemorial in a pre-established place. He went straight to the

hat. I personally had no say in the matter, nor had the hatter. I have often wondered if my father's purpose was not to humiliate me, if he was not jealous of me who was young and handsome, fresh at least, while he was already old and all bloated and purple. It was forbidden me, from that day forth, to go out bareheaded, my pretty brown hair blowing in the wind. Sometimes, in a secluded street, I took it off and held it in my hand, but trembling. I was required to brush it morning and evening. Boys my age with whom, in spite of everything, I was obliged to mix occasionally, mocked me. But I said to myself, it is not really the hat, they simply make merry at the hat because it is a little more glaring than the rest, for they have no finesse. I have always been amazed by my contemporaries' lack of finesse, I whose soul writhed from morning to night, in the mere quest of itself. But perhaps they were simply being kind, like those who make game of the hunchback's big nose. When my father died I could have got rid of this hat, there was nothing more to prevent me, but not I. But how describe it? Some other time, some other time.

This precious youth turns slowly into a bum. In "Premier Amour" (which remains unpublished) he is living in an abandoned stable and devoted to "cerebral supinity, the deadening of the idea of the me and the idea of that small residue of exasperating trifles known as the not-me." Near the canal he comes to be frequented by a certain Lulu.

Yes, I loved her, that was the name which I gave, and which alas I still give, to what I did, at that period. I possessed no data on the subject, not having previously loved, but I had heard the thing spoken of, naturally, at home, at school, in the brothel, and at church, and I had read romances, in prose and in verse, under the direction of my tutor, in English, French, Italian and German, in which it was spoken highly of. I was therefore well prepared to give a name to what I did, when I discovered myself writing the word Lulu on an old cowpad, or lying in the mud beneath the moon trying to pull up dandelions without breaking the stems.

His idyll, like Molloy's, is of short duration. All he really wants of her is a peaceable shelter, and he finds her clients disturbing. At the beginning of "Le Calmant" he (if it is still he) announces that he no longer knows when he died (whatever that means). He is quite likely in a hospital ("among these assassins, in a bed of terror"), but prefers to imagine himself in his distant refuge, hands clasped, head down, feeble, panting, calm, free, and "older than I could ever have been, if my calculations are correct." He tells himself a story of a nighttime ramble, maybe a real one, in which people came up against him like apparitions and talked no sense that he could follow, and a vision finally came to him of asphalt bursting into infinite flower, while he lay on the pavement immersed in his dream, and people took care not to step on him ("a considerateness which touched me"). In "The End" he is thrown out of the institution which has been harboring him, and after bizarre wanderings takes refuge at last in an abandoned canoe, where he dreams of slowly foundering in the open main, as the water rises slowly through a hole from which with his penknife he has extracted the cork.

All this is capital material for fiction, but not for drama. Since its point is that the protagonist has sundered all relation, so far as he can, with other persons and things, there is simply no way to exhibit him on the stage. The only thing to exhibit is other folks' curiosity about him, which grows tedious. And since Beckett's unwavering concern is with the twilight man, who does not inhabit the rational domain, whom you cannot see with Pythagorean eyes and for whom our moral vocabulary contains only the summary provided in the last sentence of "The End," that he has neither "the courage to stop nor the strength to go on," it would seem clear that for Beckett the drama was a hopeless form. But we know our man by this time; nothing makes him prick up his ears like the word "hopeless." Jettisoning *Eleutheria*, he gave over trying to dramatize the *Nouvelles* and commenced turning them instead into the trilogy. There is no telling whether it was pondering Molloy and Moran that suggested raising the number of idlers to two, for dialogue, and reducing the number of busy folk to two, for concision, and playing a waiting against a journeying, for structure. At any rate, after finishing *Molloy*, perhaps also *Malone Dies*, he commenced the impossible play, its two twilight men and much of the quality of their talk transposed from another jettisoned fiction, *Mercier et Camier*.

III

The two men waiting for Godot to come (or for night to fall) are very similar to the two men who were seeking to retrieve a bicycle and a haversack, on the off chance that these articles might prove relevant to their needs. Hear them one rainy morning discoursing of their umbrella:

For myself, said Camier, I would not open it.
And might we hear the reason? said Mercier. It is raining steadily, it seems to me. You are all wet.
Your advice would be to open it? said Camier.
I do not say that, said Mercier. I only ask when we are going to open it if we do not open it now.

This futile parasol deserves a moment's attention; there is nothing like it in *Godot*. Formerly red, tipped by a betasseled amber ball, it had floated down time's stream for nearly a half century before getting lodged in the junkshop where Mercier gave ninepence for it.

> It must have made its debut about 1900, said Camier. That was I think the year of Ladysmith, on the Klip. Do you remember it? A splendid time. Garden parties every day. Life opened before us, radiant. All hopes were permissible. We played at sieges. People die like flies. Hunger. Thirst. Bang! Bang! The last cartridges. Surrender! Never! We eat corpses. We drink our own urine. Bang! Bang! We kept two in reserve. What do we hear? A cry of wonder. Dust on the horizon. The column! Tongues are black. Hurrah anyhow! Rah! Rah! We sounded like ravens. A garrison marshal died of joy. We are saved. The century was two months old.
>
> Look at it now, said Mercier.

Look at the parasol now, or look at the century. Or look at us:

> How are you feeling? said Camier. I keep forgetting to ask.
> I felt well coming downstairs, said Mercier. Now I feel less well. Screwed up, if you like, but not to the sticking-place. And you?
> A chip, said Camier, in the midst of the limitless ocean.

Souvenir from the great dawn of an ampler day, when garden parties and rescue parties bespoke man's limitless hope, our parasol (bits of fringe still ornamenting its perimeter) is irrelevant to a time of rain, middle age, and doubt. For two pages they debate throwing it away, a course for which, Mercier concludes, it will perhaps be time "when it can no longer serve us for shelter, because of wear, or when we have achieved the certainty that between it and our present distress there has never existed the least relationship."

> Very well, said Camier. But it is not sufficient to know that we shall not throw it away. It is equally needful to know whether we are to open it.
> Since it is in part with a view to opening it that we are not throwing it away, said Mercier.
> I know, I know, said Camier, but are we to open it immediately or wait until the weather has characterized itself more fully?
> Mercier scrutinized the impenetrable sky.
> Go and take a look, he said. Tell me what you think.
> Camier went out into the street. He pressed on to the corner, so that Mercier lost sight of him. On returning, he said,
> There may be clearing patches lower down. Would you like me to go up on the roof?
> Mercier concentrated. Finally he said, impulsively,

Open it, for the love of God.

But Camier could not open it. The bitch, he said, it is stuck again.

Give it here, said Mercier.

But Mercier was no more fortunate. He brandished it. But he got himself in hand just in time. Proverb.

What have we done to God? he said.

We have denied him, said Camier.

You will not make me believe that his rancor goes to these lengths, said Mercier.

Tatter their clothing, divest the surrounding space of streets and houses, empty their hands of objects boasting assignable provenance, and they turn easily into Vladimir and Estragon. Between this dialogue and Didi's account of opportunities missed "il y a une éternité, vers 1900" (the less elegiac English text has "a million years ago, in the nineties")—

Hand in hand from the top of the Eiffel Tower, among the first. We were respectable in those days. Now it's too late. They wouldn't even let us up.

—between Camier's mock Ladysmith and this, what differences of feeling we may discover radiate from the fact that Mercier and Camier have actually in their hands a relic of those times, whereas Didi must make do with memory, and Gogo (who can barely remember the previous day) with Didi's account. Their only possessions are their clothes. Certain of these are involved in the action: two hats (exchanged), one pair of boots (substituted for another), one pair of trousers (falling down), one rope, serving Estragon as a belt (broken). None of them has any history, none bespeaks any past. Indeed all are interchangeable with substitutes in some economy exterior to the action on the stage, as it seems clear that Estragon's trousers served someone of ampler build before they came to him. So much for objects. We may note the presence of food (turnips, carrots, radishes). The universe is also furnished with natural splendors (one tree) and natural phenomena (twilight, darkness, moonlight). Consequently its inhabitants are thrown completely on their own resources:

VLADIMIR: You must be happy, too, deep down, if you only knew it.
ESTRAGON: Happy about what?
VLADIMIR: To be back with me again.
ESTRAGON: Would you say so?
VLADIMIR: Say you are, even if it's not true.
ESTRAGON: What am I to say?
VLADIMIR: Say, I am happy.
ESTRAGON: I am happy.
VLADIMIR: So am I.

ESTRAGON: So am I.
VLADIMIR: We are happy.
ESTRAGON: We are happy. (*Silence.*) What do we do, now that we are happy?
VLADIMIR: Wait for Godot. (*Estragon groans. Silence.*)

There is one other difference between this world and that of Mercier and Camier. The difference is named Godot: another person, who matters. Whether or not he appears, he supplies tensions no umbrella, bicycle, or haversack can exert. In the play before us these tensions are barely sketched; Beckett was not to concern himself with them until more than a decade later, in *Embers* and *Comment C'est*.

It is more our present business to note why, in transforming the ambiguously aimless journey of the novel into the ambiguously empty waiting of the play, Beckett has emptied the protagonists' world of objects. Objects, in his universe, go with a journey: bicycles, for instance, crutches, a hat secured by a string; in *Comment C'est*, a jute sack, tins of fish, a can opener, used in the journeying, absent in the waiting. The objects Malone inventories in his immobility—a needle stuck into two corks, the bowl of a pipe, equipped with a little tin lid, a scrap of newspaper, a photograph of an ass wearing a boater—these constitute no exception, for Malone's immobility is not a waiting but by definition a terminal phase in a journey, toward nothingness. Thus Malone's objects have histories. Since they joined his entourage they have made a journey through time in his company, undergoing modifications not always at random (he knows under what circumstances the brim came off his hat; he removed it himself, so that he might keep the hat on while he slept). It is even possible to speculate concerning their pre-Malone history; the pipe bowl which he found in the grass must have been thrown away by a man who said, when the stem broke, "Bah, I'll buy myself another." ("But all that is mere supposition.") Thus the static object, like Malone's own immobility, is a momentary cross section of a duration, the present index of a movement in time which may parallel or continue movement in space, as the Beckett journey is apt to become identical with the process of being alive.

But the scanty tale of objects that concern the bums in *Waiting for Godot* contains no item owning a past, a future, or a duration with which our vital sentiments may feel empathy. Like the elements at the beginning of a mathematical problem, the bowler hats, the boots, the pants, the rope, the tree are simply *given*, and the operations that are performed on them do not modify them (as, at the end of the most prolonged computation, x is still x).

There are, it is true, in the play a few things that undergo changes of a different order. These are irreversible changes, the sort prescribed by the Second Law of Thermodynamics, the law with whose gross effects Lucky's great speech is concerned. Reversible events are trivial, like rearrangements of furniture, or of the terms in an equation. By this criterion the status of most of the events in the play is slight, or at most ambiguous. Irreversible things are the ones that *happen*, that declare something more than a system of tautologies, or an economy of displacements. It is the sum of those happenings, however small, whose terms and agents can never again be put back the way they were—the carrot uneaten, the leaves unbudded—that advances by today's quantum the system's articulation, or perhaps its entropy. Of these *Waiting for Godot* contains a real but insignificant number.

Though this is the play in which, as Vivian Mercier wittily observed, "nothing happens, twice," things at the fall of the final curtain are not precisely as they were. Before our eyes a carrot has come into visibility out of Didi's pocket and vanished again into Gogo's mouth; its subsequent decomposition may be conjectured. Before our eyes, also, the rope has been broken, into two pieces whose combined length will equal the original length, but which can never again be combined. These are both irreversible actions; the world is now poorer by one carrot and one rope. In the interval between the acts there have been three organic changes: the tree has acquired leaves, and Pozzo has lost his sight and Lucky his speech. (We have only Pozzo's word for the latter two.) It is not clear whether these count as irreversible events, though certainly the leaves cannot be expected to go back into the tree. In the same interval Gogo's boots have been taken, and a pair of a different color substituted. Didi ventures an explanation of this, inaccurate because based on inadequate data. With the benefit of our later knowledge that the new boots are larger than the old, we can readily amend his hypothesis. The play's other substitution occurs before our eyes: as a result of a sequence of permutations too long to reconstruct, Didi midway through Act II has Lucky's hat on his head, and Didi's hat has replaced Lucky's on the ground. And one further item comes from outside the visible economy of the play, viz. Lucky's second hat, the hat he is wearing on his reappearance in Act II, after having left his first hat on the ground before his exit in Act I. These substitutions are presumably reversible, though it is not clear how Lucky's second hat would have to be disposed of.

Nor can the tedium of two evenings be said to redeem its own nullity by enhancing the experience of Didi and Gogo, as one may learn by watching bees move about. They exist in an eternity of stagnation,

Gogo's memory defective ("Either I forget immediately or I never forget"), Didi's an eventless assimilation of the same to the remembered same. They are, unlike Murphy, Mercier, Molloy, Moran, and Malone, utterly incapable of the kind of experience you can later tell a story about, and utterly detached from the least affection for objects. They have only their bodies and their clothes: hence the mathematical speed with which their situation can be exhibited. Not having chosen suicide ("sans le courage de finir ni la force de continuer"), they have grown committed, in a kind of fierce negative sanctity, to waiting for the figure with sheep, goats, many affairs, and a white beard (we need not credit any of these details). Their lives correspond exactly to St. John of the Cross's famous minimal prescription, divested of the love of created things, and the divine union is awaited beside the tree, one evening, another evening—every evening, since two terms, in the absence of indications to the contrary, imply a series, perhaps infinite. They are blessed, says Didi, in knowing the answer to the question, what it is they are doing there. They are waiting for Godot to come, or for night to fall. They have kept their appointment, that too they can claim, and it is not by accident that he refers to the saints. "We are not saints, but we have kept our appointment. How many people can boast as much?"

Lest we be tempted to take this rhetorical question for the ridge pole of the play, Gogo replies, "Billions," and Didi concedes that he may be right. The question, climaxing the longest speech either of them is to deliver, retains its torque.

Having reduced the whole of two men's lives to a waiting which epitomizes a moral issue, Beckett causes this situation to be intersected by his other key situation, a journey. Pozzo and Lucky are a little like Moran and his son, seen from the outside instead of through Moran's narrative. They are loaded, as if to emphasize the distinction between waiters and travelers, with every kind of portable property, notably a heavy bag (of sand), a folding stool, a picnic basket (with chicken and wine), a greatcoat, a whip, a watch (genuine half-hunter, with deadbeat escapement, gift of Pozzo's grandfather), a handkerchief, a pocket vaporizer, a rope, glasses, matches, and a briar pipe (by Kapp and Peterson). The watch is often consulted; there is a schedule to observe. If these two, master and servant, steadily on the move, epitomize the busy world from which Didi and Gogo have seceded, there is no record of the act of secession. Rather, the contrasting pairs appear to epitomize not ways of life so much as modes of being. Amid the great void which they contrive to fill up with exercises and conversation, Didi and Gogo circulate about one another with numb but delectable affection, Didi perpetually responsible for Gogo, enraged when Gogo is kicked, and offering to carry him (*Pause*) "if necessary." Gogo for his part rejects a proposed system for hanging themselves on the sole ground, he says, that if it fails his friend will be left alone. Both strike noble if temporary rages on behalf of Lucky, and even, when Lucky is put in the wrong, on behalf of Pozzo; and with infinite delay and ratiocination they do eventually help the blind Pozzo of the second act to his feet. Pozzo, on the other hand, absurd, theatrical, glib, patronizing ("so that I ask myself is there anything I can do in my turn for these honest fellows who are having such a dull, dull time") is capable of nothing but stage turns: the judicious stranger, the picnicker at his ease, the eulogist of twilight, the man whose heart goes pit-a-pat—very much, in each of his roles, someone we have seen before. This kaleidoscope of impostors learned all that he knows from Lucky, and we are given at some length a specimen of Lucky's capacity for imparting the things he has in his head. They live with their heads, these two, moving hither and thither, Pozzo talking of buying and selling, and imposing with his campstool and ceremonial a prissy elegance on their halts; Lucky treacherous, miserable, obeying with a precision that does not quite approximate to ritual, and dancing or thinking on command. There is no love here, and the play's waiting seems incontestably preferable to its journeying.

IV

For the stage is a place to wait. The place itself waits, when no one is in it. When the curtain rises on *Endgame*, sheets drape all visible objects as in a furniture warehouse. Clov's first act is to uncurtain the two high windows and inspect the universe; his second is to remove the sheets and fold them carefully over his arm, disclosing two ash cans and a figure in an armchair. This is so plainly a metaphor for waking up that we fancy the stage, with its high peepholes, to be the inside of an immense skull. It is also a ritual for starting the play; Yeats arranged such a ritual for *At the Hawk's Well*, and specified a black cloth and a symbolic song. It is finally a removal from symbolic storage of the objects that will be needed during the course of the performance. When the theater is empty it is sensible to keep them covered against dust. So we are reminded at the outset that what we are to witness is a dusty dramatic exhibition, repeated and repeatable. The necessary objects include three additional players (two of them in ash cans). Since none of them will move from his station we can think of them after the performance as being kept permanently on stage, and covered with their dust cloths again until tomorrow night.

The rising of the curtain disclosed these sheeted forms; the removal of the sheets disclosed the protagonist and his ash cans; the next stage is for the protagonist to uncover his own face, which he does with a yawn, culminating this three-phase strip tease with the revelation of a very red face and black glasses. His name, we gather from the program, is Hamm, a name for an actor. He is also Hamlet, bounded in a nutshell, fancying himself king of infinite space, but troubled by bad dreams; he is also "a toppled Prospero," remarking partway through the play, with judicious pedantry, "our revels now are ended"; he is also the Hammer to which Clov, Nagg and Nell (Fr. clou, Ger. Nagel, Eng. nail) stand in passive relationship; by extension, a chess player ("Me—[he yawns]—to play"); but also (since Clov must wheel him about) himself a chessman, probably the imperiled King.

Nagg and Nell in their dustbins appear to be pawns; Clov, with his arbitrarily restricted movements ("I can't sit.") and his equestrian background ("And your rounds? Always on foot?" "Sometimes on horse.") resembles the Knight, and his perfectly cubical kitchen ("ten feet by ten feet by ten feet, nice dimensions, nice proportions") resembles a square on the chessboard translated into three dimensions. He moves back and forth, into it and out of it, coming to the succor of Hamm and then retreating. At the endgame's end the pawns are forever immobile and Clov is poised for a last departure from the board, the status quo forever menaced by an expected piece glimpsed through the window, and King Hamm abandoned in check:

Old endgame lost of old, play and lose and have done with losing. . . .
Since that's the way we're playing it, let's play it that way . . . and speak
no more about it . . . speak no more.

Even if we had not the information that the author of this work has been known to spend hours playing chess with himself (a game at which you always lose), we should have been alerted to his long-standing interest in its strategy by the eleventh chapter of Murphy, where Murphy's first move against Mr. Endon, the standard P—K$_4$, is described as "the primary cause of all [his] subsequent difficulties." (The same might be said of getting born, an equally conventional opening.) Chess has several peculiarities which lend themselves to the metaphors of this jagged play. It is a game of leverage, in which the significance of a move may be out of all proportion to the local disturbance it effects ("A flea! This is awful! What a day!"). It is a game of silences, in which new situations are appraised: hence Beckett's most frequent stage direction, "Pause." It is a game of steady attrition; by the time we reach the endgame the board is nearly bare, as bare as Hamm's world where there are no more bicycle wheels, sugarplums, pain killers, or coffins, let alone people. And it is a game which by the successive removal of screening pieces constantly extends the range of lethal forces, until at the endgame peril from a key piece sweeps down whole ranks and files. The king is hobbled by the rule which allows him to move in any direction but only one square at a time; Hamm's circuit of the stage and return to center perhaps exhibit him patrolling the inner boundaries of the little nine-square territory he commands. To venture further will evidently expose him to check. ("Outside of here it's death.") His knight shuttles to and fro, his pawns are pinned. No threat is anticipated from the auditorium, which is presumably off the board; and a periodic reconnaissance downfield through the windows discloses nothing but desolation until very near the end. But on his last inspection of the field Clov is dismayed. Here the English text is inexplicably sketchy; in the French one we have,

CLOV: Aïeaïeaïe!
HAMM: C'est une feuille? Une fleur? Une toma—(il bâille)—te?
CLOV (regardant): Je t'en foutrai des tomates! Quelqu'un! C'est quelqu'un!
HAMM: Eh bien, va l'exterminer. (Clov descend de l'escabeau.) Quelqu'un!
(Vibrant.) Fais ton devoir!

In the subsequent interrogatory we learn the distance of this threat (fifteen meters or so), its state of rest or motion (motionless), its sex (presumably a boy), its occupation (sitting on the ground as if leaning on something). Hamm, perhaps thinking of the resurrected Jesus, murmurs "La pierre levée," then on reflection changes the image to constitute himself proprietor of the Promised Land: "Il regarde la maison sans doute, avec les yeux de Moïse mourant." It is doing, however, nothing of the kind; it is gazing at its navel. There is no use, Hamm decides, in running out to exterminate it: "If he exists he'll die there or he'll come here. And if he doesn't . . ." And a few seconds later he has conceded the game:

It's the end, Clov, we've come to the end. I don't need you any more.

He sacrifices his last mobile piece, discards his staff and whistle, summons for the last time a resourceless Knight and an unanswering Pawn, and covers his face once more with the handkerchief: somehow in check.

Not that all this is likely to be yielded up with clarity by any conceivable performance. It represents however a structure which, however we glimpse it, serves to refrigerate the incidental passions of a play about, it would seem, the end of humanity. It is not for nothing that the place within which the frigid events are transacted is more than once called "the shelter," outside of which is death; nor that the human race is at present reduced to two disabled parents, a macabre blind son, and an acathisiac servant. Around this shelter the universe crumbles away like an immense dry biscuit: no more rugs, no more tide, no more coffins. We hear of particular deaths:

> CLOV (harshly): When old Mother Pegg asked you for oil for her lamp and you told her to get out to hell, you knew what was happening then, no? (Pause.) You know what she died of, Mother Pegg? Of darkness.
> HAMM (feebly): I hadn't any.
> CLOV (as before): Yes, you had.

We observe particular brutalities: Hamm, of his parents: "Have you bottled her?" "Yes." "Are they both bottled?" "Yes." "Screw down the lids." What has shrunken the formerly ample world is perhaps Hamm's withdrawal of love; the great skull-like setting suggests a solipsist's universe. "I was never there," he says. "Absent, always. It all happened without me. I don't know what's happened." He has been in "the shelter"; he has also been closed within himself. It is barely possible that the desolation is not universal:

> HAMM: Did you ever think of one thing?
> CLOV: Never.
> HAMM: That here we're down in a hole. (Pause.) But beyond the hills? Eh? Perhaps it's still green. Eh? (Pause.) Flora! Pomona! (Ecstatically.) Ceres! (Pause.) Perhaps you won't need to go very far.
> CLOV: I can't go very far. (Pause.) I'll leave you.

As Hamm is both chessman and chess player, so it is conceivable that destruction is not screened off by the shelter but radiates from it for a certain distance. Zero, zero, words we hear so often in the dialogue, these are the Cartesian coordinates of the origin.

Bounded in a nutshell yet king of infinite space, Hamm articulates the racking ambiguity of the play by means of his dominance over its most persuasive metaphor, the play itself. If he is Prospero with staff and revels, if he is Richard III bloodsmeared and crying "My kingdom for a nightman!", if he is also perhaps Richard II, within whose hollow crown

> . . . Keeps Death his court, and there the Antic sits,
> Scoffing his state
> and grinning at his pomp,
> Allowing him a breath, a little scene
> To monarchize, be feared, and kill with looks—

these roles do not exhaust his repertoire. He is (his name tells us) the generic Actor, a creature all circumference and no center. As master of the revels, he himself attends to the last unveiling of the opening ritual:

(Pause. Hamm stirs. He yawns under the handkerchief. He removes the handkerchief from his face. Very red face, black glasses.)
HAMM: Me—*(he yawns)*—to play. *(He holds the handkerchief spread out before him.)* Old stancher! *(. . . He clears his throat, joins the tips of his fingers.)* Can there be misery—*(he yawns)*—loftier than mine?

The play ended, he ceremoniously unfolds the handkerchief once more (five separate stage directions governing his tempo) and covers his face as it was in the beginning. "Old Stancher! *(Pause.)* You . . . remain." What remains, in the final brief tableau specified by the author, is the immobile figure with a bloodied Veronica's veil in place of a face: the actor having superintended his own Passion and translated himself into an ultimate abstraction of masked agony.

Between these termini he animates everything, ordering the coming and going of Clov and the capping and uncapping of the cans. When Clov asks, "What is there to keep me here?" he answers sharply, "The dialogue." A particularly futile bit of business with the spyglass and the steps elicits from him an aesthetic judgment, "This is deadly." When it is time for the introduction of the stuffed dog, he notes, "We're getting on," and a few minutes later, "Do you not think this has gone on long enough?" These, like comparable details in *Godot*, are sardonic authorizations for a disquiet that is certainly stirring in the auditorium. No one understands better than Beckett, nor exploits more boldly, the kind of fatalistic attention an audience trained on films is accustomed to place at the dramatist's disposal. The cinema has taught us to suppose that a dramatic presentation moves inexorably as the reels unwind or the studio clock creeps, until it has consumed precisely its allotted time which nothing, no restlessness in the pit, no sirens, no mass exodus can hurry. "Something is taking its course," that suffices us. Hence the vast leisure in which the minimal business of *Godot* and *Endgame* is transacted; hence (transposing into dramatic terms the author's characteristic pedantry of means) the occasional lingering over points of technique, secure in the knowledge that the clock-bound patience of a twentieth-century audience will expect no inner urgency, nothing in fact but the actual time events consume, to determine the pace of the exhibition. Clov asks, "Why this farce, day after day?" and it is sufficient for Hamm to reply, "Routine. One never knows." It is the answer of an actor in an age of films and long runs. In *Endgame* (which here differs radically from *Godot*) no one is supposed to be improvising; the script has been well committed to memory and well rehearsed. By this means doom is caused to penetrate the most intimate crevices of the play. "I'm tired of going on," says Clov late in

the play, "very tired," and then, "Let's stop playing!" (if there is one
thing that modern acting is not it is playing). In the final moments
theatrical technique, under Hamm's sponsorship, rises into savage
prominence.

> HAMM: . . . And me? Did anyone ever have pity on me?
> CLOV *(lowering the telescope, turning towards Hamm)*: What? *(Pause.)* Is it
>   me you're referring to?
> HAMM *(angrily)*: An aside, ape! Did you never hear an aside before?
>   *(Pause.)* I'm warming up for my last soliloquy.

Ten seconds later he glosses "More complications!" as a technical term:
"Not an underplot, I trust." It is Clov who has the last word in this vein:

> HAMM: Clov! *(Clov halts, without turning.)* Nothing. *(Clov moves on.)*
>   Clov! *(Clov halts, without turning.)*
> CLOV: This is what we call making an exit.

By this reiterated stress on the actors as professional men, and so on the
play as an occasion within which they operate, Beckett transforms Hamm's
last soliloquy into a performance, his desolation into something prepared
by the dramatic machine, his abandoning of gaff, dog, and whistle into a
necessary discarding of props, and the terminal business with the handkerchief into, quite literally, a curtain speech. *Endgame* ends with an unex-
pected lightness, a death rather mimed than experienced; if it is "Hamm
as stated, and Clov as stated, together as stated," the mode of statement
has more salience than a paraphrase of the play's situation would lead one
to expect.

The professionalism also saves the play from an essentially sentimental committment to simpliste "destiny." Much of its gloomy power it
derives from contact with such notions as T. H. Huxley's view of man as
an irrelevance whom day by day an indifferent universe engages in chess.
We do not belong here, runs a strain of Western thought which became
especially articulate in France after the War; we belong nowhere; we are
all surds, ab-surd. There is nothing on which to ground our right to exist,
and we need not be especially surprised one day to find ourselves nearly
extinct. (On such a despair Cartesian logic converges, as surely as the
arithmetic of Pythagoras wedged itself fast in the irrationality of $\sqrt{2}$.) Whatever we do, then, since it can obtain no grip on our radically pointless
situation, is *behavior* pure and simple; it is play acting, and may yield us
the satisfaction, if satisfaction there be, of playing well, of uttering our *cris
du coeur* with style and some sense of timing. We do not trouble deaf
heaven, for there is only the sky ("Rien," reports Clov, gazing through his

telescope; and again, "Zéro.") We stir and thrill, at best, ourselves. From such a climate, miscalled existentialist, Beckett wrings every available *frisson* without quite delivering the play into its keeping; for its credibility is not a principle the play postulates but an idea the play contains, an idea of which it works out the moral and spiritual consequences. The despair in which he traffics is a conviction, not a philosophy. He will even set it spinning like a catharine wheel about a wild point of logic, as when he has Hamm require that God be prayed to in silence ("Where are your manners?") and then berate him ("The bastard!") for not existing.

The play contains whatever ideas we discern inside it; no idea contains the play. The play contains, moreover, two narrative intervals, performances within the performance. The first, Nagg's story about the trousers, is explicitly a recitation; Nell has heard it often, and so, probably, has the audience; it is a vaudeville standby. Nagg's performance, like a production of *King Lear*, whose story we know, must therefore be judged solely as a performance. Its quality, alas, discourages even him ("I tell this story worse and worse."), and Nell too is not amused, being occupied with thoughts of her own, about the sand at the bottom of Lake Como. The other is Hamm's huffe-snuffe narrative, also a recitation, since we are to gather that he has been composing it beforehand, in his head. This time we do not know the substance of the tale, but contemplate in diminishing perspective an actor who has memorized a script which enjoins him to imitate a man who has devised and memorized a script:

> The man came crawling towards me, on his belly. Pale, wonderfully pale and thin, he seemed on the point of—(*Pause. Normal tone.*) No, I've done that bit.

Later on he incorporates a few critical reflections: "Nicely put, that," or "There's English for you." This technician's narcissism somewhat disinfects the dreadful tale. All Hamm's satisfactions come from dramatic self-contemplation, and as he towers before us, devoid of mercy, it is to some ludicrous stage villain that he assimilates himself, there on the stage, striking a stage-Barabbas pose ("Sometimes I go about and poison wells.") It is to this that life as play-acting comes.

> In the end he asked me would I consent to take in the child as well—if he were still alive. (*Pause.*) It was the moment I was waiting for. (*Pause.*) Would I consent to take in the child. . . . (*Pause.*) I can see him still, down on his knees, his hands flat on the ground, glaring at me with his mad eyes, in defiance of my wishes.

"It was the moment I was waiting for": the satisfaction this exudes is considerably less sadistic than dramatic, and the anticlimax into which the long performance immediately topples would try a creator's soul, not a maniac's:

> I'll soon have finished with this story. *(Pause.)* Unless I bring in other characters. *(Pause.)* But where would I find them? *(Pause.)* Where would I look for them? *(Pause. He whistles. Enter Clov.)* Let us pray to God.

So the hooks go in. There is no denying what Beckett called in a letter to Alan Schneider "the power of the text to claw." It strikes, however, its unique precarious balance between rage and art, immobilizing all characters but one, rotating before us for ninety unbroken minutes the surfaces of Nothing, always designedly faltering on the brink of utter insignificance into which nevertheless we cannot but project so many awful significances: theater reduced to its elements in order that theatricalism may explore without mediation its own boundaries: a bleak unforgettable tour de force and probably its author's single most remarkable work.

THEODOR W. ADORNO

Trying to Understand "Endgame"

Beckett's *oeuvre* has several elements in common with Parisian existentialism. Reminiscences of the category of "absurdity," of "situation," of "decision" or their opposite permeate it as medieval ruins permeate Kafka's monstrous house on the edge of the city: occasionally, windows fly open and reveal to view the black starless heaven of something like anthropology. But form—conceived by Sartre rather traditionally as that of didactic plays, not at all as something audacious but rather oriented toward an effect—absorbs what is expressed and changes it. Impulses are raised to the level of the most advanced artistic means, those of Joyce and Kafka. Absurdity in Beckett is no longer a state of human existence thinned out to a mere idea and then expressed in images. Poetic procedure surrenders to it without intention. Absurdity is divested of that generality of doctrine which existentialism, that creed of the permanence of individual existence, nonetheless combines with Western pathos of the universal and the immutable. Existential conformity—that one should be what one is—is thereby rejected along with the ease of its representation. What Beckett offers in the way of philosophy he himself also reduces to culture-trash, no different from the innumerable allusions and residues of education which he employs in the wake of the Anglo-Saxon tradition, particularly of Joyce and Eliot. Culture parades before him as the entrails of *Jugendstil* ornaments did before that progress which preceded him, modernism as the obsolescence of the modern. The regressive language demolishes it. Such objectivity in Beckett obliterates the meaning that was culture, along with its rudiments. Culture thus begins to

Translated by Michael T. Jones. From *New German Critique* 26, (Summer 1982). Copyright © 1982 by *New German Critique*.

fluoresce. He thereby completes a tendency of the recent novel. What was decried as abstract according to the cultural criterion of aesthetic immanence—reflection—is lumped together with pure representation, corroding the Flaubertian principle of the purely self-enclosed matter at hand. The less events can be presumed meaningful in themselves, the more the idea of aesthetic *Gestalt* as a unity of appearance and intention becomes illusory. Beckett relinquishes the illusion by coupling both disparate aspects. Thought becomes as much a means of producing a meaning for the work which cannot be immediately rendered tangible, as it is an expression of meaning's absence. When applied to drama, the word "meaning" is multivalent. It denotes: metaphysical content, which objectively presents itself in the complexion of the artifact; likewise the intention of the whole as a structure of meaning which it signifies in itself; and finally the sense of the words and sentences which the characters speak, and that of their progression—the sense of the dialogue. But these equivocations point toward a common basis. From it, in Beckett's *Endgame*, emerges a continuum. It is historio-philosophically supported by a change in the dramatic *a priori*: positive metaphysical meaning is no longer possible in such a substantive way (if indeed it ever was), such that dramatic form could have its law in such meaning and its epiphany. Yet that afflicts the form even in its linguistic construction. Drama cannot simply seize on to negative meaning, or its absence, as content, without thereby affecting everything peculiar to it—virtually to the point of reversal to its opposite. What is essential for drama was constituted by that meaning. If drama were to strive to survive meaning aesthetically, it would be reduced to inadequate content or to a clattering machinery demonstrating world views, as often happens in existentialist plays. The explosion of metaphysical meaning, which alone guaranteed the unity of an aesthetic structure of meaning, makes it crumble away with a necessity and stringency which equals that of the transmitted canon of dramaturgical form. Harmonious aesthetic meaning, and certainly its subjectification in a binding tangible intention, substituted for that transcendent meaningfulness, the denial of which itself constituted the content. Through its own organized meaninglessness, the plot must approach that which transpired in the truth content of dramaturgy generally. Such construction of the senseless also even includes linguistic molecules: if they and their connections were rationally meaningful, then within the drama they would synthesize irrevocably into that very meaning structure of the whole which is denied by the whole. The interpretation of *Endgame* therefore cannot chase the chimera of expressing its meaning with the help of philosophical mediation. Understanding it can mean nothing other than understanding its

incomprehensibility, or concretely reconstructing its meaning structure—
that it has none. Isolated, thought no longer pretends, as the Idea once
did, to be itself the structure's meaning—a transcendence which would be
engendered and guaranteed by the work's own immanence. Instead, thought
transforms itself into a kind of material of a second degree, just as the
philosophemes expounded in Thomas Mann's *The Magic Mountain* and
Doctor Faustus, as novel materials, find their destiny in replacing that
sensate immediacy which is diminished in the self-reflective work of art. If
such materiality of thought was heretofore largely involuntary, pointing to
the dilemma of works which perforce confused themselves with the Idea
they could not achieve, then Beckett confronts this challenge and uses
thoughts *sans phrase* as phrases, as those material components of the *monologue intérieur* which mind itself has become, the reified residue of education. Whereas pre-Beckett existentialism cannibalized philosophy for poetic
purposes as if it were Schiller incarnate, Beckett, as educated as anyone,
presents the bill: philosophy, or spirit itself, proclaims its bankruptcy as
the dreamlike dross of the experiential world, and the poetic process
shows itself as worn out. Disgust (*dégoût*), a productive force in the arts
since Baudelaire, is insatiable in Beckett's historically mediated impulses.
Everything now impossible becomes canonical, freeing a motif from the
prehistory of existentialism— Husserl's universal annihilation of the world—
from the shadowy realm of methodology. Totalitarians like Lukács, who
rage against the—truly terrifying—simplifier as "decadent," are not ill
advised by the interests of their bosses. They hate in Beckett what they
have betrayed. Only the nausea of satiation—the tedium of spirit with
itself—wants something completely different: prescribed "health" nevertheless makes do with the nourishment offered, with simple fare. Beckett's
dégoût cannot be forced to fall in line. He responds to the cheery call to
play along with parody, parody of the philosophy spit out by his dialogues
as well as parody of forms. Existentialism itself is parodied; nothing
remains of its "invariants" other than minimal existence. The drama's
opposition to ontology—as the sketch of a first or immutable principle—is
unmistakable in an exchange of dialogue which unintentionally garbles
Goethe's phrase about "old truths," which has degenerated to an arch-
bourgeois sentiment:

> HAMM: Do you remember your father.
> CLOV: (wearily) Same answer. (Pause.) You've asked me these questions
>   millions of times.
> HAMM: I love the old questions. (With fervor.) Ah the old questions, the
>   old answers, there's nothing like them.

Thoughts are dragged along and distorted like the day's left-overs, *homo homini sapienti sat*. Hence the precariousness of what Beckett refuses to deal with, interpretation. He shrugs his shoulders about the possibility of philosophy today, or theory in general. The irrationality of bourgeois society on the wane resists being understood: those were the good old days when a critique of political economy could be written which took this society by its own *ratio*. For in the meantime it has thrown this *ratio* on the junk-heap and virtually replaced it with direct control. The interpretive word, therefore, cannot recuperate Beckett, while his dramaturgy— precisely by virtue of its limitation to exploded facticity—twitches beyond it, pointing toward interpretation in its essence as riddle. One could almost designate as the criterion of relevant philosophy today whether it is up to that task.

French existentialism had tackled history. In Beckett, history devours existentialism. In *Endgame*, a historical moment is revealed, the experience which was cited in the title of the culture industry's rubbish book *Corpsed*. After the Second War, everything is destroyed, even resurrected culture, without knowing it; humanity vegetates along, crawling, after events which even the survivors cannot really survive, on a pile of ruins which even renders futile self-reflection of one's own battered state. From the marketplace, as the play's pragmatic precondition, that fact is ripped away:

> CLOV: (He gets up on ladder, turns the telescope on the without.) Let's see. (He looks, moving the telescope.) Zero . . . (he looks) . . . zero . . . (he looks) . . . and zero.
> HAMM: Nothing stirs. All is—
> CLOV: Zer—
> HAMM: (violently) Wait till you're spoken to. (Normal voice.) All is . . . all is . . . all is what? (Violently.) All is what?
> CLOV: What all is? In a word. Is that what you want to know? Just a moment. (He turns the telescope on the without, looks, lowers the telescope, turns toward Hamm.) Corpsed. (Pause.) Well? Content?

That all human beings are dead is covertly smuggled in. An earlier passage explains why the catastrophe may not be mentioned. Vaguely, Hamm himself is to blame for that:

> HAMM: That old doctor, he's dead naturally?
> CLOV: He wasn't old.
> HAMM: But he's dead?
> CLOV: Naturally. (Pause.) *You* ask *me* that?

The condition presented in the play is nothing other than that in which "there's no more nature." Indistinguishable is the phase of com-

pleted reification of the world, which leaves no remainder of what was not
made by humans; it is permanent catastrophe, along with a catastrophic
event caused by humans themselves, in which nature has been extinguished and nothing grows any longer.

> HAMM: Did your seeds come up?
> CLOV: No.
> HAMM: Did you scratch round them to see if they had sprouted?
> CLOV: They haven't sprouted.
> HAMM: Perhaps it's still too early.
> CLOV: If they were going to sprout they would have sprouted.
> (Violently.) They'll never sprout!

The *dramatis personae* resemble those who dream their own death, in a
"shelter" where "it's time it ended." The end of the world is discounted,
as if it were a matter of course. Every supposed drama of the atomic age
would mock itself, if only because its fable would hopelessly falsify the
horror of historical anonymity by shoving it into the characters and
actions of humans, and possibly by gaping at the "prominents" who decide
whether the button will be pushed. The violence of the unspeakable is
mimicked by the timidity to mention it. Beckett keeps it nebulous. One
can only speak euphemistically about what is incommensurate with all
experience, just as one speaks in Germany of the murder of the Jews. It
has become a total *a priori*, so that bombed-out consciousness no longer
has any position from which it could reflect on that fact. The desperate
state of things supplies—with gruesome irony—a means of stylization that
protects that pragmatic precondition from any contamination by childish
science fiction. If Clov really were exaggerating, as his nagging, "common-
sensical" companion reproaches him, that would not change much. If
catastrophe amounted to a partial end of the world, that would be a bad
joke: then nature, from which the imprisoned figures are cut off, would be
as good as nonexistent; what remains of it would only prolong the
torment.

This historical *nota bene* however, this parody of the Kierkegaardian
one of the convergence of time and eternity, imposes at the same time a
taboo on history. What would be called the *condition humaine* in existentialist jargon is the image of the last human, which is devouring the earlier
ones—humanity. Existential ontology asserts the universally valid in a
process of abstraction which is not conscious of itself. While it still—
according to the old phenomenological doctrine of the intuition of essence—
behaves as if it were aware, even in the particular, of its binding
determinations, thereby unifying apriority and concreteness, it nonethe-

less distills out what appears to transcend temporality. It does so by
blotting out particularity—what is individualized in space and time, what
makes existence existence rather than its mere concept. Ontology appeals
to those who are weary of philosophical formalism but who yet cling to
what is only accessible formally. To such unacknowledged abstraction,
Beckett affixes the caustic antithesis by means of acknowledged subtraction. He does not leave out the temporality of existence—all existence,
after all, is temporal—but rather removes from existence what time, the
historical tendency, attempts to quash in reality. He lengthens the escape
route of the subject's liquidation to the point where it constricts into a
"this-here," whose abstractness—the loss of all qualities—extends ontological abstraction literally *ad absurdum*, to that Absurd which mere
existence becomes as soon as it is consumed in naked self-identity. Childish foolishness emerges as the content of philosophy, which degenerates to
tautology—to a conceptual duplication of that existence it had intended
to comprehend. While recent ontology subsists on the unfulfilled promise
of concretion of its abstractions, concreteness in Beckett—that shell-like,
self-enclosed existence which is no longer capable of universality but
rather exhausts itself in pure self-positing—is obviously the same as an
abstractness which is no longer capable of experience. Ontology arrives
home as the pathogenesis of false life. It is depicted as the state of
negative eternity. If the messianic Myshkin once forgot his watch because
earthly time is invalid for him, then time is lost to his antipodes because it
could still imply hope. The yawn accompanying the bored remark that the
weather is "as usual" gapes like a hellish abyss:

> HAMM: But that's always the way at the end of the day, isn't it, Clov?
> CLOV: Always.
> HAMM: It's the end of the day like any other day, isn't it, Clov?
> CLOV: Looks like it.

Like time, the temporal itself is damaged; saying that it no longer exists
would already be too comforting. It is and it is not, like the world for the
solipsist who doubts its existence, while he must concede it with every
sentence. Thus a passage of dialogue hovers:

> HAMM: And the horizon? Nothing on the horizon?
> CLOV (lowering the telescope, turning towards Hamm, exasperated):
>   What in God's name would there be on the horizon? (Pause.)
> HAMM: The waves, how are the waves?
> CLOV: The waves? (He turns the telescope on the waves.) Lead.
> HAMM: And the sun?
> CLOV: (looking) Zero.
> HAMM: But it should be sinking. Look again.

CLOV: (looking) Damn the sun.
HAMM: Is it night already then?
CLOV: (looking) No.
HAMM: Then what is it?
CLOV: (looking) Gray. (Lowering the telescope, turning towards Hamm, louder.) Gray! (Pause. Still louder.) GRRAY!

History is excluded, because it itself has dehydrated the power of consciousness to think history, the power of remembrance. Drama falls silent and becomes gesture, frozen amid the dialogues. Only the result of history appears—as decline. What preens itself in the existentialists as the once-and-for-all of being has withered to the sharp point of history which breaks off. Lukács' objection, that in Beckett humans are reduced to animality, resists with official optimism the fact that residual philosophies, which would like to bank the true and immutable after removing temporal contingency, have become the residue of life, the end product of injury. Admittedly, as nonsensical as it is to attribute to Beckett—as Lukács does—an abstract, subjectivist ontology and then to place it on the excavated index of degenerate art because of its worldlessness and infantility, it would be equally ridiculous to have him testify as a key political witness. For urging the struggle against atomic death, a work that notes that death's potential even in ancient struggles is hardly appropriate. The simplifier of terror refuses—unlike Brecht—any simplification. But he is not so dissimilar from Brecht, insofar as his differentiation becomes sensitivity to subjective differences, which have regressed to the "conspicuous consumption" of those who can afford individuation.

Therein lies social truth. Differentiation cannot absolutely or automatically be recorded as positive. The simplification of the social process now beginning relegates it to "incidental expenses" (faux frais), somewhat as the formalities of social forms, from which emerged the capability for differentiation, are disappearing. Differentiation, once the condition of humanity, glides into ideology. But the non-sentimental consciousness of that fact does not regress itself. In the act of omission, that which is omitted survives through its exclusion, as consonance survives in atonal harmony. The idiocy of Endgame is recorded and developed with the greatest differentiation. The unprotesting depiction of omnipresent regression protests against a disposition of the world which obeys the law of regression so obligingly, that a counter-notion can no longer be conceived to be held against it. That it is only thus and not otherwise is carefully shown; a finely-tuned alarm system reports what belongs to the topology of the play and what does not. Delicately, Beckett suppresses the delicate elements no less than the brutal ones. The vanity of the individual who indicts society, while his rights themselves merge in the accumulation of the injustice of all individuals—disaster itself—is manifest in embarrassing declamations like the "Germany" poem of Karl Wolfskehl. The "too-late," the missed moment condemns such bombastic rhetoric to phraseology. Nothing of that sort in Beckett. Even the view that he negatively presents the negativity of the age would fit into a certain kind of conception, according to which people in the eastern satellite countries—where the revolution is carried out by bureaucratic decree—need only devote themselves happily to reflecting a happy-go-lucky age. Playing with elements of reality—devoid of any mirror-like reflection—, refusing to take a "position," and finding joy in such freedom as is prescribed: all of this reveals more than would be possible if a "revealer" were partisan. The name of disaster can only be spoken silently. Only in the terror of recent events is the terror of the whole ignited, but only there, not in gazing upon "origins." Humankind, whose general species-name fits badly into Beckett's linguistic landscape, is only that which humanity has become. As in utopia, the last days pass judgment on the species. But this lamentation— within mind itself—must reflect that lamenting has become impossible. No amount of weeping melts the armor; only that face remains on which the tears have dried up. That is the basis of a kind of artistic behavior denounced as inhuman by those whose humanity has already become an advertisement for inhumanity, even if they have as yet no notion of that fact. Among the motives for Beckett's regression to animal-like man, that is probably the deepest. By hiding its countenance, his poetic work participates in the absurd.

The catastrophies that inspire *Endgame* have exploded the individual whose substantiality and absoluteness were the common elements between Kierkegaard, Jaspers, and the Sartrian version of existentialism. Even to the concentration camp victims, existentialism had attributed the freedom either inwardly to accept or reject the inflicted martyrdom. *Endgame* destroys such illusions. The individual as a historical category, as the result of the capitalist process of alienation and as a defiant protest against it, has itself become openly transitory. The individualist position belonged, as polar opposite, to the ontological tendency of every existentialism, even that of *Being and Time*. Beckett's dramaturgy abandons it like an obsolete bunker. In its narrowness and contingency, individual experience could nowhere locate the authority to interpret itself as a cipher of being, unless it pronounced itself the fundamental characteristic of being. Precisely that, however, is untrue. The immediacy of individuation was deceptive: what particular human experience clings to is mediated, determined. *Endgame* insinuates that the individual's claim of autonomy and of being has become incredible. But while the prison of individuation is revealed as a prison and simultaneously as mere semblance—the stage scenery is the image of such self-reflection—art is unable to release the spell of fragmented subjectivity; it can only depict solipsism. Beckett thereby bumps up against art's contemporary antinomy. The position of the absolute subject, once it has been cracked open as the appearance of an overarching whole through which it first matures, cannot be maintained: Expressionism becomes obsolete. Yet the transition to the binding universality of objective reality, that universality which could relativize the semblance of individuation, is denied art. For art is different from the discursive cognition of the real, not gradually but categorically distinct from it; in art, only what is transported into the realm of subjectivity, commensurable to it, is valid. It can conceive reconciliation—its idea— only as reconciliation of that which is alienated. If art simulated the state of reconciliation by surrendering to the mere world of things, then it would negate itself. What is offered in the way of socialist realism is not—as some claim—beyond subjectivism but rather lags behind it and is at the same time its pre-artistic complement; the expressionist "Oh Man" and ideologically spiced social reportage fit together seamlessly. In art, unreconciled reality tolerates no reconciliation with the object; realism, which does not reach the level of subjective experience, to say nothing of reaching further, merely mimics reconciliation. The dignity of art today is not measured by asking whether it slips out of this antinomy by luck or cleverness, but whether art confronts and develops it. In that regard, *Endgame* is exemplary. It yields both to the impossibility of dealing with materials and of representation according to nineteenth-century practice, as well as to the insight that subjective modes of reaction, which mediate the laws of form rather than reflecting reality, are themselves no absolute first principle but rather a last principle, objectively posited. All content of subjectivity, which necessarily hypostatizes itself, is trace and shadow of the world, from which it withdraws in order not to serve that semblance and conformity the world demands. Beckett responds to that condition not with any immutable "provisions" (*Vorrat*), but rather with what is still permitted, precariously and uncertainly, by the antagonistic tendencies. His dramaturgy resembles the fun that the old Germany offered—knocking about between the border markers of Baden and Bavaria, as if they fenced in a realm of freedom. *Endgame* takes place in a zone of indifference between inner and outer, neutral between—on the one hand—the "materials" without which subjectivity could not manifest itself or even exist, and—on the other—an animating impulse which blurs the materials, as if that impulse had breathed on the glass through which they are viewed. These materials are so meager that aesthetic formalism is ironically rescued— against its adversaries hither and thither, the stuff-pushers of dialectical materialism and the administrators of authentic messages. The concrete- ness of the lemurs, whose horizon was lost in a double sense, is trans- formed directly into the most extreme abstraction; the level of material itself determines a procedure in which the materials, by being lightly touched as transitory, approximate geometrical forms; the most narrow becomes the general. The localization of *Endgame* in that zone teases the spectator with the suggestion of a symbolism which it—like Kafka—refuses. Because no state of affairs is merely what it is, each appears as the sign of interiority, but that inward element supposedly signified no longer exists, and the signs mean just that. The iron ration of reality and people, with whom the drama reckons and keeps house, is one with that which remains of subject, mind (*Geist*), and soul in the face of permanent catastrophe: of the mind, which originated in mimesis, only ridiculous imitation; of the soul—staging itself—inhumane sentimentality; of the subject its most abstract determination, actually existing and thereby already blaspheming. Beckett's figures behave primitively and behavioristically, corresponding to conditions after the catastrophe, which has mutilated them to such an extent that they cannot react differently—flies that twitch after the swatter has half smashed them. The aesthetic *principium stilisationis* does the same to humans. Thrown back completely upon themselves, subjects— anti-cosmism become flesh—consist in nothing other than the wretched realities of their world, shrivelled down to raw necessities; they are empty *personae*, through which the world truly can only resound. Their "phonyness" is the result of mind's disenchantment—as mythology. In order to under- cut history and perhaps thereby to hibernate, *Endgame* occupies the nadir of what philosophy's construction of the subject-object confiscated at its zenith: pure identity becomes the identity of annihilation, identity of subject and object in the state of complete alienation. While meanings in Kafka were beheaded or confused, Beckett calls a halt to the bad infinity of intentions: their sense is senselessness. Objectively and without any polemical intent, that is his answer to existential philosophy, which under the name of "thrownness" and later of "absurdity" transforms senselessness itself into sense, exploiting the equivocations inherent in the concept of sense. To this Beckett juxtaposes no world view, rather he takes it at its word. What becomes of the absurd, after the characters of the meaning of existence have been torn down, is no longer a universal—the absurd would then be yet again an idea—but only pathetic details which ridicule conceptuality, a stratum of utensils as in an emergency refuge: ice boxes, lameness, blindness, and unappetizing bodily functions. Everything awaits evacuation. This stratum is not symbolic but rather the post-psychological state, as in old people and torture victims.

Removed from their inwardness, Heidegger's states of being (Befindlichkeiten) and Jaspers' "situations" have become materialistic. With them, the hypostasis of individual and that of situation were in harmony. The "situation" was temporal existence itself, and the totality of living individuals was the primary certainty. It presupposed personal identity. Here, Beckett proves to be a pupil of Proust and a friend of Joyce, in that he gives back to the concept of "situation" what it actually says and what philosophy made vanish by exploiting it: dissociation of the unity of consciousness into disparate elements—non-identity. As soon as the subject is no longer doubtlessly self-identical, no longer a closed structure of meaning, the line of demarcation with the exterior becomes blurred, and the situations of inwardness become at the same time physical ones. The tribunal over individuality—conserved by existentialism as its idealist core—condemns idealism. Non-identity is both: the historical disintegration of the subject's unity and the emergence of what is not itself subject. That changes the possible meaning of "situation." It is defined by Jaspers as "a reality for an existing subject who has a stake in it." He subsumes the concept of situation under a subject conceived as firm and identical, just as he insinuates that meaning accrues to the situation because of its relationship to this subject. Immediately thereafter, he also calls it "not just a reality governed by natural laws. It is a sense-related reality," a reality moreover which, strangely enough, is said by Jaspers to be "neither psychological nor physical, but both in one." When situation becomes—in Beckett's view—actually both, it loses its existential-ontological constituents: personal identity and meaning. That becomes striking in the concept of "boundary situation" (Grenzsituation). It also stems from Jaspers: "Situations like the following: that I am always in situations; that I cannot live without struggling and suffering; that I cannot avoid guilt; that I must die—these are what I call boundary situations. They never change, except in appearance; with regard to our existence, they are final." The construction of Endgame takes that up with a sardonic "Pardon me?" Such wise sayings as that "I cannot live without suffering, that I cannot avoid guilt, that I must die" lose their triviality the moment they are retrieved back from their apriority and portrayed concretely. Then they break to pieces—all those noble, affirmative elements with which philosophy adorns that existence that Hegel already called "foul" (faul). It does so by subsuming the non-conceptual under a concept, which magically disperses that difference pompously characterized as "ontological." Beckett turns existential philosophy from its head back on its feet. His play reacts to the comical and ideological mischief of sentences like: "Courage in the boundary situation is an attitude that lets me view death as an indefinite opportunity to be myself," whether Beckett is familiar with them or not. The misery of participants in the *Endgame* is the misery of philosophy.

These Beckettian situations which constitute his drama are the negative of meaningful reality. Their models are those of empirical reality. As soon as they are isolated and divested of their purposeful and psychological context through the loss of personal unity, they assume a specific and compelling expression—that of horror. They are manifest already in the practice of Expressionism. The dread disseminated by Leonhard Frank's elementary school teacher Mager, the cause of his murder, becomes evident in the description of Mager's fussy manner of peeling an apple in class. Although it seems so innocent, such circumspection is the figure of sadism: this image of one who takes his time resembles that of the one who delays giving a ghastly punishment. Beckett's treatment of these situations, that panicky and yet artificial derivation of simplistic slapstick comedy of yesteryear, articulates a content noted already in Proust. In his posthumous work *Immediacy and Sense-Interpretation*, Heinrich Rickert considers the possibility of an objective physiognomy of mind, rather than of a merely projected "soul" of a landscape or a work of art. He cites a passage from Ernst Robert Curtius, who considers it "only partially correct to view Proust only or primarily as a great psychologist. A Stendhal is appropriately characterized in this manner. He is indeed part of the Cartesian tradition of the French mind. But Proust does not recognize the division between thinking and the extended substance. He does not sever the world into psychological and physical parts. To regard his work from the perspective of the 'psychological novel' is to misunderstand its significance. In Proust's books, the world of sensate objects occupies the same space as that of mind." Or: "If Proust is a psychologist, he is one in a completely new sense—by immersing all reality, including sense perception, in a mental fluid." To show "that the casual concept of the psychic is not appropriate here," Rickert again quotes Curtius: "But here the concept of the psychological has lost its opposite—and is thereby no longer a useful characterization." The physiognomy of objective expression however retains an enigma. The situations say something, but what? In this regard, art itself, as the embodiment of situations, converges with that physiognomy. It combines the most extreme determinacy with its radical opposite. In Beckett, this contradiction is inverted outward. What is otherwise entrenched behind a communicative facade is here condemned merely to appear. Proust, in a subterranean mystical tradition, still clings affirmatively to that physiognomy, as if involuntary memory disclosed a secret language of things; in Beckett, it becomes the physiognomy of what is no longer human. His situations are counterparts to the immutable elements conjured by Proust's situations; they are wrested from the flood of schizophrenia, which fearful "health" resists with murderous cries. In this realm Beckett's drama remains master of itself, transforming even schizophrenia into reflection:

> HAMM: I once knew a madman who thought the end of the world had come. He was a painter—and engraver. I had a great fondness for him. I used to go and see him, in the asylum. I'd take him by the hand and drag him to the window. Look! There! All that rising corn! And there! Look! The sails of the herring fleet! All that loveliness! (Pause.) He'd snatch away his hand and go back into his corner. Appalled. All he had seen was ashes. (Pause.) He alone had been spared. (Pause.) Forgotten. (Pause.) It appears the case is . . . was not so . . . so unusual.

The madman's perception would approximate that of Clov peering on command through the window. *Endgame* draws back from the nadir through no other means than by calling to itself like a sleepwalker: negation of negativity. There sticks in Beckett's memory something like an apoplectic middle-aged man taking his midday nap, with a cloth over his eyes to keep out the light or the flies; it makes him unrecognizable. This image—average and optically barely unusual—becomes a sign only for that gaze which perceives the face's loss of identity, sees the possibility that being concealed is the face of a dead man, and becomes aware of the repulsive nature of that physical concern which reduces the man to his body and places him already among corpses. Beckett stares at such aspects until that family routine—from which they stem—pales into irrelevance. The tableau begins with Hamm covered by an old sheet; at the end, he places near his face the handkerchief, his last possession:

> HAMM: Old Stancher! (Pause.) You . . . remain.

Such situations, emancipated from their context and from personal character, are reconstructed in a second autonomous context, just as music joins together the intentions and states of expression immersed in it until its sequence becomes a structure in its own right. A key point in the drama—"If I can hold my peace, and sit quiet, it will be all over with sound, and motion, all over and done with"—betrays the principle, perhaps as a reminiscence of how Shakespeare employed his principle in the actors' scene of *Hamlet*.

HAMM: Then babble, babble, words, like the solitary child who turns himself into children, two, three, so as to be together, and whisper together, in the dark. (Pause.) Moment upon moment, pattering down, like the millet grains of . . . (he hesitates) that old Greek, and all life long you wait for that to mount up to a life.

In the tremors of "not being in a hurry," such situations allude to the indifference and superfluity of what the subject can still manage to do. While Hamm considers riveting shut the lids of those trashcans where his parents reside, he retracts that decision with the same words as when he must urinate with the tortuous aid of the catheter: "Time enough." The imperceptible aversion to medicine bottles, dating back to the moment one perceived one's parents as physically vulnerable, mortal, deteriorating, reappears in the question:

HAMM: Is it not time for my pain-killer?

Speaking to each other has completely become Strindbergian grumbling:

HAMM: You feel normal?
CLOV: (irritably) I tell you I don't complain.

And another time:

HAMM: I feel a little too far to the left. (Clov moves chair slightly.) Now I feel a little too far to the right. (Clov moves chair slightly.) Now I feel a little too far forward. (Clov moves chair slightly.) Now I feel a little too far back. (Clov moves chair slightly.) Don't stay there, (i.e. behind the chair) you give me the shivers. (Clov returns to his place beside the chair.)
CLOV: If I could kill him I'd die happy.

The waning of a marriage is the situation where one scratches the other:

NELL: I am going to leave you.
NAGG: Could you give me a scratch before you go?
NELL: No. (Pause.) Where?
NAGG: In the back.
NELL: No. (Pause.) Rub yourself against the rim.
NAGG: It's lower down. In the hollow.
NELL: What hollow?
NAGG: The hollow! (Pause.) Could you not? (Pause.) Yesterday you scratched me there.
NELL: (elegiac) Ah yesterday!
NAGG: Could you not? (Pause.) Would you like me to scratch you? (Pause.) Are you crying again?
NELL: I was trying.

After the dismissed father—preceptor of his parents—has told the Jewish joke, metaphysically famous, about the trousers and the world, he himself bursts into laughter. The shame which grips the listener when someone laughs at his own words becomes existential; life is merely the epitome of everything about which one must be ashamed. Subjectivity is frightening when it simply amounts to domination, as in the situation where one whistles and the other comes running. But what shame struggles against has its social function: in those moments when the bourgeois (*Bürger*) acts like a real bourgeois, he besmirches the concept of humanity on which his claim rests. Beckett's archaic images (*Urbilder*) are also historical, in that he shows as humanly typical only those deformations inflicted on humans by the form of their society. No space remains for anything else. The rudeness and ticks of normal character, which *Endgame* inconceivably intensifies, is that universality of the whole that already preforms all classes and individuals; it merely reproduces itself through bad particularity, the antagonistic interests of single individuals. Because there was no other life than the false one, the catalogue of its defects becomes the mirror image of ontology.

This shattering into unconnected, non-identical elements is nevertheless tied to identity in a theater play, which does not abandon the traditional cast of characters. Only against identity, by dismantling its concept, is dissociation at all possible; otherwise, it would be pure, unpolemical, innocent pluralism. For the time being, the historical crisis of the individual runs up against the single biological being, its arena. The succession of situations in Beckett, gliding along without resistance from individuals, thus ends with those obstate bodies to which they have regressed. Measured by a unit, such as the body, the schizoid situations are comical like optical illusions. That explains the *prima vista* clowning evident in the behavior and constellations of Beckett's figures. Psychoanalysis explains clownish humor as a regression back to a primordial ontogenetic level, and Beckett's regressive play descends to that level. But the laughter it inspires ought to suffocate the laughter. That is what happened to humor, after it became—as an aesthetic medium—obsolete, repulsive, devoid of any canon of what can be laughed at; without any place for reconciliation, where one could laugh; without anything between heaven and earth harmless enough to be laughed at. An intentionally idiotic *double entendre* about the weather runs:

> CLOV: Things are livening up. (He gets up on ladder, raises the telescope, lets it fall.) It did it on purpose. (He gets down, picks up the telescope, turns it on auditorium.) I see . . . a multitude . . . in

> transports . . . of joy. (Pause.) That's what I call a magnifier. (He
> lowers the telescope, turns toward Hamm.) Well? Don't we laugh?

Humor itself has become foolish, ridiculous—who could still laugh
at basic comic texts like *Don Quixote* or *Gargantua*—and Beckett carries
out the verdict on humor. The jokes of the damaged people are themselves damaged. They no longer reach anybody; the state of decline,
admittedly a part of all jokes, the *Kalauer*, now covers them like a rash.
When Clov, looking through the telescope, is asked about the weather
and frightens Hamm with the word "gray," he corrects himself with the
formulation "a light black." That smears the punchline from Molière's
Miser, who describes the allegedly stolen casket as gray-red. The marrow
has been sucked out of the joke as well as out of the colors. At one point,
the two anti-heroes, a blind man and a lame man—the stronger is already
both while the weaker will become so—come up with a "trick," an
escape, "some kind of plan" à la *Three Penny Opera*; but they do not know
whether it will only lengthen their lives and torment, or whether both are
to end with absolute obliteration:

> CLOV: Ah good. (He starts pacing to and fro, his eyes fixed on the ground,
>   his hands behind his back. He halts.) The pains in my legs! It's
>   unbelievable! Soon I won't be able to think any more.
> HAMM: You won't be able to leave me. (Clov resumes his pacing.) What
>   are you doing?
> CLOV: Having an idea. (He paces.) Ah. (He halts.)
> HAMM: What a brain! (Pause.) Well?
> CLOV: Wait! (He meditates. Not very convinced.) Yes . . . (Pause.
>   More convinced.) Yes! (He raises his head.) I have it! I set the
>   alarm!

That is probably associated with the originally Jewish joke from the Busch
circus, when stupid August, who has caught his wife with his friend on
the sofa, cannot decide whether to throw out his wife or the friend,
because they are both so dear to him, and comes up with the idea of
selling the sofa. But even the remaining trace of silly, sophistic rationality
is wiped away. The only comical thing remaining is that along with the sense
of the punchline, comedy itself has evaporated. That is how someone suddenly
jerks upright after climbing to the top step, climbing further, and stepping
into the void. The most extreme crudity completes the verdict on laughter, which has long since participated in its own guilt. Hamm lets his
stumps of parents completely starve, those parents who have become
babies in their trashcans—the son's triumph as a father. There is this
chatter:

NAGG: Me pap!

HAMM: Accursed progenitor!

NAGG: Me pap!

HAMM: The old folks at home! No decency left! Guzzle, guzzle, that's all they think of. (He whistles. Enter Clov. He halts beside the chair.) Well! I thought you were leaving me.

CLOV: Oh not just yet, not just yet.

NAGG: Me pap!

HAMM: Give him his pap.

CLOV: There's no more pap.

HAMM: (to Nagg) Do you hear that? There's no more pap. You'll never get any more pap.

To the irreparable harm already done, the anti-hero adds his scorn—the indignation at the old people who have no manners, just as the latter customarily decry dissolute youth. What remains humane in this scene— that the two old people share the zwieback with each other—becomes repulsive through its contrast with transcendental bestiality; the residue of love becomes the intimacy of smacking. As far as they are still human, they "humanize":

NELL: What is it, my pet? (Pause.) Time for love?

NAGG: Were you asleep?

NELL: Oh no!

NAGG: Kiss me.

NELL: We can't.

NAGG: Try. (Their heads strain towards each other, fail to meet, fall apart again.)

Dramatic categories as a whole are treated just like humor. All are parodied. But not ridiculed. Emphatically, parody entails the use of forms in the epoch of their impossibility. It demonstrates this impossibility and thereby changes the forms. The three Aristotelian unities are retained, but drama itself perishes. Along with subjectivity, whose final epilogue (Nachspiel) is Endgame, the hero is also withdrawn; the drama's freedom is only the impotent, pathetic reflex of futile resolutions. In that regard, too, Beckett's drama is heir to Kafka's novels, to whom he stands in a similar relation as the serial composers to Schönberg: he reflects the precursor in himself, altering the latter through the totality of his principle. Beckett's critique of the earlier writer, which irrefutably stresses the divergence between what happens and the objectively pure, epic language, conceals the same difficulty as that confronted by contemporary integral composition with the antagonistic procedure of Schönberg. What is the raison d'être of forms when the tension between them and what is not homogeneous to them disappears, and when one nevertheless cannot halt the progress of mastery over aesthetic material? *Endgame* pulls out of the fray, by making that question its own, by making it thematic. That which prohibits the dramatization of Kafka's novels becomes subject matter. Dramatic components reappear after their demise. Exposition, complication, plot, peripeteia, and catastrophe return as decomposed elements in a post-mortem examination of dramaturgy: the news that there are no more pain-killers depicts catastrophe. Those components have been toppled along with that meaning once discharged by drama; *Endgame* studies (as if in a test-tube) the drama of the age, the age that no longer tolerates what constitutes drama. For example, tragedy, at the height of its plot and with antithesis as its quintessence, manifested the utmost tightening of the dramatic thread, stychomythia—dialogues in which the trimeter spoken by one person follows that of the other. Drama had renounced this technique, because its stylization and resulting pretentiousness seemed alien to secular society. Beckett employs it as if the detonation had revealed what was buried in drama. *Endgame* contains rapid, monosyllabic dialogues, like the earlier question-and-answer games between the blinded king and fate's messenger. But where the bind tightened then, the speakers now grow slack. Short of breath until they almost fall silent, they no longer manage the synthesis of linguistic phrases; they stammer in protocol sentences that might stem from positivists or Expressionists. The boundary value (*Grenzwert*) of Beckett's drama is that silence already defined as "the rest" in Shakespeare's inauguration of modern tragedy. The fact that an "act without words" follows *Endgame* as a kind of epilogue is its own *terminus ad quem*. The words resound like merely makeshift ones because silence is not yet entirely successful, like voices accompanying and disturbing it.

What becomes of form in *Endgame* can be virtually reconstructed from literary history. In Ibsen's *The Wild Duck*, the degenerate photographer Hjalmar Ekdal—himself a potential anti-hero—forgets to bring to the teenager Hedwig the promised menu from the sumptuous dinner at old Werle's house, to which he had been invited without his family. Psychologically, that is motivated by his slovenly egotistical character, but it is symbolically significant also for Hjalmar, for the course of the plot, and for the play's meaning: the girl's futile sacrifice. That anticipates the later Freudian theory of "parapraxis," which explicates such slip-ups by means of their relation to past experiences and wishes of an individual, to the individual's identity. Freud's hypothesis, "all our experiences have a sense," transforms the traditional dramatic idea into psychological realism, from which Ibsen's tragi-comedy of the *The Wild Duck* incomparably extracts the spark of form one more time. When such symbolism liberates itself from its psychological determination, it congeals into a being-in-itself, and the symbol becomes symbolic as in Ibsen's late works like *John Gabriel Borkmann*, where the accountant Foldal is overcome by so-called "youth." The contradiction between such a consistent symbolism and conservative realism constitutes the inadequacy of the late plays. But it thereby also constitutes the leavening ferment of the Expressionist Strindberg. His symbols, torn away from empirical human beings, are woven into a tapestry in which everything and nothing is symbolic, because everything can signify everything. Drama need only become aware of the ineluctably ridiculous nature of such pan-symbolism, which destroys itself; it need only take that up and utilize it, and Beckettian absurdity is already achieved as a result of the immanent dialectic of form. Not meaning anything becomes the only meaning. The mortal fear of the dramatic figures, if not of the parodied drama itself, is the distortedly comical fear that they could mean something or other:

> HAMM: We're not beginning to . . . to . . . mean something?
> CLOV: Mean something! You and I, mean something! (Brief laugh.) Ah
> that's a good one!

With this possibility, long since crushed by the overwhelming power of an apparatus in which individuals are interchangeable and superfluous, the meaning of language also disappears. Hamm, irritated by the impulse of life which has regressed to clumsiness in his parents' trashcan conversations, and nervous because "it doesn't end," asks: "Will you never finish? Will this never finish?" The play takes place on that level. It is constructed on the ground of a proscription of language, and it articulates that in its own structure. However, it does not thereby avoid the aporia of Expressionist drama: that language, even where it tends to be shortened to mere sound, yet cannot shake off its semantic element. It cannot become purely mimetic or gestural, just as forms of modern painting, liberated from referentiality (*Gegenständlichkeit*), cannot cast off all similarity to objects. Mimetic values, definitively unloosed from significative ones, then approach arbitrariness, contingency, and finally a mere secondary convention. The way *Endgame* comes to terms with that differentiates it from *Finnegans Wake*. Rather than striving to liquidate the discursive element of language through pure sound, Beckett turns that element into an instrument of its own absurdity and he does that according to the ritual of clowns, whose babbling becomes nonsensical by presenting itself as sense. The objective disintegration of language—that simultaneously stereotyped and faulty chatter of self-alienation, where word and sentence melt together in human mouths—penetrates the aesthetic arcanum. The second language of those falling silent, a conglomeration of insolent phrases, pseudo-logical connections, and galvanized words appearing as commodity signs—as the desolate echo of the advertising world—is "refunctioned" (umfunktioniert) into the language of a poetic work that negates language. Beckett thus approximates the drama of Eugène Ionesco. Whereas a later work by him is organized around the image of the tape recorder, the language of Endgame resembles another language familiar from the loathsome party game, where someone records the nonsense spoken at a party and then plays it back for the guests' humiliation. The shock, overcome on such an occasion only by stupid tittering, is here carefully composed. Just as alert experience seems to notice everywhere situations from Kafka's novels after reading him intensely, so does Beckett's language bring about a healing illness of those already ill: whoever listens to himself worries that he also talks like that. For some time now, the accidental events on the street seem to the movie-goer just leaving the theater like the planned contingency of a film. Between the mechanically assembled phrases taken from the language of daily life, the chasm yawns. Where one of the pair asks with the routine gesture of the hardened man, certain of the uncontestable boredom of existence, "What in God's name could there be on the horizon?" then this shoulder-shrugging in language becomes apocalyptic, particularly because it is so familiar. From the bland yet aggressive impulse of human "common sense," "What do you think there is?" is extracted the confession of its own nihilism. Somewhat later, Hamm the master commands the soi-disant servant Clov, in a circus-task, to undertake the vain attempt to shove the chair back and forth, to fetch the "gaff." There follows a brief dialogue:

CLOV: Do this, do that, and I do it. I never refuse. Why?
HAMM: You're not able to.
CLOV: Soon I won't do it any more.
HAMM: You won't be able to any more. (Exit Clov.) Ah the creatures, everything has to be explained to them.

That "everything has to be explained to the creatures" is drummed daily by millions of superiors into millions of subordinates. However, by means of the nonsense thus supposedly established in the passage—Hamm's explanation contradicts his own command—the cliché's inanity, usually hidden by custom, is garishly illuminated, and furthermore, the fraud of speaking with each other is expressed. When conversing, people remain hopelessly distant from each other no more reaching each other than the two old cripples in the trash bins do. Communication, the universal law of clichés, proclaims that there is no more communication. The absurdity of all speaking is not unrelated to realism but rather develops from it. For communicative language postulates—already in its syntactic form, through logic, the nature of conclusions, and stable concepts—the principle of sufficient reason. Yet this requirement is hardly met any more: when people speak with each other, they are motivated partly by their psychology or pre-logical unconscious, and partly by their pursuit of purposes. Since they aim at self-preservation, these purposes deviate from that objectivity deceptively manifest in their logical form. At any rate, one can prove that point to people today with the help of tape recorders. In Freud's as in Pareto's understanding, the *ratio* of verbal communication is always also a rationalization. *Ratio* itself emerged from the interest in self-preservation, and it is therefore undermined by the obligatory rationalizations of its own irrationality. The contradiction between the rational facade and the immutably irrational is itself already the absurd. Beckett must only mark the contradiction and employ it as a selective principle, and realism, casting off the illusion of rational stringency, comes into its own.

Even the syntactic form of question and answer is undermined. It presupposes an openness of what is to be spoken, an openness which no longer exists, as Huxley already noted. In the question one hears already the anticipated answer, and that condemns the game of question and answer to empty deception, to the unworkable effort to conceal the unfreedom of informative language in the linguistic gesture of freedom. Beckett tears away this veil, and the philosophical veil as well. Everything radically called into question when confronted by nothingness resists—by virtue of a pathos borrowed from theology—these terrifying consequences, while insisting on their possibility; in the form of question and answer, the answer is infiltrated with the meaning denied by the whole game. It is not for nothing that in fascism and pre-fascism such destructionists were able heartily to scorn destructive intellect. But Beckett deciphers the lie of the question mark: the question has become rhetorical. While the existential-philosophical hell resembles a tunnel, where in the middle one can already discern light shining at the end, Beckett's dialogues rip up the railroad tracks of conversation; the train no longer arrives at the bright end of the tunnel. Wedekind's old technique of misunderstanding becomes total. The course of the dialogues themselves approximates the contingency principle of literary production. It sounds as if the laws of its continuation were not the "reason" of speech and reply, and not even their psychological entwinement, but rather a test of listening, related to that of a music which frees itself from preformed types. The drama attends carefully to what kind of sentence might follow another. Given the accessible spontaneity of such questions, the absurdity of content is all the more strongly felt. That, too, finds its infantile model in those people who, when visiting the zoo, wait attentively for the next move of the hippopotamus or the chimpanzee.

In the state of its disintegration, language is polarized. On the one hand, it becomes Basic English, or French, or German—single words, archaically ejected commands in the jargon of universal disregard, the intimacy of irreconcilable adversaries; on the other hand, it becomes the aggregate of its empty forms, of a grammar that has renounced all reference to its content and therefore also to its synthetic function. The interjections are accompanied by exercise sentences, God knows why. Beckett trumpets this from the rooftops, too: one of the rules of the *Endgame* is that the unsocial partners—and with them the audience—are always eyeing each other's cards. Hamm considers himself an artist. He has chosen as his life maxim Nero's *qualis artifex pereo*. But the stories he undertakes run aground on syntax:

> HAMM: Where was I? (Pause. Gloomily.) It's finished, we're finished. (Pause.) Nearly finished.

Logic reels between the linguistic paradigms. Hamm and Clov converse in their authoritative, mutually cutting fashion:

> HAMM: Open the window.
> CLOV: What for?
> HAMM: I want to hear the sea.
> CLOV: You wouldn't hear it.
> HAMM: Even if you opened the window?
> CLOV: No.
> HAMM: Then it's not worthwhile opening it?
> CLOV: No.
> HAMM: (violently) Then open it! (Clov gets up on the ladder, opens the window. Pause.) Have you opened it?
> CLOV: Yes.

One could almost see in Hamm's last "then" the key to the play. Because it is not worthwhile to open the window, since Hamm cannot hear the sea—perhaps it is dried out, perhaps it no longer moves—, he insists that Clov open it. The nonsense of an act becomes a reason to accomplish it—a late legitimation of Fichte's free activity for its own sake. That is how contemporary actions look, and they arouse the suspicion that things were never very different. The logical figure of the absurd, which makes the claim of stringency for stringency's contradictory opposite, denies every context of meaning apparently guaranteed by logic, in order to prove logic's own absurdity: that logic, by means of subject, predicate, and copula, treats non-identity as if it were identical, as if it were consumed in its forms. The absurd does not take the place of the rational as one world view of another; in the absurd, the rational world view comes into its own.

The pre-established harmony of despair reigns between the forms and the residual content of the play. The ensemble—smelted together—counts only four heads. Two of them are excessively red, as if their vitality were a skin disease; the two old ones, however, are excessively white, like sprouting potatoes in a cellar. None of them still has a properly functioning body; the old people consist only of rumps, having apparently lost their legs not in the catastrophe but in a private tandem accident in the Ardennes, "on the road to Sedan," an area where one army regularly annihilates another. One should not suppose that all that much has changed. Even the memory of their own particular (*bestimmt*) misfortune becomes enviable in relation to the indeterminacy (*Unbestimmtheit*) of universal misfortune—they laugh at it. In contrast to Expressionism's fathers and sons, they all have their own names, but all four names have one syllable, "four-letter words" like obscenities. Practical, familiar abbreviations, popular in Anglo-Saxon countries, are exposed as mere stumps of names. Only the name of the old mother, Nell, is somewhat common even if obsolete; Dickens uses it for the touching child in *Old Curiosity Shop*. The three other names are invented as if for bill-boards. The old man is named Nagg, with the association of "nagging" and perhaps also a German association: an intimate pair is intimate through "gnawing" (*Nagen*). They talk about whether the sawdust in their cans has been changed; yet it is not sawdust but sand. Nagg stipulates that it used to be sawdust, and Nell answers boredly: "Once!"—a woman who spitefully exposes her husband's frozen, repetitive declarations. As sordid as the fight about sawdust or sand is, the difference is decisive for the residual plot, the transition from a minimum to nothing. Beckett can claim for himself what Benjamin praised in Baudelaire, the ability to "express something extreme with extreme discretion;" the routine consolation that things could be worse becomes a condemnation. In the realm between life and death, where even pain is no longer possible, the difference between sawdust and sand means everything. Sawdust, wretched by-product of the world of things, is now in great demand; its removal becomes an intensification of the life-long death penalty. The fact that both lodge in trash bins—a comparable motif appears, moreover, in Tennessee Williams' *Camino Real*, surely without one play having been influenced by the other—takes the conversational phrase literally, as in Kafka. "Today old people are thrown in the trashcan" and it happens. *Endgame* is the true gerontology. According to the measure of socially useful labor, which they can no longer perform, old people are superfluous and must be discarded. That is extracted from the scientific ruckus of a welfare system that accentuates what it negates. *Endgame* trains the viewer for a condition where everyone involved expects—upon lifting the lid from the nearest dumpster—to find his own parents. The natural cohesion of life has become organic refuse. The national socialists irreparably overturned the taboo of old age. Beckett's trashcans are the emblem of a culture restored after Auschwitz. Yet the sub-plot goes further than too far, to the old people's demise. They are denied children's fare, their pap, which is replaced by a biscuit they—toothless—can no longer chew; and they suffocate, because the last man is too sensitive to grant life to the next-to-last ones. That is entwined with the main plot, because the old pair's miserable end drives it forward to that exit of life whose possibility constitutes the tension in the play. Hamlet is revised: croak or croak, that is the question.

The name of Shakespeare's hero is grimly foreshortened by Beckett—the last, liquidated dramatic subject echoing the first. It is also associated with one of Noah's sons and thereby with the flood: the progenitor of blacks, who replaces the white "master race" in a Freudian negation. Finally, there is the English "ham actor." Beckett's Hamm, the key to power and helpless at the same time, plays at what he no longer is, as if he had read the most recent sociological literature defining *zoon politikon* as a role. Whoever cleverly presented himself became a "personality" just like helpless Hamm. "Personality" may have been a role originally—nature pretending to transcend nature. Fluctuation in the play's situations causes one of Hamm's roles: occasionally, a stage direction drastically suggests that he speak with the "voice of a rational being;" in a lengthy narrative, he is to strike a "narrative tone." The memory of what is irretrievably past becomes a swindle. Disintegration retrospectively condemns as fictional that continuity of life which alone made life possible. Differences in tone—between people who narrate and those who speak directly—pass judgment on the principle of identity. Both alternate in Hamm's long speech, a kind of inserted aria without music. At the transition points he pauses—the artistic pauses of the veteran actor of heroic roles. For the norm of existential philosophy—people should be themselves because they can no longer become anything else—, *Endgame* posits the antithesis, that precisely this self is not a self but rather the aping imitation of something non-existent. Hamm's mendacity exposes the lie concealed in saying "I" and thereby exhibiting substantiality, whose opposite is the content dis-closed by the "I." Immutability, the epitome of transience, is its ideology. What used to be the truth content of the subject—thinking—is only still preserved in its gestural shell. Both main figures act as if they were reflecting on something, but without thinking.

> HAMM: The whole thing is comical, I grant you that. What about having
>   a good guffaw the two of us together?
> CLOV: (after reflection) I couldn't guffaw today.
> HAMM: (after reflection) Nor I.

According to his name, Hamm's counterpart is what he is, a truncated clown, whose last letter has been severed. An archaic expression for the devil sounds similar—cloven foot; it also resembles the current word "glove." He is the devil of his master, whom he has threatened with the worst, leaving him; yet at the same time he is also the glove with which the master touches the world of things, which he can no longer directly grasp. Not only the figure of Clov is constructed through such associations, but also his connection with the others. In the old piano edition of Stravinsky's "Ragtime for Eleven Instruments," one of the most significant works of his Surrealist phase, there was a Picasso drawing which—probably inspired by the title "rag"—showed two ragged figures, the ancestors of those vagabonds Vladimir and Estragon, who are waiting for Godot. This virtuoso sketch is a single entangled line. The double-sketch of *Endgame* is of this spirit, as well as the damaged repetitions irresistibly produced by Beckett's entire work. In them, history is cancelled out. This compulsory repetition is taken from the regressive behavior of someone locked up, who tries it again and again. Beckett converges with the newest musical tendencies by combining, as a Westerner, aspects of Stravinsky's radical past—the oppressive stasis of disintegrating continuity—with the most advanced expressive and constructive means from the Schönberg school. Even the outlines of Hamm and Clov are one line; they are denied the individuation of a tidily independent monad. They cannot live without each other. Hamm's power over Clov seems to be that only he knows how to open the cupboard, somewhat like the situation where only the principal knows the combination of the safe. He would reveal the secret to Clov, if Clov would swear to "finish" him—or "us." In a reply thoroughly characteristic of the play's tapestry, Clov answers: "I couldn't finish you;" as if the play were mocking the man who feigns reason, Hamm says: "Then you won't finish me." He is dependent on Clov, because Clov alone can accomplish what keeps both alive. But that is of questionable value, because both—like the captain of the ghostly ship—must fear not being able to die. The tiny bit that is also everything—that would be the possibility that something could perhaps change. This movement, or its absence, is the plot. Admittedly, it does not become much more explicit than the repeated motif "Something is taking its course," as abstract as the pure form of time. The Hegelian dialectic of master and slave, mentioned by Günther Anders with reference to *Godot*, is derided rather than portrayed according to the tenets of traditional aesthetics. The slave can no longer grasp the reins and abolish domination. Crippled as he is, he would hardly be capable of this, and according to the play's historico-philosophical sundial, it is too late for spontaneous action anyway. Clov has no other choice than to emigrate out into the world that no longer exists for the play's recluses, with a good chance of dying. He cannot even depend on freedom unto death. He does manage to make the decision to go, even comes in for the farewell: "Panama hat, tweed coat, raincoat over his arm, umbrella, bag"—a strong, almost musical conclusion. But one does not see his exit, rather he remains "impassive and motionless, his eyes fixed on Hamm, till the end." That is an allegory whose intention has evaporated. Aside from some differences, which may be decisive or completely irrelevant, this is identical with the beginning. No spectator and no philosopher can say if the play will not begin anew. The dialectic swings to a standstill.

As a whole, the play's plot is musically composed with two themes, like the double figure of earlier times. The first theme is that it should end, a Schopenhauerian negation of the will to live become insignificant. Hamm strikes it up; the persons, no longer persons, become instruments of their situation, as if they were playing chamber music. "Of all of Beckett's bizarre instruments, Hamm, who in *Endgame* sits blindly and immovably in his wheelchair, resounds with the most tones, the most surprising sound." Hamm's non-identity with himself motivates the course of the play. While he desires the end of the torment of a miserably infinite existence, he is concerned about his life, like a gentleman in his ominous "prime" years. The peripheral paraphernalia of health are utmost in his mind. Yet he does not fear death, rather that death could miscarry; Kafka's motif of the hunter Grachus still resonates. Just as important to him as his own bodily necessities is the certainty that Clov, ordered to gaze out, does not espy any sail or trail of smoke, that no rat or insect is stirring, with whom the calamity could begin anew; that he also does not see the perhaps surviving child, who could signify hope and for whom he lies in wait like Herod the butcher for the *agnus dei*. Insecticide, which all along pointed toward the genocidal camps, becomes the final product of the domination of nature, which destroys itself. Only this content of life remains: that nothing be living. All existence is levelled to a life that is itself death, abstract domination. The second theme is attributed to Clov the servant. After an admittedly obscure history he sought refuge with Hamm; but he also resembles the son of the raging yet impotent patriarch. To give up obedience to the powerless is most difficult; the insignificant and obsolete struggles irresistibly against its abolition. Both plots are counterpointed, since Hamm's will to die is identical with his life principle, while Clov's will to live may well bring about the death of both; Hamm says: "Outside of here it's death." The antithesis of the heroes is also not fixed, rather their impulses converge; it is Clov who first speaks of the end. The scheme of the play's progression is the end game in chess, a typical, rather standard situation, separated from the middle game and its combinations by a caesura; these are also missing in the play, where intrigue and "plot" are silently suspended. Only artistic mistakes or accidents, such as something growing somewhere, could cause unforeseen events, but not resourceful spirit. The field is almost empty, and what happened before can only be poorly construed from the positions of the few remaining figures. Hamm is the king, about whom everything turns and who can do nothing himself. The incongruity between chess as pastime and the excessive effort involved becomes on the stage an incongruity between athletic pretense and the lightweight actions that are performed. Whether the game ends with stalemate or with perpetual check, or whether Clov wins, remains unclear, as if clarity in that would already be too much meaning. Moreover, it is probably not so important, because everything would come to an end in stalemate as in checkmate. Otherwise, only the fleeting image of the child breaks out of the circle, the most feeble reminder of Fortinbras or the child king. It could even be Clov's own abandoned child. But the oblique light falling from thence into the room is as weak as the helplessly helping arms extending from the windows at the conclusion of Kafka's *Trial*.

The history of the subject's end becomes thematic in an intermezzo, which can afford its symbolism, because it depicts the subject's own decrepitude and therefore that of its meaning. The hubris of idealism, the enthroning of man as creator in the center of creation, has entrenched itself in that "bare interior" like a tyrant in his last days. There man repeats with a reduced, tiny imagination what man was once supposed to be; man repeats what was taken from him by social strictures as well as by today's cosmology, which he cannot escape. Clov is his male nurse. Hamm has himself shoved about by Clov into the middle of that *intérieur* which the world has become but which is also the interior of his own subjectivity:

> HAMM: Take me for a little turn. (Clov goes behind the chair and pushes
> it forward.) Not too fast! (Clov pushes chair.) Right round the

> world! (Clov pushes chair.) Hug the walls, then back to the center again. (Clov pushes chair.) I was right in the center, wasn't I?

The loss of the center, parodied here because that center itself was a lie, becomes the paltry object of carping and powerless pedantry:

> CLOV: We haven't done the round.
> HAMM: Back to my place. (Clov pushes chair back to center.) Is that my place?
> CLOV: I'll measure it.
> HAMM: More or less! More or less!
> CLOV: (moving chair slightly) There!
> HAMM: I'm more or less in the center?
> CLOV: I'd say so.
> HAMM: You'd say so! Put me right in the center!
> CLOV: I'll go and get the tape.
> HAMM: Roughly! Roughly! (Clov moves chair slightly.) Bang in the center!

What is paid back in this ludicrous ritual is nothing originally perpetrated by the subject. Subjectivity itself is guilty; that one even is. Original sin is heretically fused with creation. Being, trumpeted by existential philosophy as the meaning of being, becomes its antithesis. Panic fear of the reflex movements of living entities does not only drive untiringly toward the domination of nature: it also attaches itself to life as the ground of that calamity which life has become:

> HAMM: All those I might have helped. (Pause.) Helped! (Pause.) Saved. (Pause.) Saved! (Pause.) The place was crawling with them! (Pause. Violently.) Use your head, can't you, use your head, you're on earth, there's no cure for that!

From that he draws the conclusion: "The end is in the beginning and yet you go on." The autonomous moral law reverts antinomically from pure domination over nature into the duty to exterminate, which always lurked in the background:

> HAMM: More complications! (Clov gets down.) Not an underplot, I trust. (Clov moves ladder nearer window, gets up on it, turns telescope on the without.)
> CLOV: (dismayed) Looks like a small boy!
> HAMM: (sarcastic) A small . . . boy!
> CLOV: I'll go and see. (He gets down, drops the telescope, goes toward door, turns.)
> HAMM: No! (Clov halts.)
> CLOV: No? A potential procreator?

Such a total conception of duty stems from idealism, which is judged by a question the handicapped rebel Clov poses to his handicapped master:

CLOV: Any particular sector you fancy? Or merely the whole thing?

That sounds like a reminder of Benjamin's insight that an intuited cell of reality counterbalances the remainder of the whole world. Totality, a pure postulate of the subject, is nothing. No sentence sounds more absurd than this most reasonable of sentences, which bargains "the whole thing" down to "merely," to the phantom of an anthropocentrically dominated world. As reasonable as this most absurd observation is, it is nevertheless impossible to dispute the absurd aspects of Beckett's play just because they are confiscated by hurried apologetics and a desire for easy disposal. *Ratio*, having been fully instrumentalized, and therefore devoid of self-reflection and of reflection on what it has excluded, must seek that meaning it has itself extinguished. But in the condition that necessarily gave rise to this question, no answer is possible other than nothingness, which the form of the answer already is. The historical inevitability of this absurdity allows it to seem ontological; that is the veil of delusion produced by history itself. Beckett's drama rips through this veil. The immanent contradiction of the absurd, reason terminating in senselessness, emphatically reveals the possibility of a truth which can no longer even be thought; it undermines the absolute claim exercised by what merely is. Negative ontology is the negation of ontology: history alone has brought to maturity what was appropriated by the mythic power of timelessness. The historical fiber of situation and language in Beckett does not concretize—*more philosophico*—something unhistorical: precisely this procedure, typical of existential dramatists, is both foreign to art and philosophically obsolete. Beckett's once-and-for-all is rather infinite catastrophe; only "that the earth is extinguished, although I never saw it lit" justifies Clov's answer to Hamm's question: "Do you not think this has gone on long enough?" "Yes." Pre-history goes on, and the phantasm of infinity is only its curse. After Clov, commanded to look outside, reports to the totally lame man what he sees of earth, Hamm entrusts to him his secret:

CLOV: (absorbed) Mmm.
HAMM: Do you know what it is?
CLOV: (as before) Mmm.
HAMM: I was never there.

Earth was never yet tread upon; the subject is not yet a subject.

Determinate negation becomes dramaturgical through consistent reversal. Both social partners qualify their insight that there is no more nature with the bourgeois "You exaggerate." Prudence and circumspection are the tried-and-true means of sabotaging contemplation. They cause only melancholy reflection:

> CLOV: (sadly) No one that ever lived ever thought so crooked as we.

Where they draw nearest to the truth, they experience their consciousness—doubly comical—as false consciousness; thus a condition is mirrored that reflection no longer reaches. The entire play is woven with the technique of reversal. It transfigures the empirical world into that world desultorily named already by the late Strindberg and in Expressionism. "The whole house stinks of corpses . . . The whole universe." Hamm, who then says "to hell with the universe," is just as much the descendant of Fichte, who disdains the world as nothing more than raw material and mere product, as he is the one without hope except for the cosmic night, which he implores with poetic quotes. Absolute, the world becomes a hell; there is nothing else. Beckett graphically stresses Hamm's sentence: "Beyond is the . . . OTHER hell." With a Brechtian commentary, he lets the distorted metaphysics of "the here and now" shine through:

> CLOV: Do you believe in the life to come?
> HAMM: Mine was always like that. (Exit Clov.) Got him that time!

In his conception, Benjamin's notion of the "dialectic at a standstill" comes into its own:

> HAMM: It will be the end and there I'll be, wondering what can have brought it on and wondering what can have (he hesitates) . . . why it was so long coming. (Pause.) There I'll be, in the old shelter, alone against the silence and . . . (he hesitates) . . . the stillness. If I can hold my peace, and sit quiet, it will be all over with sound and motion, all over and done with.

That "stillness" is the order which Clov supposedly loves and which he defines as the purpose of his functions:

> CLOV: A world where all would be silent and still and each thing in its last place, under the last dust.

To be sure, the Old Testament saying "You shall become dust (Staub) again" is translated here into "dirt" (Dreck). In the play, the substance of life, a life that is death, is the excretions. But the imageless image of death is one of indifference. In it, the distinction disappears: the distinction between absolute domination, the hell in which time is banished into space, in which nothing will change any more—and the messianic condition where everything would be in its proper place. The ultimate absurdity is that the repose of nothingness and that of reconciliation cannot be distinguished from each other. Hope creeps out of a world in which it is no more conserved than pap and pralines, and back where it came from, back into death. From it, the play derives its only consolation, a stoic one:

> CLOV: There are so many terrible things now.
> HAMM: No, no, there are not so many now.

Consciousness begins to look its own demise in the eye, as if it wanted to survive the demise, as these two want to survive the destruction of their world. Proust, about whom the young Beckett wrote an essay, is said to have attempted to keep protocol on his own struggle with death, in notes which were to be integrated into the description of Bergotte's death. *Endgame* carries out this intention like a mandate from a testament.

RUBY COHN

"Comment c'est" par le bout

*Heureusement il ne s'agit
pas de dire ce qui n'a pas
encore été dit, mais de redire,
le plus souvent possible dans
l'espace le plus réduit, ce
qui a été dit déjà.*
—from "Peintres de l'empêchement"

Perhaps the initial irony concerning *Comment c'est*, published in 1961, is that it is called a novel. On the dust jacket of Beckett's first extended nondramatic writing in a decade, the designation *roman* appears between the title and the blue star-and-m of Les Editions de Minuit. Yet this work, stripping away plot and character further than ever before, is as close to poetry as to fiction; even typographically the narrative appears in irregular verses. Plot and character virtually coincide in a narrator who crawls naked through the mud, sack tied around his neck, until he meets another character who crawls naked through the mud, sack tied around *his* neck, until he in turn meets still another character who crawls naked through the mud, sack, etc., from the beginning "comment c'était" to the ending "comment c'est." This spareness of situation is paralleled by a bareness of language that even Beckett has not achieved before. With skeletal phrases, he attains the precision, control, and condensation of poetry. Rhythmic repetition, symbolic imag-

From *Samuel Beckett: The Comic Gamut.* Copyright © 1962 by Rutgers University Press.

ery, and formal structure are exploited for cosmic resonance that is constantly heightened by the comic colloquialisms of the discourse.

Not only is *Comment c'est* divided into three approximately equal parts—1. "Before Pim or the Voyage," 2. "With Pim or the Couple," 3. "After Pim or the Abandonment"—but the tripartite structure is incessantly recapitulated. Such hysterical insistence on division renders it ludicrous, whether the units be of time, place, language, or humanity. And indeed, there is frequent violation of the designated divisions. During the course of the book, nothing and no one emerges from the mud; the hero-narrator is little more than a compulsive movement in the mud, arbitrarily and absurdly imposing his trinity: "d'une seule éternité en faire trois pour plus de clarté" ("to make three eternities from a single one for greater clarity").

Since, like all Beckett's French fiction, *Comment c'est* takes the form of a monologue, the style is consistent in all three parts. Colloquial, unpunctuated phrases are grouped in uneven verses. Usually staccato, these phrases are sometimes linked syntactically; contrast, for example, two verses on the same page, the first choppy, the second containing a more consecutive linguistic flow achieved through participles and relative pronouns:

> dans le sac donc jusqu'à présent les boîtes l'ouvre-boîte la corde mais le désir d'autre chose on ne semble pas me l'avoir donné cette fois l'image d'autres choses là avec moi dans la boue le noir dans le sac à ma portée non on ne semble pas avoir mis ça dans ma vie cette fois

> (in the sack up to now I recapitulate the tins the opener the cord but the wish for something else no that doesn't seem to have been given me this time the image of other things with me here in the mud in the dark in the sack within reach no that doesn't seem to have been put in my life this time)

> qu'ayant cherchées en vain parmi les boîtes tantôt l'une tantôt l'autre suivant le désir l'image du moment que m'étant fatigué à chercher ainsi je pourrais me promettre de chercher de nouveau plus tard quand je serais moins fatigué un peu moins fatigué ou tâcher d'oublier en me disant c'est vrai c'est vrai n'y pense plus

> (which having sought in vain among the tins now one now another according to the wish the image of the moment which having thus sought till I am tired I promise myself to seek again when less tired with perhaps a little more success or to try and quite banish from my mind saying true true think no more about it)

Certain word groups, permuted and combined and recombined, constitute the burdens of this narration. Never has a "novel" been built with fewer words, but the parsimonious verbal threads are woven into a tough comic texture. Conscious of the comic tone, the narrator even invokes Thalia, muse of Comedy.

The most frequent chorus in the book—whether as an integral and pithy verse line, or as part of the more usual longer verses—is "quelque chose là qui ne va pas" ("something wrong there") (B). Reflecting doubt on the matter that precedes, or follows, or both, the colloquial phrase casts its wavering, indefinite shadow over the entire monologue. Most noticeably, it appears as a complete verse in a series of complete verses, and thus comments upon the entire series:

au couple	(at the couple
en passant par l'abandon	passing by the abandonment
ou par le voyage	or by the voyage
q'est juste	it is just
quelque chose là qui ne va pas	something wrong there)

In the middle of a verse, the refrain line reflects both backward and forward:

la boîte entamée remise dans le sac gardée à la main j'y pense l'appétit revenu ou n'y pense plus en ouvre une autre c'est l'un ou l'autre quelque chose là qui ne va pas c'est le début de ma vie présente rédaction

(the tin broached put back in the sack or left in the hand I remember when I go to eat again or forget open another it's one or the other something wrong there it's the beginning of my life latest version)

The "something wrong there" may be the cans, or forgetting where the opened can has been placed; more significantly, the "something wrong" is the beginning of the narrator's life.

Towards the end of the book, the tenses of grammar and the times of life are embraced in the summary rejection of the refrain line, this time concluding a verse.

à moins qu'elle ne me l'apprenne la voix ma vie lors de cette autre solitude qu'est le voyage c'est-à-dire au lieu d'un premier passé d'un second passé et d'un présent un passé un présent et un futur quelque chose là qui ne va pas

(unless it teaches me the voice my life during that other solitude that is the voyage that is to say instead of a first past from a second past and from a present a past a present and a future something wrong there)

Within the verses, the narrator is redundantly careful to absolve himself of responsibility for the words he mouths. On almost every page he reiterates, "je cite" ("I quote") (B), or "je le dis comme je l'entends" ("I say it as I hear it") (B). Impatient with words, questions, and thoughts, he lumps them together as "cette famille" ("that family"). Although the same phrases have been sporadically uttered by earlier Beckett narrators, notably the Unnamable and the "I's" of the thirteen Textes, the monologuist of *Comment c'est* is more resigned to ignorance. He scarcely seeks to know the original source of his words: "pas question" and "ça s'enchaîne," he shrugs. Vaguely but emphatically, he affirms, "on parle de." From "on," from somewhere, once without but now within him even if not his, the incessant, compulsive "murmure à la boue" ("murmur to the mud") is tantamount to breath. Perhaps there will be silence "quand ça cesse de haleter" ("when the panting stops") (B). Always there is the mud, the dark, and "un temps énorme" ("vast stretch of time") (B). Into that "temps énorme," world without end, the narrator attempts to interject his tripartite division: "comment c'était comment c'est comment ce sera" ("how it was how it is how it will be"). But rigid rubrics are constantly and comically flouted, since time is as continuous and pervasive as the mud.

To another time or world or life—of light up above (as in Texte II and Texte XI)—belongs all knowledge, evoked now only in self-mockery. Ironically, the narrator twists the French proverb "tout comprendre c'est tout pardonner" to "tout compris et rien su pardonner" ("to understand everything is to pardon everything"; "I understood everything and didn't know how to pardon anything"). At irregular intervals, the narrator recalls "l'anatomie" or "la géographie" or "les lettres" or "les humanités" or even "l'âme" that he used to have. By now, however, there is only the "present version" of his life, related presumably by the interminable "brefs mouvements du bas du visage" ("brief movements of the lower face") (B), frequently and cryptically summarized as "quaqua."

Other than this soundless monologue, existence consists of crawling through the slime in a straight line towards the East. Earlier Beckett heroes were unable, alternatively, to sit or to stand (Cooper and Neary of *Murphy*, Hamm and Clov of *Endgame*). Molloy, Malone, and Mahood were all reduced to reptation; Estragon of *Waiting for Godot* complains, "All my lousy life I've crawled about in the mud!" Similarly, the narrator of *Comment c'est* crawls on his belly through the mud: "dix mètres quinze mètres pied droit main droite pousse tire" ("ten yards fifteen yards right foot right hand push pull"). In different contexts, the same numbers recur; they may shift from space to time, "dix secondes quinze secondes"; to the

Beckett description of thought, "dix coups quinze coups sur le crâne"; to language, "dix mots quinze mots"; to hypothetical people, "dix autres quinze autres." But whatever the temporary substantive, the numbers constantly return to the mud in which they were conceived. The movement through the mud may vary slightly: "jambe droite bras droit pousse tire dix mètres quinze mètres halte" ("right leg right arm push pull ten yards fifteen yards stop"). Occasionally, right is replaced by left, or a side or a thigh may enter the description of the motion, but the motion itself is dully repetitive, peristaltic, caricaturing man into a worm.

Obsessed as he is with the minutiae of his movements, the narrator-hero is also sporadically aware of the chaos in which he is immersed; valiantly if vainly, he persists in his attempt to trisect eternity. In the printed text, moreover, the three parts of the book are separated by half-title pages and introduced by large Arabic numbers. Within each chapter recur several phrases that lack the raucous insistence of the book-long repetitions, but that also add to the comic tone. In Part 1, "Before Pim or the Voyage," when the narrator is alone, he chants an old Beckett theme, "moi si c'est moi" ("I if it is I"); an old Beckett irony, "dans l'ordre" ("in the natural order") (B); and an old Beckett approximation, "plus ou moins" ("more or less"). In Part 2, "With Pim or the Couple," the narrator harps on the fact that Pim "n'est pas bête seulement lent" ("is not stupid merely slow"). Since Part 2 contains a kind of marriage between the narrator and Pim, happiness is comically conjugated: At intervals, we find "ce sont de bons moments"; less frequently, "c'était de bons moments"; still less frequently, "ce sera de bons moments" and "ce serait de bons moments"; more incongruously in this "temps énorme," "ce serait de bonnes secondes."

In the third, last, and most desperate part, appear references to "les jours de grande gaîté" ("days of great gaiety"). In the final chapter, a new verse refrain appears: "c'est juste" ("it is just"). But by that time, the cumulative evidence of the entire work denies both "justice" and "justesse" in the human sentence. In Part 3, too, the book-long refrains are climactically varied so as to highlight the hopeless absurdity of human fate. Thus, the "mouvements du bas du visage" that result in the compulsive monologue are modified to "mouvements pour rien du bas du visage" ("movements for nothing of the lower face"). "Quelque chose là qui ne va pas" is intensified to "quelque chose là qui ne va pas du tout" ("something completely wrong there"). The irony is patent when "comment c'était comment c'est comment ce sera" becomes "comment c'était comment c'est comment ce très certainement sera" ("how it was how it is how it most certainly will be"). The beat of "je cite" explodes into "qu'est-ce que ça peut bien foutre je cite" ("what the hell can it matter I quote").

Having no voice, the narrator knows he speaks only when he feels his face move. With some surprise he wonders what there can be to say, but we can scarcely be surprised at the comic contradictions that tumble out of his lower face:

> on est là quelque part en vie quelque part un temps énorme puis c'est fini on n'y est plus puis de nouveau on est là de nouveau ce n'était pas fini une erreur c'est à recommencer plus ou moins au même endroit à un autre

> (one is there somewhere alive somewhere a vast stretch of time then it's finished one isn't there any more then again one is there again it wasn't finished an error it's to begin again more or less in the same place in another)

Frequently, the narrator reiterates, "j'entends dire que oui puis que non" ("I hear it say yes then no"). Towards the end of Part 2, virtually every short phrase within each verse is punctuated by a "oui" or a "non" that emphasizes with comic (and pathetic) literalness the permanent contradictions of the human situation. Towards the end of Part 3, Beckett again uses the powerfully rhythmic "oui's" and "non's," but to them he adds a frequent and vituperative "de la foutaise," as well as the final Beckett answer to all questions, "pas de réponse" ("no answer").

Although it is primarily recapitulation of these phrases that establishes the distinctive comic lyricism of Comment c'est, Beckett also uses such lesser poetic embellishments as repetition of sound—rhyme, alliteration, and pun. The comic repercussions are evident in the play between sound and sense (which is untranslatable): "santé de fer que faire que faire," "à en avoir la peau en eau," "à quoi croire," "la fin enfin," "ils passent à pas pesants," "coi dans mon coin," "jamais vu ça sa vie ici," "il coupe court par le coup," "l'entendre dire dire l'entendre da la bouche à la boue bref baiser du bout des lèvres."

Such peripheral sound play prepares the muddy ground for the focal puns of the book, those upon the two most frequently mentioned proper names, Pim and Bom. The monosyllables pain and bon are rich in pleasurable connotations: staff of life, bread of the Presence, central sustenance; God's world, ethical goal, practical use. But Pim and Bom, puns on pain and bon, are destitute and desperate, not knowing which of them creates the other—in the habit of Beckett's fictions. Perhaps Beckett's most bitter irony lies in his naming these cruel and dwindling solipsists "bread" and "good." Moreover, Beckett generalizes these ironic proper names, to represent the human species. Individual identity is virtually canceled in the reciprocal puns in the second of the following verses.

la même voix les mêmes choses aux noms propres près et encore deux suffisent chacun attend sans nom son Bom va sans nom vers son Pim

Bom à l'abandonné pas moi Bom toi Bom nous Bom mais moi Bom toi Pim moi à l'abandonné pas moi Pim toi Pim nous Pim mais moi Bom toi Pim quelque chose là qui ne va pas du tout

(the same voice the same things with nearly the same proper names and even then two suffice each awaiting nameless his Bom goes nameless toward his Pim

Bom abandoned not I Bom you Bom but I Bom you Pim I abandoned not I Pim you Pim we Pim but I Bom you Pim something completely wrong there)

Other puns are only subtly implied through the course of the book. The reiterated title, "Comment c'est," puns on "commencer" ("to begin"). And just as "how it is" is a perpetual beginning that can never be extrapolated all the way back to point zero, so the ubiquitous mud is a perpetual end that never terminates at a given goal; "bout" ("end") is implicit in and denied by "boue" ("mud").

Part 3, "After Pim," entitled "l'abandon," contains in the single French word the solitude of English "abandonment" and the unrestrained quality of English "abandon." At a cruder level, the verbiage of the monologue is constantly summed up as "quaqua," presumably pronounced "caca."

Contributing to the ironic tone is Beckett's use of repetition to link various verses, as in the following example.

quoi sur elle ma mémoire on parle de ma mémoire peu de chose qu'elle s'améliore elle empire qu'il me revient des choses il ne me revient rien mais de là à être sûr

à être sûr que personne ne viendra plus jamais braquer sa lampe sur moi et plus jamais rien d'autres jours d'autres nuits non

(my memory I say I quote that it is getting better it is getting worse that things are coming back to me nothing is coming back to me but to conclude from that that no one

to conclude from that that no one will ever come again shine his lamp on me and nothing ever again of the old days and nights no)

The repetition and climactic positions of "à être sûr" serve as ironic preparation for the final and contradictory "non." Nothing is sure in Beckett's world.

In another example, by slightly varying the linking repetition, Beckett intensifies the ironic portrayal of the narrator's predicament.

ce sera de bons moments puis de moins bons ça aussi il faut s'y attendre ce sera la nuit présente rédaction je pourrai dormir et si jamais je me réveille

et si jamais rire muet je me réveille dare-dare catastrophe Pim fin de première partie plus que la deuxième puis la troisième et dernière

(there will be good moments then less good that too must be expected there will be night present version I will be able to sleep and if ever I awaken

and if ever dumb laugh I awaken sudden catastrophe Pim end of the first part only the second to go then the third only the third and last)

By the end of the book, a comic and cosmic cruelty is conveyed in the single word "bon," repeated to link the final verses.

alos ça peut changer pas de réponse finir pas de réponse je pourrais suffoquer pas de réponse m'engloutir pas de réponse plus souiller la boue pas de réponse le noir pas de réponse plus troubler le silence pas de réponse crever pas de réponse CREVER hurlements JE POURRAIS CREVER hurlements JE VAIS CREVER hurlements bon

bon bon fin de la troisième partie et dernière voilà comment c'était fin de la citation après Pim comment c'est

(then it can change no answer end no answer I could suffocate no answer sink no answer no longer pollute the mud no answer the dark no answer no longer trouble the silence no answer croak no answer CROAK howls I COULD CROAK howls I AM GOING TO CROAK howls good

good good end of the third and last part there is how it was end of quotation after Pim how it is)

The entire work denies the "bon," both by virtue of the constantly repeated "mal" and the anguish that accumulates from verse to verse, and from chapter to chapter. From past to future, "un temps énorme," man grovels on his belly in the mud, with a sack tied around his neck, making brief movements of the lower face. In characterizing his condition, God's word, "Good," is cruelly ironic.

Unlike other heroes of Beckett's French fiction, the "I" of *Comment c'est* is relatively intact physically, for he lacks only a right thumb and a voice. But he is not clad in the picturesque costumes of earlier Beckett creations, for he crawls through his mud as naked as the proverbial worm. Yet he takes pride of possession, notably in a sack, which contains cans, cord, and can opener. As in other Beckett works, the very sparseness of specific objects is comic, and virtually demands symbolic interpretation.

The four objects fall at once into pairs: can and can opener, sack and cord. The first two are modern and smack of industrialization; the second two are as old as civilization—"vieux sac vieille corde vous je vous garde" ("old sack old cord I'm keeping you"). The can and can opener are rigid, the sack and cord pliable. Can and can opener are essentially unifunctional; sack and cord are multipurpose. But it is mainly in their linguistic connotations that the two pairs of objects differ; can and can opener are only meagerly suggestive, but sack and cord figure in many French expressions that would seem to have comic relevance to the human situation in *Comment c'est*.

Perhaps the heart of the matter is contained in "homme de sac et de corde" ("thorough scoundrel"). He may be a scoundrel, but his sentence—to be stuffed into a sack that is tied up with a cord—is crueler than his crime. So, Beckett's heroes may be scoundrels, but they are condemned to a punishment that is antecedent and irrelevant to their crimes.

Of the two objects, sack and cord, the former is of prime importance since, initially at least, it contains the other objects—perhaps, on occasion, the narrator himself. The sack is explicitly and insistently described as a fifty-kilo coalsack of wet jute. Trivially domestic though this may seem, the Coalsack is also the starless center of the Milky Way (near the Southern Cross), a black hole in the heavens. In *Murphy*, Beckett specifically links Murphy's dark center with that of our galaxy: "The sad truth was that the skylight commanded only that most dismal patch of night sky, the galactic coalsack, which would naturally look like a dirty night to any observer in Murphy's condition, cold, tired, angry, impatient and out of conceit with a system that seemed the superfluous cartoon of his own." Similarly, since the coalsack is mandatory in order for the hero of *Comment c'est* to move, "sac à charbon" may be Beckett's comic shorthand for relating his crawling creature to the center of the galaxy. Of possible relevance to the dampness of the sack is the fact that amphibian life existed on a carboniferous earth a cosmic year (or 225,000,000 years) ago.

The coalsack or "sac à charbon" also suggests "sac et cendres," or sackcloth and ashes, the traditional garb of the penitent sinner. In Part 3, which is much concerned with justice, this connotation is particularly ironic. That such justice may be divine is implied in the distinction between full and empty sacks—"une histoire de grâce." A possible almighty power is characterized as "celui qui fournit les sacs" ("the one who furnishes the sacks") and "une intelligence . . . un amour qui . . . dépose nos sacs" ("an intelligence . . . a love which . . . leaves our sacks for us").

In various French phrases, the sack can stand for either belly or brain. Although the crawling hero tends to insist upon the former and to ignore the latter, Beckett paints their chaotic combination. Since "sac," as in "avoir le sac" or "être au sac" implies riches, the meager contents of the sack of *Comment c'est* are ludicrous. Nothing, during the course of the book, is acquired to fill the sack ("remplir le sac" is "to eat copiously"), and the narrator's appetite decreases to zero. As early as Part 1, the narrator's sack is literally emptied of cord, can opener, and cans. Metaphorically, "vider son sac" is to have one's say, and the phrase is entirely fitting for the way the Beckett hero spews forth his monologue.

Within the book itself, Beckett implies that the meaning of the sack is to be extended, for we read: "mon sac seul variable," "le sac premier vrai signe de vie," "le sac seul bien," "le sac ma vie," "la mort du sac," "ce sac sans quoi pas de voyage" ("my sack only variable," "the sack first real sign of life," "the sack only possession," "the sack my life," "the death of the sack," "the sack without which no voyage"). Sacks figure comically at cross-purposes: "nous laissons nos sacs à ceux qui n'en ont pas besoin nous prenons leurs sacs à ceux qui vont en avoir besoin nous partons sans sac nous en trouvons un nous pouvons voyager" ("we leave our sacks to those who don't need them we take the sacks from those who will need them we set off without sacks we find one we can voyage").

When, early in the book, the narrator slips the sack over his head, we may think of "voir le fond du sac"—an effort to get to the bottom of things. Since the sack is wet, we need scarcely be astonished by the narrator's perpetual excuses; "se couvrir d'un sac mouillé" is "to be full of excuses." When the hand of the hero is seen in the sack, we recall that "prendre quelqu'un la main dans le sac" implies human guilt. Even more appropriate for the Beckett hero is "avoir la tête dans un sac" ("to be ignorant"); for this narrator belongs to the Beckett family in loudly protesting his absolute ignorance.

Less central than the sack—but then "Il ne faut point parler de corde dans la maison d'un pendu" ("one mustn't talk about rope in the house of the hanged")—the cord suggests two different lines of connotation, the one centered on poverty and the other on hanging. In the first group are such expressions as "usé jusqu'à la corde" ("thoroughly hackneyed"), "être au bout de sa corde" ("to be at the end of one's tether"), "montrer sa corde" ("to be played out"). In the second group are such locutions as "friser la corde" ("to escape danger"), and literally describing the situation of the narrator, "la corde au cou" ("condemned").

Moving from objects to people—barely distinguishable in *Comment c'est*—we note Beckett's continued comedy of names. In the French trilogy, Beckett had already indicated, by unceremoniously changing proper names, that such appellations were completely arbitrary, and did not confer identity. The last narrator of the trilogy is nameless and unnamable, but he can still name his creations Mahood and Worm. So, too, the hero of *Comment c'est* is finally nameless and unnamable, but he insists from the start upon the "beau nom de Pim" for the creature of Part 2, with whom he will form a temporary couplement. When the meeting takes place, however, the narrator suggests that he, too, may appropriate the fine name of Pim, then decides he prefers Bom, or perhaps Bim or Bem—"m à la fin et une syllabe le reste égal" ("m at the end and one syllable the rest doesn't matter"). A fleeting image of a wife becomes Pam Prim, and the phonetic similarity of Pam and Pim suggests that the narrator's partner in the Couple may be of either sex. An intermittently evoked witness and a scribe are called Krim and Kram, with suggestions of "crin," "cran," and "crâne." A maimed dog is called Skom Skum, with a phonetic odor of "sconse." The phonetic stipulation is somewhat ridiculous, since final m is "un-French," occurring in such borrowed words as tram, macadam, and Sam.

Sam himself is not present in *Comment c'est*, as he was in *Watt*, and yet he comes inevitably to mind through the repetition of "m à la fin et une syllabe le rest égal." Phonetically "homme" and "femme" would also meet these specifications, contributing to Beckett's usual metaphysical tendency of generalizing man to Man. Moreover, Beckett's comic penchant for humanizing things—Molloy's fondness for pebbles, Malone's for his pencil, Worm for his vase—culminate in *Comment c'est*, where the voyager is inseparable from his sack. The phrase, "le sac ma vie," occurs often in *Comment c'est*. By Part 3, Beckett generalizes humanity to "une syllabe m à la fin," and phenomena to "une syllabe c à la fin." Thus, man and thing take similar form, distinguishable by a single consonant.

In contrast to the various linguistic connotations of sack and cord, can and can opener seem confined to their phenomenological aspects. The cans are plural, the can opener singular. The cans fulfill their function of containing sustenance, but the can opener does not open a single can.

The cans, doing what they were designed to do, are soon thrown away in the mud; the can opener, not used for what it was intended, becomes the prime instrument in training Pim to speak. (In the one instance wherein cans are opened, it is an "outil" rather than "ouvre-boîte" that accomplishes the deed.) Once the narrator asserts "l'ouvre-boîte qui est ma vie" ("the can opener that is my life") but retracts to "mais de quoi ne puis-je en dire autant" ("but of what can't I say as much"). Can and can opener become the principals in a comedy of incongruous functions.

Within the text, it is ambivalent as to whether can opener, cans, cord, sack, and the pervasive mud are objects, metaphors, or images. Cord, comb, and can opener are specifically designated as objects, and yet their meaning can be extended. In the description of a crocus, "une main l'y maintient cette fleur jaune dans le soleil au moyen d'une corde de vois la main longue image," is it the entire ridiculous still life that constitutes the image? Or the living hand? Or the condensation in this image of a longer description in "La Fin"?

In *Comment c'est*, the heralding of the first image is in comic contrast to the vagueness of the image itself:

vie dans la lumière première image un quidam quelconque je le regardais à ma manière de loin en dessous dans un miroir la nuit par la fenêtre première image

(life in the light first image someone anyone I watched him after my fashion from afar stealthily in mirrors at night through windows lighted windows first image)

For the heroes of Beckett's French fiction, perception becomes increasingly difficult, and the "I" of *Comment c'est* sees his first image darkly, through several glasses. Gradually, however, as the narrator warms to his narration, the images grow clearer—a parodic picture of the narrator's mother hearing his childhood prayers, brief mention of the narrator regaining consciousness in the dark in a hospital up above in the world of light, the memory of a wife in another life. Towards the middle of Part 1 occurs the most extended narration or "image" of *Comment c'est*, which was published separately under the title "L'Image."

Wallowing in the slime, mouth open and tongue in the mud, the narrator takes up some mud on his tongue and rolls it around in his mouth. Gradually, he sees himself at the age of sixteen; he is with a girl in a pastoral scene of April or May. In most un-Beckettian fashion, boy and girl hold hands and swing arms, the boy carrying a pack of sandwiches in his free arm, the girl leading her little dog by the leash. But soon, characteristically ironic strokes color the picture: The hero neglects his girl friend (who is only less hideous full-face than in profile) to concentrate on himself; among his grotesque features are pimples, large stomach, gaping fly, splay feet, spindle legs, and sanctimonious smile. The pet dog trots along behind the couple, "rien à voir avec nous il a eu la même idée au même instant du Malebranche en moins rose les lettres que j'avais" ("nothing to do with us he had the same idea at the same instant Malebranche a little more pale the education I had").

The only proper name in the slight narrative refers to the seventeenth-century Occasionalist philosopher, Nicolas Malebranche, who carried Cartesian dualism of mind and matter to its most extreme form, so that any action of the one upon the other was the occasion for divine intervention. In literal context—that human and canine minds should be able to act upon human and canine bodies, respectively, only by miracle— the comic depends upon incongruous disproportion. Incongruous, too, are the overtones of Malebranche's asceticism in this "love story." In its larger concern with the mind-matter dichotomy, the mention of Malebranche recalls Beckett's earliest work. Particularly apposite in this section where an image arises from mud, where a kind of matter is created by a kind of mind, the naming of Malebranche precedes the bitterest phrase in the narration, "s'il pisse il pissera sans s'arrêter je crie aucun son plaque-la là et cours t'ouvrir les veines" ("if he pees he will pee without stopping I cry no sound leave her there and run to open your veins").

Although the vulgarity attaches primarily to the dog, it looks forward metaphorically to the spurt of blood that would follow "sans s'arrêter" ("without stopping") from the opening of the veins, and this in turn would lead to silence, "aucun son." The crying also follows the "sans s'arrêter" that would make agony continuous, and it precedes the suggestions of abandonment and death. The traditional French sounds of comfort, "là, là," contrast cruelly with the suicidal final phrase.

In the next verse, the lovers are suddenly at the summit of a mountain. By the positional ambiguity of the short phrases, Beckett reduces the couple to comic animality. Like the dog, the lovers concentrate on physical pleasures. Endearments mingle with mastication: "mon amour je mords elle avale mon trésor elle mord j'avale" ("my love I bite she swallows my treasure she bites I swallow"). Although the biting and swallowing act upon the sandwich at a literal level, the movements also suggest love-making and chastising; they prefigure Part 2, "the Couple," with its sustained and deliberate ambiguity as to whether the members of the couple are lovers or victim and executioner.

Leaving the mountain, the narrator loses the scene. Still smiling, though "depuis longtemps ce n'est plus la peine" ("for a long time now it hasn't been worth the trouble"), he finds himself face down in the familiar mud. This time, when his tongue reaches out, he is no longer thirsty. Empty, the tongue re-enters his mouth, and the mouth closes.

elle doit faire une ligne droite à présent c'est fini c'est fait j'ai eu l'image

(it must make a straight line at present it's done it's made I've had the image)

As originally published in three pages of unpunctuated prose, the closing words were "j'ai fait l'image." Changing the verb from *make* to *have* shifts the connotation from creation to parturition, and places the narrator at a further remove from God, who made man in His own image.

In the sixth text, Beckett had already reduced to mud the "limon" upon which God breathed on the Sixth day: "la nostalgie de cette boue où souffla l'esprit de l'Eternel" ("nostalgia for that mud where the Eternal spirit breathed"). In *Comment c'est*, it is the narrator who breathes into the mud, and who draws the image from mud which he rolls on his tongue. Thus, the mouth's straight line in the last verse of the image, links to the straight line towards the East, which is the human voyage in *Comment c'est.*

Who makes the voyage? Who forms the couple? Who abandons and is abandoned? As in all Beckett's French fiction, the answer is "I." This "I" is shrunk to twenty or thirty kilograms, indistinguishable from his "image," often indistinguishable from Pim, scarcely distinguishable from the mud through which he crawls. Nameless and voiceless, the "I" formulates words as compulsively as he moves towards the East, and his words are focused on his meeting with another—with Pim. It is Pim who will situate him in space and time.

At first the expectation is set up that Pim is different from "I." The constantly repeated "Before Pim, With Pim, After Pim" indicates a joining with and separation from another being. The prevision of a contact between flesh and flesh is hilarious in its abrupt physicality.

crochue pour la prise la main plonge au lieu de la fange familière une fesse sur le ventre lui aussi avant ça quoi encore ça suffit je pars

(hooked for the grasp the hand plunges instead of the familiar mud a buttock on his belly he also before that what else that's enough I set out)

A few pages later, the narrator foreshadows a second meeting: "sur toi soudain une main comme sur Pim la tienne deux cris le sien muet" ("on you suddenly a hand like yours on Pim two cries his silent"). Virtually from the beginning, roles are interchangeable; the toucher of a buttock becomes in turn the one whose buttock is touched.

Even in Part 1, before the section that deals overtly and explicitly with "the couple," we learn that the narrator will plunge his can opener into Pim's buttock, that Pim has a chronometer and a voice. But it is in Part 2 that the relationship between Pim and the narrator is detailed in all its comic cruelty. Making their way through the mud, hand, head, and foot of the narrator explore those of Pim, who seems to be even smaller than the narrator since he weighs twenty to thirty kilograms; Pim faces in the same direction, lies also on his belly, and either wears a wrist watch or carries a watch and chain which has announced its presence by its ticking. This creature must have been named by the narrator, and since Pim is such a fine name, the narrator indicates to Pim that he too is named Pim. Pim is momentarily confused, but the narrator is aware that at his next encounter Pim will give him the fine name of Bom. The narrator will learn his name when it is written in Roman capital letters by a fingernail across his own buttocks, precisely as he will teach Pim's name to him.

But before Pim learns to read in this fashion, he undergoes an arduous apprenticeship at the hands of the narrator. Since Pim has a voice, he is taught to speak by having the can opener plunged into his buttocks. Pim becomes a can to disgorge its contents; "c'est mécanique."

A blow on the head is the command that Pim be silent, and we may recall the blows on the head that Molloy delivered to his mother and to the charcoal-burner, that Moran dealt the dim man, that Malone's visitor used to frighten Malone, and that Malone's fiction Lemuel hammered at himself.

Pim learns other lessons besides that of silence; he learns to sing when fingernails scratch his armpit, to recite words when the can opener is plunged into his buttocks, to speak louder when the handle of the can opener strikes the small of his back; each lesson is meticulously numbered *ad infinitum* and *ad absurdum*:

> cinq moins fort index dans l'anus six bravo claque à cheval sur les fesses sept mauvais même que trois huit encore même que un ou deux selon

> (five softer index in the anus six bravo whack on the buttocks seven bad same as three eight again same as one or two according

As earlier fictions of Beckett's narrators teach them about love and reason, so the narrator learns by teaching Pim. Briefly recalling wife, father, and mother from the world of light, the narrator then denies that there has ever been anyone but himself: "moi on parle de moi pas Pim Pim est fini" ("me we're talking about me not Pim Pim is finished"). The intermittently evoked Krim and Kram, witness and scribe, reverse their roles, even as the narrator prepares to become the Pim of Bom or Bem. Only the maimed dog seems to contain his dualism from the start, in the double name Skom Skum. At the end of Part 2, the narrator plies Pim with his own questions, supplying the "oui's" and "non's" from the texture of his own experience.

Part 3, "the Abandonment," opens a new orgy of solitude: "cette solitude où la voix la raconte seul moyen de la vivre" ("this solitude where the voice tells it only way to live it"). Yet the narrator foresees that his solitude will be interrupted again, that he will undergo the training of Pim of Part 2. After an indefinite period, he may become the trainer again, as his trainer may become trainee. Every creature becomes, in turn, trainer and trainee, lover and loved one, a dumb and stationary executioner and a speaking, voyaging victim. The generalization of the human predicament is accomplished by an old Beckett comic device—merciless permutation, combination, and statistics, which belie the promise at the beginning of Part 2, "plus le moindre chiffre désormais" ("not the least little number from now on"). Similarly, although no more images were to be evoked after Part 1, the same matter continues to figure through Part 3: "le sac les bras le corps la boue le noir cheveux et ongles qui vivent tout ça" ("the sack the arms the body the mud the dark hair and nails that are living all that"). At the end, Kram and Krim dissolve into a single ear; Pim and Bem dissolve into a single "I." With verbal and numerical abandon, the narrator insists that man is abandoned.

> et qu'ainsi reliés directement les uns aux autres chacun d'entre nous est en même temps Bom et Pim bourreau victime pion cancre demandeur défendeur muet et théâtre d'une parole retrouvée dans le noir la boue là rien à corriger

> (and that bound directly to one another each of us is at the same time Bom and Pim executioner victim schoolmaster dunce plaintiff defendant dumb and theater of a word found again in the dark the mud there nothing to correct)

Apparent opposites are only temporary aspects of a basic human substance, perpetually in the dark and the mud. "Pim Bim nom propre" ("Pim Bim proper name") are voiceless and voiced aspects of the same absurd, explosive name. (Molloy, too, confused B and P, as does Estragon in Waiting for Godot.)

Bim and Bom, the Russian clowns, have been haunting Beckett's work through the years from *More Pricks Than Kicks* (1935). In "Yellow," the story in which the hero dies, an unexplained Bim and Bom are grouped with Grock, the clown whose comedy depended on human failure, and with Democritus, the laughing philosopher of antiquity. In choosing to laugh at death, Beckett's first hero, Belacqua, sides with this company of comedians. In *Murphy* (1938) Bim and Bom (the nicknames, respectively, of Tom and Tim Clinch) are the sadistic attendants of the Magdalen Mental Mercyseat. In the very first published version of *En Attendant Godot* (1952), the cruel and comic aspects of Bim and Bom are briefly but explicitly synthesized:

> ESTRAGON: On se croirait au spectacle. (You'd think you were at a show.)
> VLADIMIR: Au music-hall. (At the vaudeville.)
> ESTRAGON: Avec Bim. (With Bim.)
> VLADIMIR:. Et Bom. (And Bom.)
> ESTRAGON: Les comiques staliniens. (The Stalinist comedians.)

In this passage, the two friends react to the antics of Pozzo and Lucky, Beckett's most sharply delineated victim-executioner couple. But by paralleling them with Bim and Bom, Beckett levels Pozzo and Lucky, and virtually identifies them with one another as "Stalinist comedians."

Both victims and perpetrators of comic cosmic cruelty, Bim and Bom as Pim and Bom indicate the limits of "comment c'est"—victim and executioner, turn and turn about. The narrator, wallowing in slime, meeting first Pim and then Bom, perhaps creating them through his vague movements of the lower face, perhaps being each one of them in turn, finally comes to deny them both:

> non jamais eu de Pim non ni de Bom non jamais eu personne non que moi pas de réponse que moi oui ça alors c'était vrai oui moi c'était vrai oui et moi je m'appelle comment pas de réponse MOI JE M'APPELLE COMMENT hurlements bon

> (no never any Pim no nor Bom no never anybody but me no answer but me yes so that was true yes me that was true yes and me my name is no answer ME MY NAME IS howls good)

Ironically, the final "bon," approval of anguished howling at nameless-ness, has the same sound as Bom, a name. But the human destiny is ironic, and only suffering is real. Creation and creator are conceivable, believable, only as aspects of anguish. The narrator, hearing his creation howl, utters God's judgment of his own creation: "good."

Structurally, *Comment c'est* is divided, like the Bible, into chapter and verse. The monologue of the narrator is sprinkled with casually colloquial "mon Dieu's"; the protagonist recalls praying at his mother's knee, and seeing a Bible in her hand; while crawling through the slime, he blesses or curses God. Pim believes in God (though not every day), but the narrator prays for prayer without specifying his own state of belief; in a long passage on an unnamed God occurs the phrase, "ma foi je cite toujours" ("my faith I'm still quoting"). On the other hand, the narrator frequently evokes himself on his knees, whereas this position is impossible for Pim. The narrator names Christian holidays; he is obsessed by nails in the palms of the hands; he sees traces of crosses in the mud, and leaves his arms crossed at the end of the book. The puns Pim-pain and Bom-bon have biblical resonance.

These Christian remnants rise incongruously from a crawler through primeval slime. In a verse of extraordinary comic compression, Beckett implies a contrast between his semi-amphibian hero and divine creation:

> fou ou pis transformé à la Haeckel né à Potsdam où vécut également Klopstock entre autres et oeuvra quoique enterré à Altona l'ombre qu'il jette

> (mad or worse transformed à la Haeckel born at Potsdam where Klopstock among others also lived and worked though buried at Altona the shadow he casts)

Although Klopstock and Haeckel lived over a century apart, Beckett couples the atheist popularizer of evolution with the Romantic poet who devoted his life to writing a *Messiah*. It is Haeckel (best remembered, probably, for his capsule phrase, "Ontogeny recapitulates phylogeny") who is buried at Altona, but the ambiguity of phrasal position embraces Klopstock as well, and it is deliberately ambivalent as to which of the two men, scientist or poet, heretic or believer, is the "il" who casts his shadow over "comment c'est." The verse thus summarizes a tension between science and religion, logic and inspiration, evolution and creation, a naked worm in primeval slime and man in God's own image.

This worm-like being, the heir of Molloy who crawled like a worm, and of the Unnamable who created a fictional Worm, feeds on fish, in comic reversal of the natural order. Nibbling occasionally as he crawls, the human worm partakes mainly of sardines:

> ou une boîte celeste sardines miraculeuses envoyées par Dieu à la nouvelle de mon infortune de quoi le vomir huit jours de plus

> (a heavenly tin miraculous sardines sent by God at the news of my misfortune so that I can vomit it for another week)

Crawling through the mud, he also eats from tins of tuna, shrimp, sprat, prawn, herring, and cod liver—all vacuum-packed and hermetically sealed in this primitive substratum.

Fish has long been a pagan fertility symbol. Since the first letters of Jesus Christ, Son of God, Saviour, spell *fish* in Greek ('Ιχθύς), fish became the symbol of Christ. In Beckett's early story, "Dante and the Lobster," there is ironic reference to this symbol: "Fish had been good enough for Jesus Christ, Son of God, Saviour. It was good enough for Mlle Glain."

The worm-like hero of *Comment c'est* nibbles at morsels of the body of Christ, taken from a vacuum-packed tabernacle, until he loses his appetite and discards his canned sustenance into the ubiquitous mud. At the end, he flings away his fictions too—Pim-pain and Bom-bon. The only Christian remainder is the compulsive journey to the East, but stars are invisible in *Comment c'est*, as in the galactic Coalsack.

As it was in the beginning, so it is in the end. The straight-line journey to the East is beset with circularity—constantly repeated phrases, gestures, and events. Life is the old, traditional, and ruthless voyage; briefly, a couple may be formed, and then the voyage continues in solitude, until there is another brief coupling, with the partners reversing their roles. In spite of that reversal, in spite of a straight-line momentum, and although he may deny it, man keeps going round in circles, repeating a few ridiculous phrases, a few ridiculous gestures.

JACQUES GUICHARNAUD

Existence Onstage

Since the 1952–53 season, during which Samuel Beckett was in danger of being eclipsed by more established names, critics and a great majority of the public have almost unanimously recognized the importance of his first play, *En Attendant Godot (Waiting for Godot)*, which is now considered *the* play par excellence of the "new theatre"—the masterpiece of French (and perhaps English) postwar drama. It is original, it lives, it not only represents a true insight into a way of feeling typical of our times but formulates a definition of man that transcends our times, and it introduces a new form of dramatic expression. Indeed, *Godot* would seem the end result of a long and searching endeavor—through the bitterness of naturalistic plays, the mysticism of Catholic drama, and the transcendency of poetic theatre—to express man's fundamental drama.

Certain critics have described *Godot* as an "allegorical play," whereas it is in fact altogether symbolic without being traditionally allegorical. Allegory implies analysis, exteriorization, and a concrete representation of the elements of the analysis. In *Godot* the elements of waiting (psychological, symbolic, or metaphysical), which remain *within* the characters, are not even individually conceptualized but are continuously and synthetically experienced by the characters. Moreover, there are no personifications of the abstract or the imaginary: Vladimir is not the personification of the soul or of the thirst for God; Estragon is not the personification of material hunger. Although the subject of *Godot* is the waiting for what never comes, and although the play, from beginning to end, evokes that gaping emptiness within man which, according to the play, is his very condition,

From *Modern French Theatre.* Copyright © 1967 by Yale University Press.

it does not contain the intermediary that is characteristic of allegory: the reduction to abstract elements.

The play also avoids the traps of expressionism and the dangers of the "play of ideas," since there is no question of abstract qualities or intellectual analyses. Although Vladimir and Estragon sometimes "philosophize," they are in no way like those profound and lucid tramps occasionally found in theatre or films. *Godot* does not imply that out of the mouths of tramps comes wisdom. What they say is not explicit and is immediately transposed into poetry; it is chiefly an effort in the direction of ideas, memories, and a crude intellectualization of feelings or impressions—so that the interest lies not in their reasoning but in the effort they make to reason. The vague ideas they express are not given for themselves, but have a purely dramatic function: they are one of the poles toward which the characters desperately strain. There is neither debate nor confrontation, as in Giraudoux, Anouilh, or Sartre, but merely a representation of the vacuum that separates the characters from what they want to attain.

The absence of any intellectual debate and the spectacle of a constant state of tension sets *Godot* radically apart from the "play of ideas" and recalls symbolist drama, in which intellectual content is not given a logical and discursive form of expression—a form unsuitable for treating a reality that in itself is experienced. The late nineteenth-century symbolist playwrights were concerned with reaffirming the reality of the Idea as against ideas—that is, the totality of an Essence grasped by intuition in contrast to analytic categories. By the same token, Mood (*Etat d'âme*) was opposed to Discourse. Whereas Discourse gradually develops in time, advancing through the moments of an action, Mood is immobilized in order to evoke an eternity. To the naturalistic discourse, to the sequence of events linked together by the relation of cause and effect, moving ahead in time which is comparable to that of an office worker, a physicist, or even Darwin, symbolist drama opposed "moments, minutes that are eternal." Almost Bergsonian in intention, it became "static drama"—a drama that does not move forward and in which nothing happens, similar to a "ball that seems inert" but is "charged with electricity." In extreme cases it has been reduced to the presentation of a painting onstage.

Rémy de Gourmont's description of symbolist drama would seem to anticipate *Godot*:

> Hidden in mist somewhere there is an island, and on that island there is a castle, and in that castle there is a great room lit by a little lamp. And in that room people are waiting. Waiting for what? They don't know! They're waiting for somebody to knock at their door, waiting for their

lamp to go out, waiting for Fear and Death. They talk. Yes, they speak words that shatter the silence of the moment. And then they listen again, leaving their sentences unfinished, their gesture uncompleted. They are listening. They are waiting. Will she come perhaps, or won't she? Yes, she will come; she always comes. But it is late, and she will not come perhaps until the morrow. The people collected under that little lamp in that great room have, nevertheless, begun to smile; they still have hope. Then there is a knock—a *knock*, and that is all there is: And it is Life Complete, All of Life.

The play itself must flow; its time is that of the performance. But within the play, time is neither that of the scientist nor that of the watch-wearing spectator: it is a synthesis of the time of the performed anecdote and the time of "All of Life." Since waiting contains both of these dimensions at every moment, it is the same whether it lasts for one hour or for fifty years. Here the similarity with *Godot* is obvious. In each act there is an anecdote that takes place in the evening and continues for a few hours. The two evenings are consecutive, yet they are situated in different seasons, and "one day we are born, one day we die, the same day, the same second" (Act II). Moreover, the inaction characteristic of static drama is closely related to that of *Godot*. Gestures or words lose their inherent finality when considered in the light of eternity: they are leveled off by the waiting, by the consciousness of a missing transcendency. Experiencing great love or eating a carrot are two "adventures" that dissolve in the same grayness, the same hollow.

A transcendency can color the world in two contrary ways: it can enrich it (two pieces of wood become the Cross; a red rag embodies the liberation of man) or it can make it appear insignificant, as in Rémy de Gourmont's description or in *Godot*. The transcendency that strips the meaning or ordinary value from an action and substitutes no glorification on any other level took a different form in Shakespeare: the sound and fury of Macbeth's adventures dissolve into a final nothingness, and life becomes no more than a tumultuous story "told by an idiot." Didi's and Gogo's clownish tricks and screams, like Macbeth's machinations, would not be insignificant were they given for themselves, but their meanings are reduced to zero by the waiting for Godot. While in *Macbeth* zero is reached at the end of a long trajectory, a long evolution, in *Godot* it is given in advance and is thus responsible for the play's apparent inaction (despite all the activity), for the fact that it marks time, and for the impeccable constancy with which the basic tension is maintained.

En Attendant Godot is a new form of static drama in which three levels are constantly juxtaposed: the words and actions (poetry, clownish tricks, embryonic scenes), the direct significance of those words and actions (love, misery, hunger, the role of the intellectual, the dialectic of master and slave, the dimness and confusion of memories, fear, bad faith, even a certain "miserabilism"), and the waiting which levels everything off. As raw material, Beckett used comedy and the drama of the bum—an art similar to Chaplin's or to Fellini's film *La Strada,* a farce about poverty and solitude, based on realistic observation, in which the spectator is asked to recognize an image of his own condition. Although *Godot* has a more universal and profound meaning, Beckett used the same foundation, the same background of observation.

As the minutes go by, Vladimir and Estragon produce an unpretentious mixture of "sound and fury": they live, they eat, they suffer, they dance, they move about. Their activities are the stylization of a kind of tramp's slice of life: they make use of the objects they find, they eat the bones left by a rich picnicker, they are cold, and they are beaten by the "others." On a psychological level Vladimir and Estragon are much more coherent and individualized than the "characterless" characters of the first absurdist plays. They are characters in the traditional sense of the word, without appearing as neo-Romantic masks of the author (as, for example, Ionesco's Bérenger does). Each of them has a coherent and original personality, a body, and a past, yet they are often treated anonymously. They are called Vladimir and Estragon only in the cast list: the young boy calls Vladimir "Monsieur Albert," Estragon introduces himself as Adam (Catulle in the French version), and between themselves they resort to the childish nicknames Gogo and Didi. Although according to Edith Kern they are as anonymous as A and B in *Molloy,* such anonymity would seem more comparable to that conferred, by the use of conventional theatricalist names, on characters in farce or in a Molière comedy than to the abstractions A and B or the numbered characters in certain expressionistic plays. Didi and Gogo are not interchangeable either between themselves or with the members of a collectivity. In fact, they strongly resemble the colorful, turbulent, and diversified fauna that desperately peoples the works of the Irish.

While in one of his radio plays, *All That Fall (Tous ceux qui tombent),* Beckett showed his gifts as an observer in the traditional style, the setting in *Godot*—a vague platform with one lonely tree—is far less precise and can hardly be said to evoke an Irish landscape. Nor are Didi and Gogo as localized as Mrs. Rooney, Mr. Tyler, Tommy, and Jerry of *All That Fall.* As tramps, they have cut all attachments to their places of origin; they come from different backgrounds and met somewhere a long time ago. Indeed, it seems as if each one's absolute uprootedness was part of his individual definition—an uprootedness accompanied by partial amnesia, and perhaps even explained by it. Yet the fact that they only dimly recall their pasts does not mean that they have none. Their former lives are suggested in illuminating flashes. We learn, for example, that their youths were more promising than their present situations. "In the nineties," says Vladimir, "hand in hand from the top of the Eiffel Tower, among the first. We were respectable in those days. Now it's too late. They wouldn't even let us up." We also learn that Estragon was a poet, that he and Vladimir harvested grapes together, that Estragon threw himself into the Durance and that Vladimir fished him out—unconnected memories in a state of uncertainty which is in keeping with the characters' general psychological confusion.

The realism of Vladimir and Estragon is increased still more by their differences. The lines of one could not be spoken by the other. Vladimir thinks more, he is more cultured, his anguish is more intellectualized, he is more hesitant and more demanding in his choice of words. Estragon is more spontaneous and more lethargic, he is more childish, he sulks more, he is more eager for protection, he is more egotistical and more obstinate, he holds to his own vocabulary and refuses Vladimir's nuances. Vladimir is more restless, more active, Estragon more inert. Vladimir has the responsibility: he is in charge of the carrots, radishes, and turnips that constitute their meals. Estragon is more the victim: he is kicked by Lucky. While Vladimir tries to make conversation with Pozzo and to seem "well-bred," Estragon listens only because he is threatened or ordered to; otherwise, he independently follows the flow of his own thoughts. Didi and Gogo clearly recall the traditional vaudeville couples. In fact, their ancestors come directly from farce: the yokel and his sly partner, transformed in the modern world into the two soldiers of the nineties in French military *vaudeville,* the comic teams in American movies, Lemmy and George in Steinbeck's *Of Mice and Men.*

On the level of anecdote the difference between the two characters creates a dramatic tension. Vladimir and Estragon are bound by a relationship that subsists on their dissimilarities. Their dialogue is not only a kind of antiphonal chant of misery but also a theatrical dialogue in which the two characters attract and repel, possess or elude, one another. Essentially, like an old married couple, they need each other. Vladimir needs someone to talk to, a soundboard for his verbal digressions, and tension is created the moment Estragon refuses to "return the ball." Estragon wants protection, and in that respect he is the feminine half. He actually demands protection, reproaches Vladimir with singing in his absence, gets angry, leaves, then is afraid and comes back—a kind of coquettish friendship. What saves this study of two tramps from being merely grotesque or clinical is the fact that their friendship is profound. It provokes emotion and recognition in that its basic element, independent of needs or habits, is tenderness. They talk about a common past, they help each other, they kiss each other, and even when their actions are somewhat farcical, they are steeped in compassion.

While the play's ultimate objective obviously transcends the anecdote and characterization, *Godot* is made up of traditional elements despite its originality as a whole. In the first production of the play in Paris those elements were stressed, with the result that the spectator's participation was increased, the misery of the characters made more striking, and the tension between a life similar to ours and an indifferent and forgetful universe made more convincing and more poignant.

The spectator also participates because this slice of tramp life is charged with human suffering. Even if he does not identify with the characters, he is bound to be sensitive to the spectacle of misery in general, for although *Godot*'s "miserabilism" (similar to Chaplin's) is one of the least important aspects of the play, it is constantly present.

In a broader sense Vladimir and Estragon symbolize man in general, and on that level the play presents a commentary on life and a definition of man. Edith Kern points out that Vladimir and Estragon are outside of society, that they are not what the existentialists would call *en situation*. Actually they are *en situation* inasmuch as they are beaten, beg, and so on, but they are detached from the machinery of society, in which they no longer have any function, and also from the historical situation. Therefore they have the time to be men. They play at the kind of purity that the classics have bestowed upon certain tragic heroes.

The tramp, then, is the modern metaphor for universal man. The King in tragedy—risen above men, conducting his politics for himself, closed within his own glory, in direct contact with Fate and Values—represented man's condition in its pure state, without intermediaries and freed from bondage. When Voltaire and the Encyclopedists defined man by his function in and his relation to the world of objects (manufacture, commerce), the bourgeois became representative of humanity. He was Sedaine's citizen of the world. By comparison, the royal hero, who did not transform either economy or materials, would seem like an abstraction. Now that bourgeois society has begun to doubt its own definitions, we have returned to the metaphor of man in the form of a detached character— the Proustian hero, for example, that bourgeois who does nothing. Leftist ideologies continue to define man by his relation to transformable materials but consider the bourgeois relation as abstract and take the proletariat as the symbol of humanity—a humanity *en situation*, defined both by its work and by the conquest of its freedom. If one believes, however, in the permanence of universal man, it is difficult to accept the proletariat as a satisfying metaphor, for at this particular moment in history the proletarian is no more than a "half-man" (Sartre). Beside him we have the tramp—a symbol of humanity considered as residue, stripped of its functions and plans for transformations, and left face to face with itself. The tramp has become the image of our condition laid bare, with everything else a mere secondary quality or anecdote. He is an image of humanity reduced to zero, about to start again from nothing. Here there are perhaps possibilities for a new classicism. A. J. Leventhal, for example, established a strict parallel between man according to Beckett and man according to Pascal.

The tramp represents man as such, as detached from society. He is in some ways the symbol of the inalienable part of every man, the irreducible element that transcends particularities and remains aloof from social, political, civic, or ideological brigades. He marks the renunciation of bourgeois participation in common values, as well as the idea of humanitarian commitment. Indeed, man now seems better defined by his solitude and his estrangement than by his participation.

One of the signs of man's solitude is physical suffering. Where sympathy is possible in the case of moral suffering, physical pain would seem to isolate the individual. When Vladimir suffers, he is no more than a spectacle for Estragon. From the very beginning of the play each tramp remains outside the other's pain:

ESTRAGON: Help me!
VLADIMIR: It hurts?
ESTRAGON: Hurts! He wants to know if it hurts!
VLADIMIR: . . . I'd like to hear what you'd say if you had what I have.
ESTRAGON: It hurts?
VLADIMIR: Hurts! He wants to know if it hurts!

No one feels physical suffering *with* another. Here again a comparison can be made with man according to Pascal—the "Man without God," who cannot even use his suffering as a means to salvation. Pascal's idea of solitude as unbearable is also exemplified in the friendship of the two tramps, which shows man's inability to remain alone with himself. The drama of the human condition thus lies in the uncertainty of each man's relationship to others. Existentialist theatre derives its basic drama from a Sartrean analysis of the "others." Similarly, man in *Godot*, in a perpetual series of rebounds, is constantly thrown back into his solitude. At one extreme there is the idea of a kind of "togetherness" in common action, thanks to which emptiness and solitude seem to be filled:

ESTRAGON: We don't manage too badly, eh Didi, between the two of us?
   . . .
   We always find something, eh Didi, to give us the impression we exist?

In contrast to Estragon's "we" is the other extreme—a total absence of communication, even an absolute rejection of the other, as when Estragon, in a moment of brief but cruel betrayal, closes his eyes and, in the depths of solitude, calls to another, infinitely more powerful than Vladimir:

ESTRAGON: (*Stopping, brandishing his fists, at the top of his voice.*) God have pity on me!
VLADIMIR: (*Vexed.*) And me?
ESTRAGON: On me! On me! Pity! On me!

Man's situation should be defined not by his communion with others, nor by an absolute absence of relations with others, but by a fluctuation between the two extremes, by his attempts at communion that are perpetually broken off, by a shifting synthesis of permanent solitude and the effort made to emerge from it. The fluctuation is characteristic of our activities and brands them as futile. Vladimir and Estragon do not act: they try to act. They invent games and then quickly tire of them. Their agitation is a kind of Pascalian diversion practiced by characters who know that they are only amusing themselves. What Beckett's man has that Pascal's freethinker lacks is lucidity, the consciousness of his own condition. Pascal's King who hunts continues to hunt because he does not know why he hunts. Vladimir and Estragon know that they act in order to avoid thinking about their condition. One acts merely to fill up a vacuum—a fact of which the King is unaware. The tragedy of their condition is circular: man's condition is unbearable, but the only apparent means of escape are illusory.

Suicide is twice considered as a possible solution. In the first act, presented as a sinister form of amusement on the same plane as the others, it is attractive only momentarily (for the sexual consequences of hanging) and then rejected because it may separate the two tramps should one of them fail to die. The idea is renounced merely because it means complications. At the very end of the play they come back to it, but they still do not commit suicide—now because of a technical accident: the cord breaks. Yet they never give up the idea, and the dialogue shows that suicide might be a solution when, at the end, Estragon declares that he "can't go on like this," suggests to Vladimir that they separate, and Vladimir answers that they will hang themselves next day. Nevertheless, there is no suicide; there are only two attempts. Here again, even in the case of suicide as a last possibility, the true condition of man is not in the realization but in the effort made toward it. Since the attempt miscarries, it makes suicide an action like any other. Moreover, it represents what is most theatrical in any action—the moment when the character tries to act and seems immobilized between two modes of being: this time, the being he is and the nonbeing he envisions. The drama is neither in the "to be" nor in the "not to be" but in the "or" that links them. Thus another tension is established in *Godot* between the importance one ordinarily attaches to the "or" and the character's apathy toward it. "Why don't we hang ourselves?" is a proposition that has neither more nor less importance than: "We could do our exercises."

Suicide is parodied in a way by the characters' inactivity or desire for inactivity in the scene in Act II in which, once they fall down, they remain lying down. That kind of "Oblomovitis"—the lethargic irresponsibility of man lying down—is made impossible by Pozzo's agitation. The world of the others, who beat Estragon, also condemns him to getting up and acting.

An intrusion into the monotonous flow of the tramps' gestures and comments is provided by the entrance of the couple Pozzo and Lucky. This type of intrusion, so frequent in theatre—the arrival or passing through of an apparently different kind of person—makes the spectator wonder whether the intruder will succeed in transforming the play's universe or whether his difference will prove to be no more than illusory. For the two tramps, Pozzo and Lucky constitute a fantastic spectacle offered by the society of men from which they are excluded. By the same token, they are treated less realistically than the two heroes, for they are a sort of metaphor of what the tramps see in the society that is foreign to them.

Their nature and the nature of their relationship are immediately clear to the spectator. Pozzo, dressed like a country gentleman, carries a whip and holds, at the end of a rope, a pale and thin creature wearing a valet's vest and heavily burdened. One is the master, the other the slave. They enter shortly after the following exchange of words:

> ESTRAGON: (*His mouth full, vacuously.*) We're not tied?
> VLADIMIR: I don't hear a word you're saying.
> ESTRAGON: (*Chews, swallows.*) I'm asking you if we're tied.
> VLADIMIR: Tied?
> ESTRAGON: Ti-ed.

VLADIMIR: How do you mean tied?
ESTRAGON: Down.
VLADIMIR: But to whom? By whom?
ESTRAGON: To your man.
VLADIMIR: To Godot? Tied to Godot? What an idea! No question of it.
(*Pause.*) For the moment.

Almost directly, Pozzo appears onstage holding the rope to which Lucky is *tied.* Is Lucky's rope similar to the bond that might possibly unite the tramps to Godot? Are they not in fact waiting for the opportunity to give themselves up to bondage? They are waiting to be taken over by Godot, they hope to be, but they never explain what they want of him. All that Vladimir and Estragon say is that they are waiting to be "saved." The idea of salvation without any concrete content is suddenly actualized by the rope that ties Lucky to Pozzo. If salvation consists in being possessed by Godot, the desire to meet Godot and the repulsion provoked by the rope would be the two poles of a fundamental hesitation, a movement back and forth comparable to that which attracts the two tramps to one another and then separates them. Here again is the tragic circle, similar to that in existentialist drama: the vacuum of freedom calls for something to fill it, for the nothingness is unbearable; but when total commitment or possession is realized, the resulting state is just as agonizing. Man is caught between the vacuum of waiting for Godot and the bondage of a Lucky (the lucky one who has found his Godot).

Neither possession nor bondage, then, would seem to be solutions. The friendship between the two tramps and Pozzo's and Lucky's rope are only sketches or parodies of a true union—both desired and feared, yet never realized. They seem to imply that we never achieve more than a pitiful or grotesque approximation of a union, just as, through action, we achieve no more than the "impression we exist." In other words, our lives are farces of Life.

The master-slave relationship and Pozzo's acts represent one aspect of the farce—the most ordinary and the least lucid. The rope is meant to reassure Pozzo, just as through his comments Estragon reassures himself by dwelling on the friendship that ties him to Vladimir. But where Vladimir and Estragon make a pretense at acting, fighting, or playing, Pozzo takes his actions seriously, and the least of his gestures becomes a whole spectacle glorified by noble language. In exaggerating the simple processes of life—having Lucky serve him his lunch, sitting down again after having got up, describing the sky, lighting his pipe—Pozzo tries to drown his life in a general atmosphere of ceremony so as to cover up its insignificance.

Either man waits for Godot or he clutters up his life with all the outer signs of importance.

In the second act Pozzo is blind. For Edith Kern, Pozzo's blindness and Lucky's muteness are signs of the inevitable degradation of the master-slave couple. Actually, Pozzo's blindness leads to a partial reversal of the relationship. He no longer drives Lucky, he follows him, and the rope has become shorter—a kind of parodic and concrete sketch of the master-slave dialectic. Besides, although the rope is shorter, Pozzo's blindness throws him into the shadows of his solitude. He thus grasps more accurately the horror of his condition, which has now become an amplification of Vladimir's and Estragon's. For even more than having doubts about time and his situation in space, Pozzo is in complete ignorance or total confusion.

Indeed, it would seem that truth lies in the depths of the confusion. Pozzo's definition of life, implied by the play as a whole, is drawn from his darkness: "One day we are born, one day we die, the same day, the same second." Since the days are all alike, they merge into one indefinite day. There is no flow, only a state. Yet the words are spoken by a character who is in perpetual motion. Beckett plays with contrasts and creates a whole network of subtle tensions between the *state* and the *effort*. Pozzo, who passes by, clings to his state. The tramps, who remain, are always making an effort to get up and do something. When Estragon almost reaches a state (the deathlike state of man lying down), it is Pozzo who, also fallen down, makes an effort to get up. That scene, in which Vladimir and Estragon call themselves "men" and Pozzo "all humanity"—with all the characters who have fallen down now trying to get up, now refusing, going from immobility to effort and vice versa—is the most developed metaphor of the human condition. It has an echo in *All That Fall*, when Mr. and Mrs. Rooney, he blind, she lamed by her obesity, try not to fall.

Pozzo tried to give his life a structure by his possession of Lucky and the visible sign of his possession—the rope. By the same token, Lucky is "saved" by that bond, by his function and his state of servitude. Servitude, however, leads to a mechanization that crushes the individual. Lucky is reduced to basic reactions: he trembles, he cries, he kicks. He has a past: he had been a better dancer, he had been Pozzo's "thinker," he had been, and still is, his valet and his jester. Lucky is more than a servant in the ordinary sense of the word. He represents other servitudes, principally that of the intellectual and the artist. He thinks *for* Pozzo, he dances *for* Pozzo. Vladimir and Estragon think and play, or try to think and play, for themselves. Their efforts are perhaps ridiculous, but Lucky's are inhuman and abstract—at least they have become so in Pozzo's service. Ultimately, both situations—independence (or solitude) and service (or union)—result in grotesque failures. Moreover, the complexity and incoherence of Lucky's long speech show his situation at that moment to be a farcical satire on the condition of professional intellectuals. Supported by a society for whom they are all valets, they "produce" thought, as they are asked to do, but exasperate their masters by their verbal delirium. The result of such deteriorization is silence: in the second act Lucky has become mute.

This new state introduces a usual notion of time. We are born and die the same day, but still the change indicates that we are born *before* we die (in *All That Fall* there is mention made of a little girl who dies because she has not been born). Pozzo and Lucky have changed from one act to the other, from one day to the next, from winter to spring. The amount of time is undetermined, but the direction of time is preserved. In the compressible but irreversible time that Vladimir and Estragon fill up in their monotonous way, the Pozzos and the Luckys "evolve":

> VLADIMIR: How they've changed!
> ESTRAGON: Who?
> VLADIMIR: Those two.
> ESTRAGON: That's the idea, let's make a little conversation.
> VLADIMIR: Haven't they?
> ESTRAGON: What?
> VLADIMIR: Changed.
> ESTRAGON: Very likely. They all change. Only we can't.

Where the two tramps are immobilized by their waiting for Godot, the couple Pozzo-Lucky, who are not waiting for anything, deteriorate in time. If they were meant to represent a society entirely concerned with itself, a kind of prophecy can be seen at that level. Desperately clinging to its present structure (the master-slave relationship) and its rites, amused by an abstract and anguished art (Lucky, who formerly danced the jig and the fandango, breaks out into a symbolic pantomime of "the net"), society, by means of an intellectual delirium that no longer has meaning, will evolve into a world of blind Pozzos and mute Luckys—or toward the world of Hamm and Clov in *Fin de partie* (*Endgame*).

The scenes that include Pozzo and Lucky show the meeting of two living durations in different modes that merge: the perpetuation of waiting, a monotonous flow experienced by men who ask for happenings and change (*Estragon:* Nothing happens, nobody comes, nobody goes, it's awful!), and the transition, change, and deterioration experienced by men who cling to their state, although conscious of the speed of destruction and the unexpectedness of events (*Pozzo:* . . . night is charging and will burst upon us—pop! like that!). In contrast to social and historic man, who is in a hurry to be something or thinks he is, in the brief decrescendo that makes up the duration of a life or a civilization, the play offers a portrait of man as withdrawn from history and society, left to his existence, and continuously yawning in the indefinite flow of monotonous time.

In both cases the activities and effort are vain and serve only to pass the time. What maintain and reinforce this particular meaning of the play, keeping the spectator from attributing an inherent finality to any one activity, are the constantly repeated references to Godot, who is awaited but never comes. Pozzo and Lucky come up to us like the person who stops and tells us the story of his life while we are impatiently awaiting a friend. The fact that we are waiting takes away all real finality from his words and relegates them to a negative universe marked by the absence of the friend we are awaiting. In the same situation the drink we are having is not drunk for itself; it is drunk-while-waiting. And it is the *waiting* that permeates all of the tramps' gestures and comments and relegates their acts to a background of nonbeing such as Sartre analyzed in *L'Être et le néant*.

Of course, besides the agitation invented to pass the time, the moments of life marked by hunger, blows, fear, or physical suffering are real and are experienced in horror. Yet even that reality is finally reduced to insignificance. It, too, becomes the negative background marked by the absence of Godot. Thus the transcendency by which suffering is negated is itself no more than an absence. In the symbolist drama the Idea—mysterious, obscure, or chaotic as it may be—is reality. In *Godot* the real remains at the level of what is directly experienced, and Godot is systematically absent; his very existence is uncertain: he is the fantasy that is satisfying because it gives content to man's desire for a frame of reference. Man is unable to accept insignificance, unable to understand that his misery and his existence are themselves devoid of meaning. Godot is that by which man both justifies and confirms the insignificance of existence. He is the Hypothesis that explains a negative phenomenon. He is the Yes dialectically necessary for life to be the No that it is. The question is not to justify being but to justify nonbeing. The development in *En Attendant Godot* consists of three movements: awareness of insignificance, the assertion of a meaning (Godot) in relation to which it is possible to conceive of an absence of meaning, and the strengthening of insignificance through an awareness of and the waiting for something that *has* meaning.

On the level of anecdote Godot is a character just like the others. His absence makes him more blurred and more uncertain, yet enough details are given to form a sketchy but concrete image. He has shepherds, agents, a family, and a bank account. He even has a beard. He is distant, capricious, and powerful, like the Masters in Kafka's world. Exactly who is he and whom does he represent? Edith Kern suggests God plus the ending "ot" of Charlot, the name given to Chaplin's Little Man by the French. C. Chadwick, on the other hand, sees a relation between Godot and certain French pejoratives, such as *godiche*, implying clumsiness or stupidity. In fact, the meaning of the play does not lie in explanations of what Godot symbolizes. Whether he signifies God or any other belief or illusion is of secondary importance. The subject of the play and its drama is not the identity of Godot but the waiting itself.

Therefore the play does not fall into any of the established categories of religion or ideology, which in themselves would suggest a definition of Godot. It represents a reversal of the Romantic attitude: instead of God coming first and then the *vague à l'âme* (a rather indefinite anguish and melancholy) as a sign of our desire for God, the desire for Godot to arrive comes first. Godot is a positive element created to correspond to man's feeling of emptiness and insignificance, which alone is real and experienced.

The play reveals a universe of insignificance, its tension created by the conflict between that insignificance and man's effort to give himself meaning despite everything. The metaphor of waiting is the best form of expression for that conflict, which is Beckett's definition of man. *En Attendant Godot* is not an allegory, an unfinished *Pilgrim's Progress*, but a concrete and synthetic equivalent of our existence in the world and our awareness of it.

Whatever Beckett's evolution in the past years, *En Attendant Godot* remains the most satisfying of his dramatic works. The others, all in the foreground of today's theatre, pick up and develop particular aspects of *Godot*, Beckett's basic play.

On the scenic level, *Godot* was written for the Italianate or picture-frame stage, and it is within that stage frame that Gogo's and Didi's endless adventure must be seen and heard. The set consists of a platform, with an audience seated in front of it and a curtain hung at the back of it. Both audience and curtain are incorporated into the play, for Beckett uses the convention of the fourth wall or breaks it at will. In *Godot*, by unexpectedly destroying the conventional illusions, he produces unoriginal but surprising effects: in Act I the audience is taken for a "bog" or is ironically considered as "inspiring prospects," and in Act II (French version) the background itself, suggesting a space alongside a road, suddenly becomes a stage set again when Estragon, in a moment of panic, rushes headlong "toward the backdrop, gets entangled in it, and falls." For his other plays as well, Beckett demands a conventional stage. It is very important, for example, when he tries to produce a full-face effect: in *Fin de Partie* Hamm in his armchair must be seen from the front, just as the figures in Giacometti's paintings, looming out of a space enclosed on three sides, are prisoners of their frames, or like one of Francis Bacon's horrifying apparitions. The play can thus be performed only in a box set, strictly limited by its frame. Both *Krapp's Last Tape* (*La Dernière Bande*) and

Happy Days (Oh! Les Beaux Jours) must also be played on the conventional stage if Krapp is to disappear into the background to drink in obscurity, and if Willie is to remain hidden behind Winnie's sandpile. For *Play (Comédie)*, too, an Italianate stage is absolutely necessary for not only the facial alignment of the three characters in urns but the lighting effects.

Indeed, it is not at all surprising that Beckett became interested in the screen—of both television and the cinema. While these relatively new media allow certain writers complete freedom of movement, they may also be conceived as limiting frames: the power of Beckett's *Eh Joe (Dis Joe)* lies in the closeup of a face that is prisoner of the frame of a television screen, while his film *Film* is the story of a character who flees until finally a frame (of both a mirror and the screen) reveals his true face to himself and to the viewer.

In other words, for Beckett the tradition of the Italianate stage, like that of the rectangular screen, offers possibilities for profoundly theatrical effects. While others seek theatricalism in complexity, in the systematic multiplicity of points of view, and in spectacular movement *around* the action, Beckett is satisfied with the elementary artificiality of a stage frame and exploits it to a maximum. Instead of merely forgetting it, as is done in realistic theatre, he makes it not only obvious but obsessing. An immobile eye is fixed on the characters—that of the spectator. They perform facing him, on occasion they acknowledge him, and sometimes they identify him with some imaginary witness. On television, as Joe listens to a woman's voice coming from nowhere, he has no choice but to stare with horror at the eye of the camera.

In explicitly confronting an audience with actors who perform for it, Beckett is not returning to the naïve devices of the Renaissance prologue or the improvised conversation with some particular spectator in the manner of the English music hall, but he never hesitates to address the spectator directly and with varying degrees of complicity. Certain lines are not only a direct expression of the character's thoughts but also comments addressed to the spectator by the playwright himself:

> VLADIMIR: This is becoming really insignificant.
> ESTRAGON: Not enough.

In *Fin de partie* the asides to the audience are more obvious. The play begins like a nineteenth-century bourgeois comedy, with the servant's pantomime of his domestic duties followed by several remarks explaining the situation. More frequent are comments to the audience on the meaning of the play itself, such as Clov's last declamatory speech. In *Happy Days* Winnie's entire soliloquy is addressed to the spectators: just as she is prisoner of a sandpile, so are they her captive audience, whether they like it or not.

Beckett's characters are like children who can act only if they feel they are performing. A child never really acts without a witness ("Look at me, daddy," "Don't look now, daddy") by whom he wants to be seen or from whom he is hiding. While Beckett's characters are adults and in no way similar to Arrabal's infantile creatures, they do exist and want to exist in that state of relativity called "play." The master in *Fin de partie*, for example, is named Hamm, and since his partner's name is Clov, the image of the hammer and the nail (*clou* in French) was immediately suggested to certain critics. Nevertheless, Hamm's first words in the play, after he is unmasked by Clov (who removes the bloody handkerchief covering his face), are: "Me—to play." Once he emerges from the immobility conferred by the mask, he begins to live—that is, he becomes a ham actor. Moreover, the characters know they are playing. All of them feel they are giving a structure to their lives by choosing particular events and telling about them in an affected style with rhetorical effects, aware not of reliving but of replaying them. "How did you find me?" asks Pozzo after his description of nightfall. Hamm demands an audience and constantly interrupts to comment on his own style: "Nicely put, that . . . A bit feeble, that." And Mr. Rooney asks, after an interruption, "Where was I in my composition?"

Such composed narratives are part of a system of rites by which Beckett's characters try to give form to life, fitting it into a framework of beautiful language or deliberately masking its horror. In *Krapp's Last Tape* the hero records the narrative of his life as it unfolds, and he listens to himself. While Proust's hero set about saving his past by making it eternal through art, Beckett's heroes try to save their lives from insignificance through narrative. On the other hand, Pozzo and particularly Hamm are aware of the vanity of their attempts, and Krapp's tape turns silently at the end of the act. Literature, then, is not necessarily salvation; it is merely an effort to save oneself, perhaps as futile as any other. Yet Beckett himself makes the effort.

Presented as theatrical "numbers," the narratives—and, by extension, literature and theatre—are games. Conscious of the aesthetic quality of their monologues, Pozzo, Hamm, Mr. Rooney, and Krapp play and watch themselves play. And just as Winnie, in *Happy Days*, interrupts her monologue to comment on her own language ("old style"), so the Man in *Play* constantly apologizes for ruining his monologues with burps. Of course, Vladimir and Estragon never succeed in taking their own actions seriously; they rapidly become aware of the fact that they are actors and spectators at the same time. Life consists in pretending to live—just as children pretend that they fly or are animals—yet we have nothing more than our lives. Thus there is a correspondence between our lives in the world and the essence of theatre, in which, paradoxically, what is performed is both reality and a game and requires both participation and detachment. Clearly, Beckett's vision of life is made for the stage.

Using all the devices involved in the art of theatrical language, Beckett has always written three-way dialogues: character 1, character 2, the spectator. The triangle may be Gogo-Didi-the spectator, Hamm-Clov-the spectator, Krapp-his tape recorder-the spectator, the Man-two Women-the eye (or spectator), or Joe-the Voice-the television camera (or spectator). Thus two clearly drawn but closely linked dramas are created—one between the characters, the other between the characters and the spectator.

While the former is obviously traditional, Beckett has given it new power by reducing it to essentials and building his whole theatre around the couple. The characters are bound two by two in varying forms of solidarity. Even the character of *Acte sans paroles I (Act without Words I)* is in contact with a kind of invisible and superior being who plays with his desires. With the greatest simplicity, each character rebounds against another; each one acts now with, now against, that other. Indeed, the relationship with another would seem necessary to the effort of playing at living, dialogue being one of the forms of the tension that constitutes man's existence. Tenderness, need, and hate are the psychological components of the bond and are always treated with a rather touching irony, for while the characters are bound by the recognition of their common misery, the bond remains unworkable, never transforming the misery, and each one uses the other, pretending to communicate with him. When Nell and Nagg *(Fin de partie)*, for example, reminisce about a boat outing on Lake Como, they realize that, for different reasons, they had experienced the happy moments each alone, and their so-called common past had not saved them from final agony in separate garbage cans. The couples Pozzo-Lucky and Hamm-Clov, aside from their affective ties, add another dimension to the drama—the master-slave relationship, as conceived since Diderot's *Jacques le fataliste* and especially since Hegel.

Beckett's language and staging has given this drama of the couple such rigor and such new form that it could well stand alone. Since it is altogether permeated with systematic theatricalism, however, the spectator is drawn in as a participant. Not only, as mentioned earlier, is he addressed directly, but he clearly becomes a witness to the characters' conflict. For the characters speak into an ear and act for an eye—both situated beyond the footlights. While the suggested or related adventures may be close to certain slices of life, as in *Happy Days* and *Play*, they are not the subjects but the objects of the plays, the real drama being that of the evidence *clamata in deserto*—that is to say, addressed to spectators who thereupon become actors. Through an obvious but subtle form of theatricalism, Beckett's plays make the entire theatre into a stage, on which man discovers that he has no witness but man.

Since life is no more than the comedy of life, no more than an attempt to play at living, no more than an embryonic farce, the often childish or capricious "games" that represent life onstage must necessarily be borrowed from genres in which the spectacle consists of failure, stumbling, and the resistance of objects—that is, circus and vaudeville sketches and their outgrowth, the motion-picture farce. Among others, the hat business in *Godot*, Mrs. Rooney's difficulties with Mr. Slocum's car in *All That Fall*, and Winnie's struggle to decipher the trademark on her toothbrush in *Happy Days* clearly establish the equivalence between daily life, made up of obstacles, repetitions, and failures, and the most elementary and crudest forms of theatrical comedy. Farce of this kind is grating, precisely because the equivalence is made so obvious and because the spectator's life is directly concerned. Beckett's characters are constantly caught between their own clumsiness and the resistance of objects (shoes that are too narrow, hats too small, car doors too low, windows too high), including their own bodies (prostate conditions, hemorrhages, itching). Moreover, they forget necessary objects or misplace them, especially in *Fin de partie* and *Krapp's Last Tape*.

In fact, Beckett's universe is one of perpetual irritation, in which nothing works—a universe of imperfections, in which things would seem to have been created not for man, nor actually against him, but merely in order to exist in a state of passive resistance to his efforts. In *Actes sans paroles*, *Happy Days*, and *Play* Beckett is more explicit. Objects literally slip away from the character in the pantomime *Actes sans paroles*, while the noticeable atmosphere of concrete uneasiness that pervades his spoken plays is replaced by an abstract notion of frustration. Winnie is prisoner of a sandpile into which she is gradually sinking, and the three characters of *Play* are reduced to immobile heads and invisible bodies compressed into urns: here the physical world is not only irritating but altogether paralyzing.

In the plays in which the characters enjoy a relative freedom of movement, all the small obstacles of daily life cause men to make a series of efforts that represents, in a way, the more general attempt to give a structure and meaning to life. The various attempts made are given a theatrical quality by means of techniques borrowed from the art of clowns and which result in pure theatricalism. In *Godot* Beckett uses a twentieth-century myth—that which best expresses man's attempt to live decently in a world of hostile objects and social groups: Charlie Chaplin's Tramp. In Act II of *Godot* the curtain rises on Estragon's boots placed "front center, heels together, toes splayed," and Lucky's bowler hat thrown somewhere in the background. Chaplin's cane is missing, as if the tramps, relatives of Chaplin's Little Man, had not managed to achieve his elegance.

Chaplin's Little Man is a modern myth and, apart from Hitler, the only modern myth sufficiently distant and individualized. Hollywood, the Party, the middle-class American and Frenchman, and the capitalist are all institutions, collectivities, or abstractions raised to the level of myth. Chaplin's Little Man emerged directly as a myth, with his own individuality and his own past. His universality is guaranteed in part by his generality. He is known, recognized, and loved by about everyone. In suggesting Charlie Chaplin, Beckett is using a contemporary tradition to give a visible sign of the play's universality, as well as to show that the universal is in the present.

In *Godot* Beckett multiplied the Little Man's family. The character closest to the source is Vladimir, with his attempts at playing a certain worldly game: "Never neglect the little things in life," he says as he buttons his fly, and when he is asked his opinion on Lucky's dance, "There's something about it . . . ," he says, "squirming like an esthete." On the other hand, Estragon's shoes most clearly recall the Little Man's classic attributes, and it is Estragon who kicks like him in order to have his revenge. All the characters, however, wear bowler hats as a sign of their participation in the myth, for Chaplin's Tramp is the myth of man who, despite everything, *plays* at being a man.

Although Beckett's other dramatic works are not concerned with the myth itself, the idea of life as a game and of man's attempt to play it remains a central theme. The titles *Fin de partie* and *Play* are themselves indicative of it. On the other hand, the physical agitation and narratives that represent those attempts to play are constantly countered by images of release through annihilation. Just as in *Godot* there are the motifs of Estragon's Oblomovitis, the characters' supine positions, and suicide as a possible solution, so in *Fin de partie* the characters waver between play and a desire for annihilation, in *All That Fall* Mrs. Rooney wants to be transformed into a "big fat jelly" or disappear into her comfortable bed, and in *Happy Days* Winnie's gradual sinking into the sand, while apparently not her fondest wish, is nevertheless representative of the theme of fusion with inert matter, of a final repose that has already been accepted by her body.

The struggle between an attempt to play and the wish for self-destruction is always accompanied by an awareness of life's absurdity and brevity: "The same day, the same second . . . ," as Pozzo says; or Mrs. Rooney's "Just one great squeak and then . . . peace. They would have slit her weasand in any case," after Mr. Slocum had squashed a hen with his car; or Hamm's "Moments for nothing, now as always, time was never and time is over, reckoning closed and story ended," which concludes *Fin de partie*. *Krapp's Last Tape* ends in a kind of stupor, with the tape recorder turning silently after Krapp's last words on the best years of his life: "I wouldn't want them back." Beckett's great feat is to make the spectator experience simultaneously the interminable series of minutes that make up his life—a game that never stops ending and in which he exists in a state of permanent tension, perpetually headed for defeat—and the somewhat objective awareness of life's brevity. "The end is in the beginning and yet you go on," says Hamm parodying T. S. Eliot. Life is a bad play performed for nothing, yet it is the only one we have. Mrs. Rooney dreams of annihilation but continues nonetheless to appreciate the landscape and makes every effort to walk without falling. Hamm and Clov call out for the end to come but continue to play the hateful game of the man who cannot sit down and the man who cannot get up.

Although the same themes and theatrical devices are found over and again from play to play, and although Beckett's general vision of life and definition of man are relatively unchanging, each play is situated in a different and shrinking universe. *All That Fall,* for example, takes place in the peopled and known world of realism: Mrs. Rooney has gone out, regrets it because of the dangers of the outside world, but persists in following the road to the station amid people, animals, and flowers; while the point of view is always hers, the people she meets are treated with an objectivity in the manner of Maupassant. If *Godot's* universe is also that of the outside world, its space is subjectively interpreted by the characters and becomes a kind of desert shot through with rare and unjustifed happenings. In *Fin de partie* the characters never go out at all, remaining voluntary prisoners of their own private dramas. The outside world, which continues to interest them, can be seen only through a telescope: it is an end-of-the-world landscape in which life has almost disappeared and the sea itself has become immobilized. "To hell with the universe," says Hamm as he resumes the interminable quarrel that binds him to his servant Clov. Just as the indefinite space of *Godot* becomes, in *Fin de partie,* a closed room, so the open image of waiting for salvation has been replaced by the closed image of waiting for annihilation. In *Krapp's Last Tape* the room itself shrinks to a shadowy hole, while in *Happy Days* and *Play* the characters' living space is reduced to almost nothing, for they exist immobilized in their containers.

Parallel to Beckett's evolving toward ever-clearer images of physical paralysis is the increasing emphasis he puts on the weight of the past. The characters in *Godot* are, on the whole, turned toward a problematic future, as those in *Fin de partie* live in relation to an end that never comes. But with *Krapp's Last Tape, Happy Days, Play,* the radio plays *Embers (Cendres), Cascando,* and *Words and Music (Paroles et musique),* and the television script *Eh Joe,* reminiscences, vague memories, and difficult plunges into the past gradually take on greater importance and create an atmosphere of general discomfort, not only because of lapses in memory, but because of the relatively obscure guilt feelings that are disclosed. Indeed, the more immobile they are, the more Beckett's characters speak about their pasts or are confronted with them by the voice of another. The language itself—difficult, hesitant, and spellbinding in its rhythms, breaks, and resumptions—is the embodiment of the tragic condition implied by Beckett's works: it signifies the effort to live and at the same time discloses the absurd sin that consists in living. As Pierre Mélèze points out in his *Beckett,* this is a theatre of impossible redemption: since Godot never came, there is nothing to be done but contemplate the fundamental sin, which is to have been born and to live.

Using certain grotesque gestures of everyday life, the buffoonery of clowns, and, above all, language, Beckett—in the wake of the successive demystifications of the postwar playwrights—attempts the supreme demystification: he attacks life itself. He does it without lengthy rationalizations and without contradictory debates. He merely places existence onstage. Existing, for Beckett, means watching oneself try to exist and, by the same token, either being fully aware of the effort it takes or attempting to blind oneself to it. The dogmatism of the Cartesian *cogito* is transformed into a skepticism tinged with Eastern philosophy: "I see myself trying to exist, therefore I exist." And, as Pozzo says, "Sometimes I wonder if I'm not still asleep." In fact, the drama that constitutes the substance of Beckett's theatre is the ironic duality of demystified man.

Beckett's characters silently struggle toward forms of being or structures that are suddenly disclosed by a gesture or in words. Lyricism, eloquence, invectives, and clichés are like fixatives, making existence intelligible and temporarily "saving" it: the words that hesitatingly move on from image to image toward the greatest possible precision or toward an enrichment or transformation of reality are punctuated by screams and swearing that also "fix" some gesture or some impression. Yet while the poetry of the language lies in its precision, in the music of intersecting voices, and in the calculated alternation of pauses and transparent words, the fixatives are ephemeral and the words fall back into silence, as water subsides to form a new wave. The pulsation of effort, forever repeated and forever vain, gives Beckett's works their rhythm, their balance, and their form. When all of life is a game, theatre, the game par excellence, has the last word.

WOLFGANG ISER

The Pattern of Negativity
in Beckett's Prose

Negativity and construction—this is Sartre's definition of the principle underlying literature. He uses this definition in order to try to establish the function of literature in the context of human society. Negativity is to be regarded as one aspect of freedom, because it is not, as Sartre says in *What Is Literature?*, a matter merely of "the abstract ability to say no, but of a concrete negativity that retains for itself that which it rejects, and is completely colored by it." As such, it gives a degree of free play to the reader of the literary text it colors, for his task is to discover that which the work suppresses. One might say, in this respect, that negativity transforms the work into a kind of suction effect: because the reader seems to be relentlessly drawn into the world, the text opens up for him.

This particular effect distinguishes negativity from simple negation, for as Kenneth Burke has shown, negation contains the imperative demand to seek the positive elsewhere than in what is negated, and this demand is nearly always accompanied by a number of signposts to point the way: what the reader has to find can be taken to be the opposite of what has been negated, and so contrasts and contradistinctions form a frame of reference within which the intention of the negation can be discovered. In this way negations enable literary texts to stimulate specific attitudes to specific social situations. However, when such frames of reference are dismantled or even deliberately suppressed, negation changes

---

From *The Georgia Review* 3, vol. 29, (Fall 1975). Copyright © 1975 by The University of Georgia.

into negativity, and instead of a demand we have what I have called a suction effect.

Negativity is the hallmark of the typical Beckett text. It is produced by a relentless process of negation, which in the novels applies even on the level of the individual sentences themselves, which follow one another as a ceaseless rejection and denial of what has just been said. The negation may relate either to a statement, or to something preceding that statement. If a statement is negated, this does not mean that nothing is left of it. A poster stamped "performance cancelled" is still a poster, and is all the more striking if, as in this case, there are no other posters to tell you what *is* on. The fewer orientations there are, the more oppressive will be the cancellation of what we *have* been given. The Beckett reader is continually being confronted by statements that are no longer valid. But as the negated statements remain present in his mind, so the indeterminacy of the text increases, thus increasing the pressure on the reader to find out what is being withheld from him. At the same time the cancellation of statements teaches him that he is not to be given any specific orientation, and this evokes in him an even greater need for finding out what the negated orientation actually drives at. Thus negativity turns out to be a basic constituent of communication. If we look at the process of negativity in this light, we will see that Beckett's work is by no means so negative or destructive as many critics would have us believe—especially those who, like Lukács, feel obliged to view his writings as the "most profound pathological debasement of man." Indeed negativity can be regarded here as a structure of bringing forth—at least potentially—infinite possibilities. This becomes clearer if we take a closer look at the other type of negation, the one that is related to what precedes a statement. If a negation can no longer be viewed in terms of any given frame of reference, it explodes into a multiplicity of possibilities. This process is as old as human society. The Ten Commandments contain a typical example: "Thou shalt not make thee *any* graven image, *or* any likeness *of any thing* that *is* in heaven above, or that *is* in the earth beneath, or that *is* in the waters beneath the earth" (Deuteronomy 5:8). The history of Christian art shows the extent to which this negative commandment has "exploded" into an endless variety of graven images and likenesses. The same applies to Beckett. The continual negation of the ideas evoked by the texts—the self and its history, the end and its ending, the demand (in *Imagination Dead Imagine*) that imagination itself be negated as the origin of such images—constitutes the massively productive force that releases all these possibilities, a force to which the very existence of Beckett's own works bears eloquent testimony.

Negativity brings into being an endless potentiality, and it is this potentiality that forms the infrastructure of Beckett's writings. By negativity we mean the hidden motive for the many negations and deformations that condition the characters we meet in these works. It stimulates communicative and constitutive activities within us by showing us that something is being withheld and by challenging us to discover what it is. If we take the term negativity to cover the deformations of Beckett's characters and also their own negative aspects which in turn lead to so many negativized situations, we may begin to understand what is actually conveyed by negativity. Merleau-Ponty has said, with reference to pictorial art, that "it is peculiar to the visible . . . that it is duplicated by something invisible which is, to a certain extent, absent and which the visible makes present." If we apply this to Beckett's works, we will find that our own imaginations are concerned not with concretizing the deformations of the characters or their constant failures, so much as with the duplication of the "invisible," for the concretizing of deformations and failures can only come about if we can discover their cause, and this is never given to us. We are compelled to try to fulfill a hidden potential, as we seek to conceive the conditions which alone can lead us to the sense of what we are reading. Thus negativity mediates between presentation and reception: it initiates those processes of imagination that are necessary to bring out the virtuality of those conditions, which—though linguistically not stated—are responsible for all the deformations of the characters and their constant failures. It is an important agent of the interaction between text and reader, and at the same time it constitutes the point at which Beckett's texts sink their roots into life itself.

Tavistock School's psychoanalytical research into communication takes as its starting-point the fact that negativity is the basic regulator of human communication. As R. D. Laing remarks, it is characteristic of human relations that we have no real knowledge of how we experience one another. This fundamental gap in our knowledge leads us first to a productive process through which we build up our own conceptions of how our partner experiences us; we base our reactions upon these projections. Our imaginary picture, then, is a product that enables us to cover the unbridgeable gap in human relations. However, we then find that this product is only the image of a reality which certainly exists—for our partner must experience us in some way or other—but which we can never know. Consequently such images can also distort human relations and even destroy them, as they tend to become reified, i.e., come to be taken for realities in themselves and not just as substitutes that we need in order to bridge the gaps of the unknowable in interpersonal relations.

Herein lies the ambivalence of negativity: the interaction might be a triumph of social creativity in which each is enriched by the other, or it might be a spiralling débâcle of increasing mutual hostility from which neither benefits.

In Beckett's dramas there is an almost total breakdown in communication. Perhaps this is because the characters spring from a consciousness of the extent to which communication can only take place by way of projected ideas, and from an awareness of the fact that these can only be revealed as projections if they are constantly made to disappear in the dialogue of the characters. Therefore these characters appear to be constantly on their guard to prevent a communicative interaction from happening. Built into their behavior is the knowledge that dialogue as a means of partners "tuning in" to each other can only produce projections; these may provide the bridge between people, but at the same time they undermine that bridge, because they are subjective ideas which can slide all too easily into psychopathological conditions. Beckett's art of negativity consists in the fact that this situation, which prevails throughout human society, is not simply conveyed to us as such; instead we are made to feel the impact of this situation for ourselves by the deliberate omission of the basic features of dialogue in the conversation of these characters.

This impression is all the more remarkable in that the titles of the plays always open up horizons of human endings—*Waiting for Godot, Endgame, Happy Days, All That Fall*—as a background against which we are to see the characters. We expect them to come to some kind of understanding in the face of such situations. However, as we are deprived of their projections, we begin to project ourselves, only to realize again and again that our conceptions fall short or lead nowhere—i.e., that they *are* projections. And yet in our everyday lives we are always guided by the conviction that our conceptions can grasp realities; we are not aware that they may represent mere fictions formulated because we find ourselves confronted by realities of whose existence we are conscious but which we can never actually know. In our human relationships we act as if we knew what our partner was experiencing from our presence. But in Beckett's dramas, we can only provide motives for the continual negation of the dialogue by realizing that our explanatory conceptions are in fact nothing more than fictions. This realization, however, does not help us in any way to solve the social or historical problems we are faced with. On the contrary, the fact that we have seen through our fictions brings forth a new and almost insoluble dilemma: we know that they are false, but at the same time we know that they are useful. They seem to provide us with knowledge wherever we are temporarily or permanently ignorant. Now if we know that, as Vaihinger puts it, they are "deliberately false," do we sacrifice their usefulness? Or do we hold onto them precisely because they are useful, and so close our eyes to what we know about them? It is this problem that we must now consider in more detail, with reference to Beckett's trilogy *Molloy, Malone Dies,* and *The Unnamable.*

II

In order to gain access to this trilogy, we must first elaborate a little on the definition of negativity. So far we have described it as a structure of bringing forth infinite possibilities, in the sense that it is a formal but at the same time central condition of communication. In Beckett, however, this structure is related not just to individual situations, but to basic features of human existence, whose reality is indisputable, although we cannot *know* what this reality consists in. We have already mentioned one such feature: interpersonal communication, which arises from what we shall have to call the inexperienceability of other people's experiences. The other features are the self and the end. In the first case we have an unknowable reality, and in the second an inexperienceable one.

Communication, the self, and the end are subjects chosen at random—they are central preoccupations of contemporary thought. But in dealing with these basic themes, Beckett discloses something that is not brought out by the current interpretations attached to these themes by present-day thought and value systems; perhaps it is not meant to be brought out, as it would otherwise cancel the validity of the explanations offered by the systems concerned. Herein lies the structural relevance and function of Beckett's negativity. It does not lead to other explanations that will vie with those already in existence, but it draws attention to those factors that condition existing explanations of self and end.

From *Murphy* right through to the end of the trilogy the dominant theme is the identity of the self; the characters are obsessed with the desire to know themselves. Murphy tries to bring himself back to an identifiable point, to what "makes him tick," by a constant withdrawal from his social environment, from his body and finally from the recognizable forms of his spiritual activities. He strives for the absolute contact of the ego with itself. This is why he releases himself from all worldly ties, in order to get to the point where, in his attitude toward himself, he can finally coincide with himself. What happens in this process has been made explicit by Merleau-Ponty in a different context: "My absolute contact with myself, the identity of being and appearance cannot be posited, but only lived as anterior to any affirmation. In both cases, therefore, we have the same silence and the same void. The experience of absurdity and that of absolute self-evidence are mutually implicatory, and even indistinguishable. The world appears absurd, only if a demand for absolute consciousness ceaselessly dissociates from each other the meanings with which it swarms, and conversely this demand is motivated by the conflict between those meanings. Absolute self-evidence and the absurd are equivalent, not merely as philosophical affirmations, but also as experiences." If the identity of the self has, at best, the character of self-evidence, identity can only exist as experience and never as knowledge. Self-evidence and knowledge exclude one another—or in other words, the certainty of self-evidence does not lend itself to be questioned. It is characteristic of Beckett's texts that from the very beginning they are concerned with those experiences of which we can never know anything. This does not satisfy Beckett's characters; on the contrary, they demonstrate what it means to have no knowledge of what is self-evident and of what consequently can only be experienced, thus setting off a process that clearly goes against the modern theme of subjectivity which has constantly defined identity in terms of historically motivated norms. But they do not stop at undermining the historical manifestations of such norms; instead they show the problematic but utterly indispensable necessity of these norms.

"Live and invent" is Malone's summary of the situation. "I'm tired of being matter, matter, pawed and pummelled endlessly in vain," says the Unnamable. Here we have a basic dilemma of life itself; though we are alive, we do not know what it is to be alive. If we try to know what it is to be alive, we are constrained to search for the meaning of something we can, in the last analysis, know nothing about. And so the constant invention of images and the immediate rejection of their claim to elucidation or to truth constitutes the only possible product of this dilemma. Malone and the Unnamable are not taken in by their own inventions, but they are able, at least to a certain degree, to satisfy their urge to know something about which there can be no knowledge. Malone goes on writing, because by nullifying what he has written he can insure that he is not inventing himself; he knows that everything he writes is a lie, because any conception of himself can only be a fiction.

This awareness is built into the Unnamable. He not only defends himself against being invented by the conceptions which he himself has formulated and which now have merged into "gestalten" whom he calls vice-existers; he also knows the conditions which have led to those self-engendering fictions continually usurping him in order to tell him what and who he is: "I don't believe in the eye . . . there's nothing . . . to see with . . . when you think what it would be, a world without spectator. . . . No spectator then, and better still, no spectacle, good riddance." The Unnamable knows the restrictedness of vision that conditions all our knowledge and in its turn is merely an indication that we are inescapably caught up in the ever-changing situations of life. Our efforts to raise ourselves above this being in the midst of ever-changing situations, while we still remain trapped within the limitations of human vision, must inevitably lead to fictions, but we hold onto these fictions because they satisfy our need for knowledge. We are like Beckett's characters to the extent that we are not content merely with the fact of being alive; but we lag behind them because we are not willing to see our conceptions of the experienceable but unknowable, or of the inexperienceable, relegated to the level of mere fiction.

III

Beckett's mode of communication makes it impossible for us to escape from this situation, and this is the reason why we often feel oppressed by his work. From *Molloy* to the *Unnamable* there is continual narration, but in this narrative process we experience an increasing erosion of what we expect from a narration: the unfolding of a story. This expectation is actually encouraged by the many fragments of stories, but these serve only to show up the narrative process as one of continual emptying out. Furthermore, the whole trilogy is littered with the empty husks of traditional literary conventions. We normally take it for granted that a story is told because of its exemplary value, so that the facts of the plot—which we can generally summarize ourselves—only take on their real function when they begin to interact with one another, thus adumbrating the meaning which is to be communicated. However, if statements are made and then instantly rejected, as happens all the time in this trilogy, then we can have nothing more than the beginnings and the rebeginnings of a plot. As a result of all this fragmentation, meaning becomes impossible to grasp, and instead there arises a massive blank—partially structured, it is true, by the rudiments of plot—and the reader finds himself almost compelled to produce a filling for this blank. A further stimulus to the reader's imagination is the fact that the first person narrators—just like Hamm and Clov in *Endgame*—are all afraid that what they say or do might mean something; their fear is that some representative value might be extracted out of what they have said and might be taken for the meaning of the whole.

The reader is continually tempted to try to fill the blank with his own projections, simply because he longs to find a plausible explanation for a narrative process that frustrates all his expectations by denying him access to any specific meaning. If any of his explanations did cover the meaning of Beckett's novels, then we should have to regard these as mere picture puzzles that one need only gaze at with a certain amount of application in order to uncover the secret message. But the structure of these novels is such that the reader himself is forced to reject all the explanations provoked by the "plot" if he is to keep up with the observations of the characters, who know all too well the value, or lack of value, of their own explanations. Of course, the reader need not follow the dictates of the structure; he may be unwilling to give up the explanation provoked by the "plot," because his one concern is to endow the story with the consistency essential for comprehension; in this case, though, he will find that the meaning he has produced and ascribed to the novels themselves is almost impossibly abstruse. The complaint is not an unfamiliar one in Beckett criticism. But if the reader does follow the dictates of the structure, in order to gain access to the conscious minds of the characters, then he will be forced to take the continual obsolescence of his own meaning-projections—which basically are conditioned by his own particular world of ideas—as the meaning of Beckett's novels.

This process can perhaps be best understood with reference to Beckett's use of language. To a high degree, Beckett has stripped language of implications: it means what it says, and nothing more. It looks as if it were pure denotation, at pains to exclude connotation. In Stanley Cavell's words, Beckett "shares with positivism its wish to escape connotation, rhetoric, the noncognitive, the irrationality and awkward memories of ordinary language in favor of the directly verifiable, the isolated and perfected present." But Beckett writes novels. Literary texts do not denote any given, empirical world, and so they ought to use the denotative function of language in order to build up instructions about how meaning is to be produced. Beckett however, constantly takes language at its word, and as words always tend to mean more than they say, all statements must be qualified or even cancelled. By turning language against itself, Beckett shows clearly how language actually functions. But as language is used here to prevent the formation of connotations, without fulfilling its alternative function of denoting an empirically existing object, inevitably the reader will find himself trying to supply those connotations denied him by the text. He has to take over the responsibility for building up a meaning, and so the language—reduced to mere utterance by the eradication of its implications—becomes conspicuously operative in the mind of the reader: he must experience the continual invalidation of the meanings he is continually formulating. This is the cause of the profound discomfort most Beckett readers have to endure; it also enables us to understand what Beckett may have meant when he spoke of the power of texts that claw their way into us. Furthermore, the way in which the reader is induced to reject the meanings he himself has formulated brings to the fore an expectation all of us have about the meaning of works of art: that meaning should bring the resolution of all the disturbances and conflicts which the work has brought into being. Both classical and psychological aesthetics have been united in their demand for the relief of tensions as the basic feature of meaning and intention of literary works. However, this view of meaning constitutes an historical but by no means normative expectation, and Beckett for one is clearly concerned with a very different sort of meaning.

IV

Beckett's novels turn upon two basic elements of human existence: the identity of the self, and the end. We have not discussed the "end" in any detail here, but suffice it to say that these are two topics one of which can only be experienced by means of self-evidence, while the other, a reality that effects us all, cannot be experienced (except, of course, in a way that is incommunicable). This "inexperienceability" and "unknowability" is profoundly disturbing for us. The extent of the disturbance can be gauged from the plethora of pictures and images produced by it, ranging from the apocalypse to the new political millennium.

Now as such pictures constitute our response to "inexperienceability" and "unknowability," they are by their very nature fictional. And yet their lack of reality does not disturb us, because they give us the illusion of access to those areas of life that are inaccessible. Beckett's novels certainly show us that fiction acts as a compensation for what our mental processes and physical actions cannot supply, but the process does not stop at revealing to us why we stand in need of fiction. Although we become aware of it, this insight does not make us act on what we know. Thus Beckett's first person narrators go on. Even though they cancel out the possible meanings of their utterances with every succeeding sentence, they still go on, so that they are clearly fascinated by the process of cancellation itself and cannot tear themselves away from it. If the unmasking of fiction as deliberate falsehood were the sole object of these novels, the time and energy spent on the unmasking would be out of all proportion.

The same purpose would have been more convincingly served by a pointed satire. The fact that these narrators cannot stop is an indication of the degree to which they are caught up in the process of fiction building and destroying. This may seem like an end in itself, but it is in fact conditioned by a self-generating structure that *cannot* be halted. The characters know that all access to the world and to themselves is subject to the restrictions of their perspective. Perspective, however, is as Merleau-Ponty says, "the invention of a controlled world, which one possesses totally in a momentary synthesis." The characters are continually frowning upon such syntheses as pragmatically oriented fictions. But as they are inescapably caught up in the midst of ever-changing situations, this mode of comprehension is the only one possible, even though real comprehension is *not* possible. Their knowledge of this fact can only retain its validity through a ceaseless production and rejection of perspective-oriented meanings.

Such an unremitting process of rejection might be expected to bore both character and reader to death, but this is not the case because the rejections never remain static. A perspective can only come into being through a situation, and the fiction can only be useful in terms of a situation. The fiction takes on its form through its reference to concrete problems which it has to solve, and that is why there can be no such thing as an abstract fiction, for without this concrete function, it would really be nothing. And so Beckett's characters reject ever-changing fictional "gestalten," each of which they have themselves invented in order to solve ever-changing, concrete problems.

Every cancellation involves a negation, but negations take longer to work out than affirmations, and as this process again can only take place through the mode of perspectives, the characters find themselves with more and more to do. As we have already observed, the negations cancel out previous fictional "gestalten," but these are not removed from the scene altogether; they remain as cancelled "gestalten," and so inevitably give rise to conjectures as to the cause and motivation of the cancellation. Thus negation leads to an unending and ever-increasing activity on the part of the characters.

This activity is by no means welcome, for it constitutes the growing compulsion to get away from something to which they are in fact permanently fixed. The perpetual effort to retract what has been stated has its counterpart in their physical existence as well: it is to be seen in the paradoxical cheerfulness that overcomes them in their increasing deformity and paralysis. For the body is the first and last hold that man has on the world; reliance on the body means recognition of an irrevocable factor to which we owe our presence in the world. And so as the body (like the language) progressively loses its functions, Beckett's characters formulate new hopes. Stanley Cavell, with reference to *Endgame*, gives the following description of these hopes: ". . . salvation lies in the ending of endgames, the final renunciation of all final solutions. The greatest endgame is Eschatology, the idea that the last things of earth will have an order and a justification, a sense. That is what we hoped for, against hope, that was what salvation would look like. Now we are to know that salvation lies in reversing the story, in ending the story of the end, dismantling Eschatology, ending this world of order in order to reverse the curse of the world laid on it in its Judeo-Christian end. Only a life without hope, meaning, justification, waiting, solution—as we have been shaped for these things—is free from the curse of God."

A rejection of hope, meaning, justification, and a simultaneous repudiation of our being caught up in the ever-changing situations of life leaves us, in fact, like nowhere men in a nowhere land. And this is precisely the position of Beckett's characters, who have rejected all the alternatives and so leave themselves without alternatives, thus revealing the insurmountable finiteness of man to be an endless or in-finite going on. They know that all connections with relations are fictional in that these are the means by which we delude ourselves that we have brought order into chaos. The only escape from this naiveté is to reject fiction, but such a rejection can then be as meaningful (and so as suspect) as the meaning we gain from establishing connections, and so on. Any meaning, any interpretation automatically carries with it the seeds of its own invalidity, for it must exclude everything that runs counter to it. Beckett's characters know this, and so with every interpretation they present the weaknesses of that interpretation, thereby invalidating it. This process is extremely ambivalent: on the one hand it shows that the indeterminacy of human existence cannot be resolved by pragmatic definitions; on the other, it does away with the coagulating demand for validity posed by all forms of interpretation.

Fiction, then, is both a symptom and a product of man's finiteness. It permits those pragmatic extensions necessitated by his entanglement in an indeterminate and undefinable life. The rejection of fiction, however, prevents us from arbitrarily following our inclinations to reify what we should so like to regard as realities—those explanations that clarify the inexplicable. But the rejection of fiction does not lead to a Utopian enlightenment of man, for what would be the use of merely fixing ourselves in the knowledge of our unknowability? What Beckett's rejection of fiction reveals is the nature of man's inescapable limitations: it is an infinite retention of the self within this insurmountable finiteness. Herein lies the true significance of Beckett's negativity, for finiteness means being without alternatives, and this intolerable condition explodes into an endless productivity, of which both the origin and the product are fictions. The game with fictions can never stop, and it is this fact that endows man's finiteness with its infinitude. Such a situation can only be conveyed through the rejection of fiction if finiteness is to be seen as itself and not as the expression of something else. The perpetuity of the process springs from the fact that a denial must be preceded by a statement, but in turn the denial itself become a statement, and this bring forth the next denial, and so on *ad infinitum*. Thus the rejection of fiction becomes a structure of communication; it conveys the ceaseless activity of man as the irremovability of his finiteness.

If finiteness is to be experienced as itself, it must be without meaning, because otherwise it would be experienced in terms of a frame of reference greater than itself from which it would receive its meaning. Beckett's novels are an attempt to show up all references as pragmatic fictions, so that ultimately we may see finiteness as the basic condition of our productivity. But the novels themselves are fiction. And herein lies both the fascination and the oppressiveness of Beckett's work, for this fiction does not help us to forget our finiteness by virtue of orderly myths and explanations; it makes us *feel* what we are inescapably caught up in. We can no longer retreat to a safe distance through such explanations, because the experience communicated here continually brings us back to their pragmatic conditionality, which in turn invalidates them. Explanations are not possible—the most we can do is experience the unknowable, and herein lies the greatness of Beckett's achievement. He has fulfilled to the letter a saying attributed to him "that art, an arrangement of the inexplicable, never explains."

JOHN FLETCHER

Beckett as Poet

As a poet, Beckett is a minor talent. To be less honest about his stature as a poet would be to invite skepticism for one's evaluation of the fiction (which I consider on a par with Kafka's and Nabokov's) or of the drama (which seems to me the greatest of any living English-language playwright). Beckett as poet is disadvantaged by an unfortunate though superficial resemblance to the richer poetic mode of T. S. Eliot. Both authors owe a great deal to Dante; both wrote the sort of verse to which publishers urged them to append explanatory notes; and both weave into their work allusions to their voluminous reading and to their private suffering. But there the resemblance ends. Eliot, the Anglican high Tory, contemplates with distaste the contemporary world and longs for a return of the golden age that he locates around the era of Lancelot Andrewes; Beckett, the lapsed Protestant atheist, has no such reactions against the modern world, since for him the greatest problem is our having been born, and that has been going on since eternity.

II

Of the dozen or so valid poems collected in Beckett's truly slim, "slim volume," nearly half are, perhaps surprisingly, narrative poems. It is true that they all date from the thirties, long before Beckett had begun doubting and subverting the very concept of "story" (as he was to do in his postwar French fiction); nevertheless, for such a reticent fabulist (or, as Robert Scholes might say, fabulator) it is curious how much of his

From *Samuel Beckett*, edited by Ruby Cohn. Copyright © 1975 by John Fletcher.

collected verse is in the narrative mode. "Enueg I" is perhaps the best of the group, and it runs to all of three pages. The title, like "Alba" and "Serena," is borrowed from Provençal or troubadour poetry, but Beckett's *enuegs* resemble those of the twelfth century only loosely. The early *enueg*—the word means something like "nuisance"—was a loose catalogue of items, some of them fairly scabrous, which annoyed or irritated the poet, such as "tough beef" or a "tight cunt in a fat broad." Beckett uses this free (in both senses of the word) form to itemize objects and concerns which bother or upset him, starting out with his "darling's red sputum" and ending with the fastidious reaction of his nose to a crush of "sweaty heroes" met upon the road. But he eschews the grossness and the triviality of the model and sets it more firmly within the fictional framework of a story told in the present tense:

> Exeo in a spasm
> tired of my darling's red sputum
> from the Portobello Private Nursing Home
> its secret things
> and toil to the crest of the surge of the steep perilous bridge

Anyone coming to Beckett's verse for the first time—indeed anyone coming to anything written by Beckett for the first time—might be forgiven for thinking this is mandarin nonsense. Mandarin it may be, nonsense it is not. The poet is writing of something that pains him personally to an extreme degree: the illness and suffering of a loved one which he has been impotently watching until he can stand it no longer, so that he flings himself out of the private hospital and starts on a bitter trudge around the suburbs of the city of Dublin, "my skull sullenly / clot of anger/skewered aloft strangled in the cang of the wind," biting "like a dog against its chastisement." Much of Beckett's writing springs directly from a private pain: but it is always well disguised. It is now known, for instance, that there was a "green girl" in his life in Dublin: she wore green, had greenish eyes, and was very Irish. Presumably she and Beckett—who has very blue eyes and is Anglo-Irish and of Huguenot origin—were fated not to succeed in their relationship. Was it like the situation so poignantly described in Joyce's story "Eveline" (in *Dubliners*), where the Catholic girl cannot bring herself, at the last moment, to run away with her sailor boy, who offers her an escape from the drabness and unhappiness of her life with her father? However that may be, years later, in the play *Krapp's Last Tape*, Beckett asked himself rhetorically, "What remains of all that misery? A girl in a shabby green coat, on a railway-station platform?" And later still, in the television piece *Eh Joe*, Beckett has the accusing voice remind

Joe of his desertion of "The green one . . . the narrow one . . . always pale . . . the pale eyes . . . the look they shed before . . . the way they opened after." It is probably the same girl. Affectionately—but also as a disguise—Beckett gives her the name Smeraldina, which is Italian for "emerald green" (and Ireland, of course, is popularly known as the Emerald Isle). Lawrence Harvey tells us that "the Smeraldina" died at the age of twenty-four. Her death certainly overshadows "Enueg II" (in the line "the green tulips"), and she may be the "darling" of "Enueg I" since her green is turning "green-black" under the influence of the disease. The darkening, lowering sky shows up green-black, "like an ink of pestilence," as if the whole world were reflecting the cruel decomposition of the loved one.

The five lines I have quoted from the opening of "Enueg I" are therefore characteristic of Beckett's habit of masking his private pain in erudite but not necessarily obscure language. It is true that he expects his reader to have a smattering of Latin (*exeo*—"I go out")—in other poems of the *Echo's Bones* cycle he requires German, French, and Italian—but no more, and perhaps even less than Eliot expects of the reader of *The Waste Land*. Like Eliot, too, he plants a quotation from Dante's *Inferno*: "secret things" is a translation of *segrete cose*, Dante's expression for the shameful arcana of Hell to which his alter ego is about to be introduced by Virgil (*Inferno*, III). Similarly Beckett's poet has left a "hell," the hell on earth of a terminal sanatorium. And again like Eliot, he speaks of a real place, the Portobello Hospital in Dublin's Richmond Street South, by the Portobello Bridge over the Grand Canal (a topographical feature that crops up continually in Beckett's writings); I am reminded of the Brighton Metropole and other real landmarks in Eliot's far from totally symbolic "waste land."

Thereafter in "Enueg I," Beckett explores his own waste land, and a drab and dreary place it is; the words "fungus," "oozing," "fetid" and "grey spew" not only give a somber emotive charge to the description of the landscape, they also elaborate the metaphor of eructation: the entire world is coughing up its polluants like the "darling" her bloody spittle. All that the "wrecked" mind of the poet can do in these circumstances is kick against the pricks (compare Beckett's contemporaneous title for his collection of short stories, *More Pricks Than Kicks*), and end hopelessly with a citation from Rimbaud's *Illuminations*:

> Ah the banner
> the banner of meat bleeding
> on the silk of the seas and the arctic flowers
> that do not exist.

"Sanies I"—despite its title, which means "pus" in Latin—is less obsessed by corruption and degeneration of the flesh, though its treatment of the subject of birth is wry and slightly sardonic rather than cheerful (we could hardly expect cheerfulness on this subject from a poet who lovingly cites Calderón in *Proust*: "Pues el delito mayor/Del hombre es haber nacido," man's worst offence is to have got himself born). The birth in question is the poet's own; he recalls how he "popped" out like the cork from the champagne which was opened to celebrate the birth and slake the midwife's thirst, while his father ("the glans") took the day off with a friend from an insurance company. This memory is aroused by the fact that the poet, who is "tired now hair ebbing gums ebbing" and "good as gold now in the prime after a brief prodigality," is cycling homeward, to the house in which he was born "with the green of the larches."

Birth is also the subject of another long narrative poem. "Serena II"; this time it is a Kerry Blue bitch which "trembles . . . in the stress of her hour." Beckett, who once owned such a dog, recalls in this piece a long walk in the Irish mountains with it, and the fascinated disgust with which he was reminded by "this clonic earth" of the bitch's spasms in labor. This sets up a chain of images to do with birth and lactation (the harbor he can see below reminds him of "a woman making to cover her breasts"), but the horror of procreation—of the manner in which the convulsions of the act of love lead inexorably to those of the act of par-turition—is brought into sharp relief by the acid phrase "the light randy slut can't be easy," followed like a refrain by the words which open the poem, "this clonic earth." If the reader was in doubt over the tone of that epithet at the outset, he is no longer so when he comes across it repeated in this context.

Of the medium-length narrative poems in the *Echo's Bones* cycle, "Sanies II" comes nearest to recalling the note of sour lament we associate most closely, in modernist poetry, with *The Waste Land*. The "American Bar/in Rue Mouffetard" is the kind of contemporary hell in which Eliot's barman shouts "HURRY UP PLEASE ITS TIME"; here a spanking takes place ("fessade à la mode"), and there we are told a sordid tale of the "pills I took, to bring it off." In Beckett we have a sardonic twist on Shakespeare's sonnet 116 ("suck is not suck that alters"); in Eliot we find the ironic juxtaposition of "Goodnight Lou" with Ophelia's exquisite and tragic farewell "Goodnight, sweet ladies." Of course to say how close Beckett is in this instance to Eliot is also to point up the differences: a whole ethic is implied in Eliot's quotations and misquotations—most characteristically, in his ironic twisting of Goldsmith's pious lines, "When lovely woman stoops to folly" in the "typist home at teatime" episode—whereas Beckett's allusions imply at most a metaphysic, perhaps no more than an aesthetic. His poetry, unlike Eliot's does not indict the modern age as such; his allusions to the great writings of the past are not nostalgic hankerings for a past era when—as in the case of the typist's act of fornication—"stooping to folly" meant something. Beckett has no such generalizing ambition. His poem about his father's funeral, "Malacoda," draws heavily on the imagery of Dante's *Inferno*: Malacoda is one of the demons in the eighth circle. In Beckett's verses, he is an "undertaker's man," his perineum (unlike Dante's demon's) muted in respect for the widow's weeds; but his presence is invoked not to make an ethical point, but in order to link the poet's father with the "bulk dead" who are the subject of the other markedly Dantean poem of the cycle, "Alba." Significantly, "Malacoda" ends with a gesture of refusal, the word "nay," and it comes immediately after the spurious cheerfulness of "all aboard all souls/ half-mast aye aye." This reminds me of the ending of the best story in *More Pricks Than Kicks*, "Dante and the Lobster," which describes how the hero Belacqua is baffled first by the fact that piety excludes pity in Hell, and then by the more homely—but for that reason the less acceptable—fact that lobsters are plunged alive into the cooking pot. Belacqua comforts himself with the reflection that "it's a quick death, God help us all"; but the narrator punctures this amiable dishonesty with the words that close the story, words that incarnate all the refusals of all the obscenity of suffering ever uttered by mankind down the ages: "It is not." Similarly the poet's voice whispers "nay" to easeful death at the end of "Malacoda." Beckett has an immense regard for Dante, as extensive as Eliot's, but unlike Eliot he will not embrace Dante's theology. The hero of *More Pricks Than Kicks* wonders seditiously: "why not piety and pity both, even down below?" Beckett's elegy for his father first assimilates the dead man with the bulk dead of Dante's vision, and then repudiates the sentence passed on them all. We are quite a distance from Eliot's fastidious detachment, although both attitudes derive from *Inferno*. For all that, Eliot is close to Beckett in the narrative poems of the *Echo's Bones* cycle; but the two poets have little in common if we turn to Beckett's short lyrics which are of distinctly higher quality.

III

The short lyrics are concerned with a number of issues: love, its extremes and paradoxes; death, either past or anticipated, especially of a loved one; mental torment; time and eternity; and what is called in "Cascando" (the poem, not the radio play of the same title) the agony of "pestling the unalterable / whey of words." These cosmic issues of life and art are handled in verse forms of great economy and concision; Beckett's tight, enigmatic poems on these themes are usually worth all the trouble it takes to unravel their meaning.

The extremes of love are the subject of two pieces printed appropriately vis-à-vis: "Alba," the subject of which is the Beatrice-type figure of the maiden beloved; and "Dortmunder," which treats of a whore, standing before the poet "in the bright stall / sustaining the jade splinters/ the scarred signaculum of purity quiet." Both, in their necessarily different ways, are love poems: Beckett has nothing (at least not at this stage in his career) of Eliot's contempt of the flesh and its lusts; even the somber phrase "mard of all sinners" (where "mard" means the same as the French word *merde*) cannot entirely efface the impression of pleasure to be had in a "night phrase" of this kind. The term "phrase" here is a musical one; it is paralleled in "Alba," which obviously treats of a much "purer" form of love, by mention of "the white plane of music / that you shall establish here before morning." We know from *Murphy* that music is a euphemism in Beckett's vocabulary for sexual intercourse: Compare this sly aside, planted to allow the censors to "commit their filthy synecdoche": "Celia said that if he did not find work at once she would have to go back to hers [i.e., prostitution]. Murphy knew what that meant. No more music." In this light we can appreciate the two forms of love described in "Alba" and "Dortmunder": the one "white" and pure as the title implies, the other "violet" and forbidden. If "Dortmunder" is a veiled confession—and it probably is—it is also a defiant one. Perhaps the Alba (Beckett's nickname for another girl in his early life) knew of and condoned the kind of lapse recorded in "Dortmunder" from the stern ethics in which the poet grew up: If so, this would explain the connection the poet establishes between Alba and the Jesus who invited the scribes and Pharisees to cast the first stone at the adulteress they had caught in the act: like Jesus, the Alba "stoop[s] with fingers of compassion / to endorse the dust"; and like Jesus's, this act of generosity cannot "add to [her] bounty."

But such delicate allusions to love in its sexual sense—either as platonic restraint or as venial debauchery—are less crucial in the poet's mind than the consideration given to the problem of whether love is possible in any sense whatever. The most extended exploration of this theme is to be found in "Cascando," which—somewhat unusually for Beckett—is a discursive, even a dialectical piece, pivoting round conjunctions like "if" and "unless," and deploying rhetorical questions such as "why not." Towards the end of the poem we find the poet's dilemma in love summed up in this way:

> terrified again
> of not loving
> of loving and not you
> of being loved and not by you
> of knowing not knowing pretending
> pretending

This rather naive utterance gives way in the later verse to more poignant and forceful explorations of the theme. "What would I do," the poet wonders, in the third of the *Four Poems* of 1937 and 1948 originally written in French.

> what would I do without this silence where the murmurs die
> the pantings the frenzies towards succour towards love
> without this sky that soars
> above its ballast dust

and he answers his own question: "what I did yesterday and the day before / peering out of my deadlight looking for another/wandering like me eddying far from all the living"; those who, like the "lost ones" of a recent prose text, inhabit "a convulsive space / among the voices voiceless"; the voices which haunt the Unnamable and "throng my hiddenness." In such a world—in the drear limbo in which all Beckett's later heroes struggle to fend off the "silence of which the universe is made"—love is hopeless, and even "those with stomach still to copulate strive in vain."

But perhaps the most beautiful—and the most enigmatic—of all Beckett's poems about love is the last of the *Four Poems* and the one which closes the collection *Poems in English*:

> I would like my love to die
> and the rain to be falling on the graveyard
> and on me walking the streets
> mourning the first and last to love me

It is likely this poem—written not long before his mother's death—is Beckett's anticipated elegy on the woman who, he realizes as he turns forty himself, may well have been "the first and last" to love him. But it is no conventional lament: the poet, like Krapp in the play, waits in anguish, "wishing she were gone"; and yet in neither context do we have the feeling of callousness and cynicism. It requires a great love, a selfless devotion, to wish the loved one gone, removed from the misery and pain of sickness and degradation. And yet (the short poem's many paradoxes force me to use that qualifier twice in three sentences) there is at the same time a flaunted masochism, a defiant hint that the poet is no stranger to the pleasures of grief. And if the poem is about a mistress and not a mother, what curious perversity it reveals! As if to say: "I love her so much I wish to wallow straight away in the anguish I know I shall experience when she dies." He who has never experienced such complex and contradictory emotions amongst you, *hypocrites lecteurs*, let him first cast a stone . . .

Compassion, tolerance, a willingness to put his own head upon the block—these are the attractive features of Beckett's poetic *persona* (and, be it noted in passing, qualities conspicuously lacking in Eliot's). The tensions arising from the paradoxes latent in a piece like "I would like my love to die" are compelling attributes of a talent otherwise slender enough in verse terms. There are naturally not the same tensions in his two short pieces about death and bereavement, but the compassion is still much in evidence. I refer to "Da Tagte Es," which Lawrence Harvey convincingly explicates as another elegy, presenting "a vision of ultimate separation" from a loved one, possibly Beckett's father again, and the title poem "Echo's Bones" itself, which broods on the fact that the grave is the only real "asylum," or—as the opening sentence of the recent text *Lessness* puts it, "True refuge long last towards which so many false time out of mind." All other sanctuaries are a cheat and an illusion: in the earth, the poet appears to be saying—in direct contrast to Marvell's point about "none do there embrace"—man experiences the only "revels," albeit "muffled" ones, which are not a sham.

The sort of elliptical utterance we are presented with in "Da Tagte Es" and "Echo's Bones," where the subject is death, comes into its own in the poems which are primarily concerned with the theme of mental torment and suffering, "The Vulture" and *Saint-Lô*. "The Vulture" adopts the same kind of ironic stance toward its source (Goethe's invocation that his verse should hover like a vulture in search of prey) which we have perceived in the Provençal-inspired poems: Beckett's poetic vulture drags his hunger "through the sky/of my skull" which is a sort of "shell of sky and earth," and the prey is unsentimentally proclaimed to be "offal." We are a long way here from Goethe's Olympian confidence in the art of poesy. But this 1935 piece is feeble stuff compared with the last poem Beckett appears to have written in English, *Saint-Lô*, which in my view is the finest he has written so far in either language (though the exquisite but as yet untranslated verses "vive morte ma seule saison" run it a close second), and which is cast in the form of a deceptively simple quatrain:

> Vire will wind in other shadows
> unborn through the bright ways tremble
> and the old mind ghost-forsaken
> sink into its havoc

Probably the only gloss which the uninformed reader needs on this poem is that the Vire is the river which runs through the Normandy town of Saint-Lô where Beckett spent some time after the end of World War II, working for the Irish Red Cross. The "other shadows" Lawrence Harvey interprets as being those that will be cast when the war-torn city is rebuilt and new walls produce new shade. However that may be, the general sense of the poem is clear enough: the town, which in rubble is a fair reflection of the metaphysical anguish the poet feels about life in general, a kind of objective correlative of his state of mind, will eventually rise again, and the Vire will wend its way through other shadows and different (yet probably not greatly dissimilar) forms of pain and grief; but the poet will continue, the more effectively for having been deserted by the "ghosts" haunting him in these ruins, to sink further into his own personal havoc, a state which no bombardment brings about and no bulldozer therefore can clear away. It is thus a poem about loneliness: the incurable sort that reconstruction and rebirth serve only to highlight and exacerbate. Once again Beckett is not callously indulging in a facile or glib cynicism: he is stating facts. Vire will wind again through a new Saint-Lô, but it will still be a place of shadows despite the fact that the "bright ways tremble"; as Hamm puts it in *Endgame*, "You're on earth, there's no cure for that." War is terrible, but life is even worse; the as yet "unborn" waters of the ever-flowing river are a deceitful promise of refreshing succor. Here Beckett's pessimism extends much further than Eliot's, since there is hope offered by the American poet that the waste land can be revitalized by spring rain. Beckett's attitude toward such a belief is probably best expressed in *Waiting for Godot* by Estragon's sour twist of the wise saw by Heraclitus, a philosopher from whom Eliot draws comfort, especially in *Four Quartets*, to the effect that one never steps twice into the same stream, that existence is a continually renewed and therefore potentially exciting phenomenon. It is hard to despair if life seems to be in constant movement, since better days may be just around the corner. Estragon deflates such happy optimism when he asserts, with characteristic forthrightness, "It's never the same pus from one second to the next."

Such "long shifting thresholds" and their deceptive comforts are the subject of the second of the *Four Poems*, "my way is in the sand flowing," which like "Dieppe" (a poem that links in paradox the words "again" and "the last ebb") wrestles with the enigma of time and eternity, though hardly as poignantly or as forcefully as *Malone Dies*, the novel which raises so acutely the issue of what constitutes living and dying, and whether the two states do not fade into each other ("It's vague, life and death," Malone thinks). But such abstract metaphysical notions are rarely a suitable topic for poetry, as Eliot shows in *Four Quartets*, from which one best remembers graphic images like the brown-edged concrete of the dry pool rather than the more prosaic meditative sequences. So, in Beckett's most didactic poem, "Cascando," what strikes the reader most forcibly is not the scholastic tossing-about of question and answer that I referred to earlier, but a fine image. Apart from its intrinsic evocative qualities it is a good fragment to end on, since it expresses limpidly and concisely the essential subject of all Beckett's better verse and indeed of his entire oeuvre: that the artist is condemned to a task of Sisyphean proportions, the obligation to say the unsayable and seek words for an experience which it is beyond the power of language to utter. In such circumstances what else can the artist do, Beckett wonders in "Cascando," but grind on remorselessly, "pestling the unalterable / whey of words?"

What indeed? Especially when Dante Alighieri, the revered *maestro di color che sanno*, the "master of those that know" (Dante's description of Aristotle which Beckett applies to Dante himself), ends his great poem on a similar note. "Just as the geometer must fail in his attempt to square the circle," Dante writes, "the description of the glorious vision of God which I was vouchsafed was a flight for which my wings were not fledged"; but, "On my desire and will prevailed the Love that moves the sun and the other stars." Such Love is tragically absent in Beckett's world: but the pressing need of it, to enable man to transcend his condition and his language, remains entire and unfulfilled.

FRED MILLER ROBINSON

Samuel Beckett: "Watt"

Samuel Beckett's comedy is far more ironic and less joyful than Stevens' or Faulkner's or his mentor Joyce's. In fact, joy does not have the relevance to Beckett's work that it has in Joyce's and Stevens'. And yet there is a dark lyricism, what Beckett would call a "nightsong," running through his work that gives his comedy its depth, its necessary ongoing human pulse. Unlike Faulkner, Beckett does not give his sense of absurd endurance the levity and charm of a folk tale. His vision is more abstract, his characters more often thinking heads than figures in a landscape. Yet despite all his protagonists' desires to *stop* thinking, to cease using words, they "go on." Although Beckett's "I'll go on" is a cry of despair over the doggedness of human consciousness, it is a signal, too, that no despair is final, that there is something like the "contradiction" in Stevens' "Long and Sluggish Lines," the comic stirring among the trappings of misery. Something is kept alive, however much that something and that life are resented. So Beckett's often bitter, often hilarious, always potent irony is never destructive, though his characters wish it were. The little kingdoms of words get contrived—and contrived beautifully—no matter how often they are shat upon. Contrivance, the fabrication of worlds through words, is—as in our other comic authors—a continual and indestructible force that carries with it a dark song of an essential reality beyond words. This ongoingness makes the irony comic: no matter how intentionally destructive or persistent it is, no matter how terrific in scope, it cannot have the last say.

From *The Comedy of Language: Studies in Modern Comic Literature.* Copyright © 1980 by University of Massachusetts Press.

It may seem strange to [compare] Beckett [and] Wallace Stevens, writers who are seldom if ever paired. Yet however different the surface characteristics of their work, there is in both a profound sense of the paradox of human consciousness: that it grows in power in its attempts to transcend or eliminate itself in an effort to express what it cannot express. In Stevens' late poem, "The Rock," he wrote these eerily Beckett-like lines, creating a scene like the one between Watt and Sam that I will discuss later.

> The lives these lived in the mind are at an end.
> They never were . . . The sounds of the guitar
>
> Were not and are not. Absurd. The words spoken
> Were not and are not. It is not to be believed.
> The meeting at noon at the edge of the field seems like
>
> An invention, an embrace between one desperate clod
> And another in a fantastic consciousness,
> In a queer assertion of humanity:

Here it is stated that words are absurd, that the mind's life is "at an end" because nothing that has been spoken has mattered. And yet it has *not* ended, human consciousness asserts itself again, and the poem gains in strength as it recognizes this vitality. Nothing is final, permanent, concluded—deep in the cold comes this "queer assertion." The paradox of the situation is rendered in the lines that follow soon after the above passage:

> As if nothingness contained a métier,
> A vital assumption, an impermanence
> In its permanent cold, an illusion so desired
>
> That the green leaves came. . . .

Out of nothingness comes a calling, a trade, a career of words. In the absence of form is contained the seed of form, illusory but necessary. But how can nothingness contain a métier? To paraphrase one of Beckett's Addenda to *Watt*, how can words enclose nothingness? The dilemma here is too somberly declared to be comic, but the unsolvable paradox that yields both Stevens' and Beckett's comedy of language is there, available.

Here is a typical example of Beckett's comic style, from the "Texts for Nothing":

> That's right, wordshit, bury me, avalanche, and let there be no more talk of any creature, nor of a world to leave, nor of a world to reach, in order to have done, with worlds, with creatures, with words, with

misery, misery. Which no sooner said, Ah, says I punctually, if only I could say, There's a way out there, there's a way out somewhere, then all would be said, it would be the first step on the long travelable road, destination tomb, to be trod without a word, tramp, tramp, little heavy irrevocable steps, down the long tunnels at first, then under the mortal skies, through the days and nights, faster and faster, no, slower and slower, for obvious reasons, and at the same time faster and faster, for other obvious reasons, or the same, obvious in a different way, or in the same way, but at a different moment of time, a moment earlier, a moment later, or at the same moment, there is no such thing, there would be no such thing, I recapitulate, impossible.

A voice calls for the end of talk while talking. It calls for an end to creatures while going about its creaturely métier, inventing a persona, an "I." It trashes its words while inventing more, faster and faster. The passage is a verbal equivalent of a clown's continually stumbling without being able to fall. The voice, in fact, imagines a way out of language only as a way out of life: just as steps tramped through mortal time are seeking a conclusion, so words are steps toward the wordless. Only "destination tomb" can end this voice, and Beckett's voices never die because they keep on talking. Their language, like the language above, becomes more comical as it tries to realize itself as language—that is, as something syntactically and substantially logical, a *form* of expression, a figuring out of things maniacally and fastidiously—because the contradiction between the logic and the absurdity and arbitrariness of language becomes more pronounced. Beckett's comedy is, in many respects, our purest example of the comedy of language because his obsessive preoccupation is with the very fact of address. Often, as in the "Texts for Nothing," there is nothing else but a voice ruminating on what issues from it: words, words.

THE APORETICAL STYLE

"What am I to do, what shall I do, what should I do, in my situation, how proceed?" Beckett's Unnamable asks himself, and immediately follows this question with another: "By aporia, pure and simple?" Aporia is the awareness of opposing and incompatible views of the same subject; it also means the doubt or skepticism implicit in such an awareness. Aporia thus connotes irresolution or impasse (the Greek *aporos* means "impassable"). One poises, in suspension, two mutually exclusive ideas, points of view, etc. This may suggest a kind of stasis, but if one is true to one's aporetics, no stasis is possible. If the Unnamable has *stated*, "By aporia pure and simple," he would have decided on an answer to how to proceed, and the issue would be, in a way, resolved. No, in aporia all answers are further questions. Indeed, the Unnamable soon says, "I say aporia without knowing what it means. Can one be ephectic otherwise than unawares?" About this, J. D. O'Hara has judiciously written, "Obviously if one is deliberately skeptical, if one deliberately suspends judgment as a matter of policy, then one's action is in itself a judgment; pretending to be skeptical, one has actually committed oneself to a belief." This is so, but O'Hara, for his own relatively unplayful purposes (his subject is not Beckett's comedy), does not quite follow through with the joke: the Unnamable obviously *does* know what aporia means, he uses it quite precisely, is obviously aware of suspending judgment (being "ephectic"). And so the problem continues in a vicious circle, the questions go on, like the voice of the Unnamable, whose refrain is "I can't go on, I'll go on."

Beckett's Malone, near the beginning of *his* novel, reveals his familiarity with aporia: "Perhaps I shall not have time to finish. On the other hand perhaps I shall finish too soon. There I am back at my old aporetics. Is that the word? I don't know." He, too, claims not to understand what he really does understand about not understanding what he really understands, and so on. The more one unravels such paradoxes, the more comic one's own prose becomes, because language, with its syntax and sentences, is designed to elucidate the elusive, not to confront the fact of elusiveness itself. Language isolates what it can out of flux and ignores flux itself. The more language attempts to fix what it cannot fix, what cannot *be* fixed, the more it parodies its own mechanism. This is how much of the comedy of *Watt* works, particularly in the extended passages in which Watt (a unit of energy asking questions) tries to fix in words a reality (the reality of Knott) that eludes him. The result is a vaudeville of language, an explosion of hectic and futile reasoning.

A visual equivalent of Watt's mental processes at work is Buster Keaton's "great infernal nutcracking machine," which Henriette Nizan has described:

The machine which stands on a table must be at least three feet high. It looks extremely complicated. This is how it works: a crane, put in motion, picks a choice nut from a gunny sack. The crane raises the nut to the top of a slide and drops it; the nut begins its slide, and after meandering from small a to big A, then from small b to big B, it drops into a basket. The basket conveys it from C to Ć to a transporter bridge. From there, after a lot of comings and goings intended to soften it, the nut crosses several canals and inclined planes, and then, suddenly set on its vertical, comes to a raised platform on which it descends, progressively, until it arrives at last beneath a kind of steam-hammer in the form of a mallet which, at the proper moment, rises, comes down, and . . . misses.

The machine, if it did crack the nut, would still be comic in a Rube Goldbergian way. It is profoundly comic because it does not crack the nut, and so realizes itself as a kind of pure machine: functionless, solipsistic, engaged solely in its own processes. Watt confronts incidents "of great formal brilliance and indeterminable purport," a phrase that also describes, necessarily, the language that issues from his thought processes—and also Keaton's machine. The "formal brilliance" of the machine is a function of its not cracking the nut. The pleasure we feel in seeing the machine operate is a function of our ironic awareness that it will not fulfill its express purpose. And vice versa: the irony of our awareness is a function of our pleasure in seeing it operate. The comic experience is two-fold and simultaneous: (1) we see, ironically, that the machine does not "work," and (2) we see, in a sudden expansive vision that is the soul of play, that it *does* work insofar as it fulfills itself on its own terms.

So too with language, which comes to comical fruition in its failed efforts to get its job of ordering done. We have left Malone at his old aporetics; if we return to them we can connect them to the idea of play. Malone, waiting to die in his room, knows that, however much his unquiet thought will be "wide of the mark," it will struggle on nevertheless. And so he conceives of his stories, his incessant language production, as "play" or "a game." So conceived, his language need no longer be burdened with "the earnestness" of seeking for some formulated truth: "What half-truths, my God. No matter. It is playtime now."

Aporia is "play" because, in the suspension of its opposing terms and consequent circularity of its reasoning, it puts us in touch with a form that is closer to the life of things, a reality that simply goes on in purposeless splendor. Eugene Fink says that "play is characterized by calm, timeless 'presence' and autonomous, self-sufficient meaning," that it "has only internal purpose, unrelated to anything external to itself." He continues, "In the autonomy of play action there appears a possibility of human timelessness in time. Time is then experienced, not as a precipitate rush of successive moments, but rather as the one full moment that is, so to speak, a glimpse of eternity." This is precisely what Didi's and Gogo's vaudeville-style "play" does for them in *Waiting for Godot*: allow them to forget the tedious round of their waiting, and prepare for whatever will come at the end of that round: God, Godot, Nothing, Knott. And yet play reflects, just as it absorbs, the presentational forms of the world outside its boundaries, just as children often enact war in their play. Malone's consciousness and the language that expresses it go on, in relentless purpose, seeking to describe what it cannot describe, seeking to cancel itself out and so avoiding the cancellation. "And I even feel a strange desire come over me, the desire to know what I am doing, and why. So I near the goal I set for myself my young days and which prevented me from living. And so on the threshold of being no more I succeed in being another. Very pretty." We can understand Malone's (and Beckett's) voice if we realize that the tone behind "very pretty" is as appreciative as it is sardonic and bitter. Indeed, it is both. The aporetical style expresses a constant contradiction between a desire to cease speaking because language is absurd, and a desire to speak because language is necessary. The contradiction is never resolved, no point of view is ever final. Henriette Nizan's response to Keaton's nutcracking machine is appropriate: "There's nothing for it but to begin all over again."

THE FORMS OF FIASCO

Before analyzing in some detail Beckett's second novel, *Watt*, I think it would be useful to sketch some of Beckett's characteristic paradoxes, as a background to the central images and ideas in the novel, and in all his work, and as a preparation for describing the comedy of these images and ideas.

Beckett's most obsessive imagery is that of light and darkness. Darkness expresses security, enclosure, refuge, silence: the state of the womb, or conditions for which the womb is paradigm. Darkness is the Paradise that has been lost, for we are expelled from it into light, into the world, the "outside" data demanding to be named. This expulsion is a Fall which Beckett's protagonists lament. They regard living in this world, the outer world, as atonement for an unknown sin, or "itself a sin, calling for more atonement," or as a series of "stations." The cross that they bear is consciousness, for as soon as they are expelled from the womb they begin to hear voices naming things. Molloy expresses this most lucidly in the passage . . . in which his consciousness is described as a disturbance of silence, a "lie." The voice inside us, with which we speak, is not truly of ourselves, but is a voice inherited, as it were, from "outside." This results in a fragmentation of our identity: "I express by saying, I said," or Molloy says, or any number of given and invented names says. Richard Coe articulates this well when he says, "we do not make our words—we learn them. From others. Others speak and we hear.

Not a thought in our heads, not a memory, not a fragment of our personality, which was not created and put there by other people."

Birth entails, then, a loss of identity, of the self we feel is ours alone, the unnamable self. We emerge from our self-enclosed being into an illusory and patterned world, a Babel of voices outside that initiates a Babel of voices within, murmuring constantly. We enter what in *Murphy* is called the "physical fiasco," the rot of living, the valley of the shadow of death. Moran gives us a feeling for it in this passage: "I get up, go out, and everything is changed. The blood drains from my head, the noise of things bursting, merging, avoiding one another, assails me on all sides, my eyes search in vain for two things alike, each pinpoint of skin screams a different message, I drown in the spray of phenomena." Change is the ruling principle of the fiasco. Change brought us outside and rots us. Moment to moment, infinite fractions of moments to infinite fractions of moments, things change, perceived or unperceived.

There is no actual light without darkness, and no actual darkness without light in Beckett's landscape, only a continual movement from one to the other, a shadowing and dawning in eternal change. For we are not only expelled onto our personal *via dolorosa*, but we long to return to the security of darkness, to the sense of our being without consciousness, to mother, to "home." "Murphy, all life is figure and ground," said Neary; "But a wandering to find home," said Murphy. At home we can experience once again "the silence of which the universe is made," and be at rest at last. In Beckett's world, one is prodded out of one's rest, and one seeks rest. The protagonist of "The Expelled," on being expelled from his home, sets out on his own, failing to stay on the sidewalk (all Beckett's protagonists find motion to be an intricate and difficult business, the life of forms a precarious affair). Soon he enters a cab like a "black box" and curls up foetally in a corner of it. In the course of most of the story he attempts to remain in the womb-like cab, and finally must leave it, making "towards the rising sun. . . . When I am abroad in the morning, I go to meet the sun, and in the evening, when I am abroad, I follow it, till I am down among the dead." Most of the scenes in Beckett's landscapes take place in the dawning or dying day. Even at midday there are shadows, and at night there is usually the moon, pouring its rays upon Watt, for example, who dislikes it. As Sam says much later, referring to the effects of the years on the colors of Watt's hat and coat," So it is with time, that lightens what is dark, and darkens what is light." Or again, of Malone's fictional creation, Sapo, it is said, "of a sudden he is off again, on his wanderings, passing from light to shadow, from shadow to light, unheedingly." Beckett's descriptions of scenic landscapes are seldom of solid objects clearly seen, but of things seen dimly and lyrically in the constant movement of light and shadow.

For Beckett's protagonists, existing in change, the movement toward light is a movement forced on them. The contingencies of the world require them to move, prodded from the foetal rest that was contentment. Analogously, the murmur of voices, the continuous babble of "intelligible sounds," makes them seek *meaning* in these sounds. Referring to the "spray of phenomena" that he encounters outside, Moran continues, "It is at the mercy of these sensations, which happily I know to be illusory, that I have to live and work. It is thanks to them that I find myself a meaning. So he whom a sudden pain awakens." Consciousness is a "pensum" assigned to us by the Generalized Other; we are obligated, for reasons unknown, or because we are human, to wrench meaning out of chaos. This painful undertaking is the "ancient labour" at which Watt labors.

The search for darkness, for refuge from phenomena, is initiated by a desire to be free of meanings, and of the voices that suggest them—to touch what lies beyond words, that which Beckett calls in his monograph on Proust "the mystery, the essence, the Idea." In *Proust* Beckett makes a distinction between "Habit" and "the suffering of being." Habit is all that we mean when we say "Life" or "living"; it is the "compromise effected between the individual and his environment," whether inner or outer, the "consecutive adaptations" to the world that we make in order to be comfortably sealed off from the "suffering of being." This suffering occurs when the individual, in rare and painful and delicious moments, comes in contact with "the real"—that is, reality stripped of the protective conceptions with which we, in self-defense, clothe it. The world then appears truly strange, and ourselves truly strangers in it.

> . . . when the object is perceived as particular and unique and not merely the member of a family, when it appears independent of any general notion and detached from the sanity of a cause, isolated and inexplicable in the light of ignorance, then and then only may it be a source of enchantment. Unfortunately Habit has laid its veto on this form of perception, its action being precisely to hide the essence—the Idea—of the object in the haze of conception—pre-conception.
>
> (*Proust*, II)

Habit, then, allows us to cope with the outside world; our voice, at the beck of the voices we inherit, formulates meanings, conceptions, categories, so that objects are classified—chair, book, pot, Molloy—by inherited words, the "icy words" that "hail down upon" us, "the icy meanings, and the world dies too, foully named." This is by now a familiar idea to us: language, which in its naming and classifying is inexorably logical, separates us both from reality and our own identity, an identity which for Beckett's protagonists is "wrapped in a namelessness often hard to penetrate." The attempt to penetrate it, which forms the main action of *Watt*, is what I am calling the movement toward darkness.

It is important to understand that the two movements, toward light and toward darkness, are simultaneous, in constant and comic contradiction. Perhaps the most abstract expression of this condition is in Beckett's first published work, his essay on Joyce's "Work in Progress" (*Finnegans Wake*), entitled "Dante . . . Bruno. Vico . . . Joyce":

> Thus we have the spectacle of a human progression that depends for its movement on individuals, and which at the same time is independent of individuals in virtue of what appears to be a preordained cyclicism. . . . the work of some superior force, variously known as Fate, Chance, Fortune, God . . . Individuality is the concretion of universality, and every individual action is at the same time superindividual. The individual and the universal cannot be considered as distinct from each other.

For Beckett, as for Vico, we live paradoxically in and out of History. As part of a "universal" structure, we are in a sense victims of its preordination, and as individual agents we are aware of our unique identities, our unique relations with a unique world. We inherit "voices" yet we realize, if we are not completely stunned by Habit, that these voices are not our own. Richard Coe, who provides us with a sort of Ariadne's thread through Beckett's abstract thought, comments on one of Watt's ruminations in this way: "For either Tom is temporal, in which case his whole existence is determined by his place in the series; or else he is a-temporal, a-spatial, and independent of the series—he cannot very well be both. *And yet*, says Beckett, *this is precisely what he is*. Human existence *is* a logical impossibility. It belongs to the series and yet evades the series; it is at once in time and out of time."

As Sartre said in his essay on Faulkner's *The Sound and the Fury*, every metaphysic implies an aesthetic, and Coe's remark bears on his thesis that Beckett's view of the human condition, and hence of art, is that they are "literally and logically *impossible*." The idea of a paradoxical aesthetic brings us to Beckett's only extended commentary on his own aesthetic, his "Three Dialogues" with the French art critic, Georges Duthuit, to which I have referred [elsewhere]. The central paradox is this: that the artist is obliged to express at the same time that he cannot express. Part of the third dialogue, on the painter Bram Van Velde, goes like this:

B.—The situation is that of him who is helpless, cannot act, in the event cannot paint, since he is obliged to paint. The act is of him who, helpless, unable to act, acts, in the event paints, since he is obliged to paint.
D.—Why is he obliged to paint?
B.—I don't know.
D.—Why is he helpless to paint?
B.—Because there is nothing to paint and nothing to paint with.

The artist is obliged to paint (to express, create, relate things) simply because he exists in the world. Born into the light, he is compelled by the light, voices compel him, inexorably, inexplicably. To ask why he is obliged to express is like asking why certain muscles contract to effect parturition. They contract involuntarily. And involuntarily we toe the line of History, and proceed along it, receiving a language, asking questions with it, seeking answers. This is our cross to bear. The artist is "helpless" to express because he is aware of "the incoercible absence of relation," the Nothing that underlies our orders, relations, conceptions, words—and so is aware that his relations are false. "The history of painting . . . is the history of its attempts to escape from this sense of failure, by means of more authentic, more ample, less exclusive relations between representer and representee, in a kind of tropism toward the light . . . and with a kind of Pythagorean terror, as though the irrationality of pi were an offense against the deity, not to mention his creature." The references to dark and light are consistent with my earlier comments. The shadowing toward darkness involves a sense of the falseness of language (whether of paint or words) and the knowledge that art, and the artist, must fail. The "tropism toward the light" involves involuntary Habit, the desire to create and possess one's conceptions, stake out one's artistic property on the vast and meaningless landscape of reality. This is the "estheticized automatism" of the individual who seeks to express and to be part of the universal. Art, to Beckett, is or should be impossible because the artist seeks or should seek to express "nothing," attempt to enclose silence in words. As Northrop Frye says at the end of his review of the Trilogy, Beckett's "final paradox is the conception of the imaginative process which underlies and informs his remarkable achievement . . . to restore silence in the role of serious writing."

The mention of the irrationality of pi in the passage from the "Three Dialogues" quoted above suggests another paradox—or, more precisely, another expression, in different terms, of an essential paradox—the fact that man exists, simultaneously, in rational and irrational worlds. The domain of rational numbers is the domain of History, of forms.

But as Hugh Kenner points out, there is another domain, "which we can think about but not enter with our minds," the domain of irrational numbers, "more numerous even than the infinitely numerous rationals. And it is the analogy between these interpenetrating but incommensurable domains that Beckett discerns his central analogy for the artist's work and the human condition." The closeness of this to Bergson's opposed world of the intellect and intuition should be noted. The work of the intellect is with stable states, forms—by analogy, rational numbers. Intuition brings us into contact with the creative evolution of constant change—by analogy, the irrational realm which the intellect cannot define, or what Beckett calls, when describing Murphy's mind, the "matrix of surds."

Beckett's description of Murphy's mind helps us to relate the imagery of light and darkness to the domains described above. Murphy's "mental experience was cut off from the physical experience. . . . It was made up of light fading into dark. . . . If felt no issue between its light and its dark, no need for its light to devour its dark. The need was now to be in the light, now in the half light, now in the dark. That was all." His mind is not ethically oriented, and so its only operative principle is constant changing from its states of light and half light and dark. In the zone of light, mental experience is "parallel" with physical experience (cause and effect being an obvious lie to all of Beckett's protagonists). This climate of light is the one in which most of us spend most of our lives. Murphy regards it as merely "a radiant abstract of the dog's life. . . . Here the whole physical fiasco became a howling success." In the zone of half light mental experience is not parallel with physical experience. This is the climate in which most of Beckett's protagonists intermittently exist, in which one contemplates one's physical experience objectively, if one contemplates it at all. Physical life is there, nevertheless, a source of Chaplinesque surprise. In the third zone mental experience is completely self-enclosed, "a closed system subject to no principle of change but its own, self-sufficient and impermeable to the vicissitudes of the body." Beckett describes it in significant detail:

> The third, the dark, was a flux of forms, a perpetual coming together and falling asunder of forms . . . nothing but forms becoming and crumbling into the fragments of a new becoming, without love or hate or any intelligible principle of change. Here there was nothing but commotion and the pure forms of commotion. Here he was not free, but a mote in the dark of absolute freedom. He did not move, he was a point in the ceaseless unconditioned generation and passing away of line.
> Matrix of surds.

This is the irrational zone. At the end of the novel, Murphy glimpses it in the eye of Mr. Endon, who is insane, and presumably achieves it in his (Murphy's) death, when the "superfine chaos" of gas soothes him to a final sleep, his body quiet at last. The third zone is not a state that can be entered except in madness or death. *Murphy* is not a comedy because, in effect, Murphy resolves his dilemma, or has it resolved for him. It is the half light in which the minds of Beckett's other protagonists play, and they play continually, their minds in a comic flux between the light of rationality and the darkness of surds.

I have been sketching some related paradoxes. Perhaps an accumulation of them is called for:

light	dark
universal	individual
words	silence
rational numbers	surds

The world of Beckett's comic fiction and drama takes place in an aporia between these poles, in which the oppositions are not resolved but are suspended in paradox. If we think of this fictional ground as, say, a magnetic field, we can imagine particles constantly ordering and reordering themselves on it. Beckett's protagonists seek rest and are compelled to move, seek silence and are compelled to speak and write their reports, are overwhelmed by a sense of the irrational yet are compelled to rationalize. Their problems are central to Beckett's problem as an artist: given that he is obliged to write, how does he write when there is nothing to write about and nothing to write with? Or, as the question is put in the Addenda to *Watt*, who may "nothingness/in words enclose?"

This is a brief sketch of Beckett's vision. How is it made the subject of comedy? Discussing *Watt*, Hugh Kenner remarks with characteristic cogency: "That things and events are extracted in self-defense from an unintelligible continuum of changes is one of philosophy's self-cancelling propositions, assailing the very fact of its own affirmation. It is thus ideally suited to Beckett's characteristic comedy of the impasse. It is first cousin to the statement, 'Every statement that I make is meaningless.' " How are such reflexively self-cancelling statements related to comedy? In *Sweet Madness: A Study of Humor*, the psychologist William Fry proposes, in discussing the "vicious-circle principle" and the role of paradox in human communication, that paradox is an inescapable and pleasurable issue of human thought processes and is the essence, the very nature of "play" or humor. The vicious-circle paradox of the lying Cretan is found by Fry to be operative, in less obvious ways, in simple statements like "This is unreal" or "This is a dream"—reflexive statements that, by cancelling themselves out, initiate a "shimmering, endless oscillation of the paradoxes or 'real-unreal.' Humor becomes a vast structure of intermeshed, revolving rings of reality-fantasy, finite-infinite, presence-void."

This speaks directly to Beckett's comic world. Take the celebrated end of *Molloy*: "Then I went back into the house and wrote, It is midnight. The rain is beating on the windows. It was not midnight. It was not raining." This calls Moran's report into question, making us realize that all his statements have been fictional creations and hence lies. And, at the same time, the seeming voice of "truth" ("It was not . . .," etc.) is only, after all, another fictional voice, as suspect as any other. If we read the passage closely enough, we are made acutely aware of the fictional nature of any voice. It might have been raining, who can know? The conventional distinction between fictional present ("It is. . . .") and fictional past ("It was not. . . .") is broken down. The voice of Moran in his report and the voice of Moran speaking to us as he writes his report, the voice of Beckett in his fiction and the voice of Beckett commenting on his fiction—all are equally real or unreal, we cannot be certain, we are suspended in uncertainty. The discovery of this is a playful discovery, the sudden understanding of a profound joke, what Freud called "the liberation of nonsense" in the discovery that "what at one moment has seemed to us to have a meaning, we now see is completely meaningless. . . ." By disembodying language from any notion of "truth," Beckett makes a game of it, or exposes it as a game—a serious and important game (for it is about a universal fiasco), but a game nevertheless.

I have discussed two basic movements in Beckett and of paradoxes generated by the simultaneity of these movements. The movement from light to dark is the expression of the meaninglessness of the world of forms, a world which exists in light. And the movement from dark to light is the expression of form through language. Near the end of *Molloy*, Moran ruminates about his bees:

> For the bees did not dance at any level, haphazard, but there were three or four levels, always the same, at which they danced. . . . I was more than ever stupefied by the complexity of this innumerable dance. . . . And all during the long journey home, when I racked my mind for a little joy in store, the thought of my bees and their dance was the nearest thing to comfort. For I was eager for my little joy, from time to time! And I admitted with good grace the possibility that the dance was after all no better than the dances of the people of the West, frivolous and meaningless . . . it would always be a noble thing to contemplate.

Here a comic balance is struck between the nobility and the meaninglessness of the dance, between its ability to give comfort and joy and its
essential obscurity and frivolity. It is "of great formal brilliance and
indeterminable purport." Beckett's protagonists seek this sense of form, of
being able, nonsensically, to measure the measurelessly "innumerable," at
the same time that they recognize the futility of the endeavor. "For I was
eager for my little joy" is at once sardonic and lyrical, a typically Beckettian
comic utterance. Beckett's world is comic in its relentless reduction of the
modes of thought, the "dances" of the Western world (particularly its
tropism toward logical meaning), and it is also comic in the strange gaiety
with which it creates and orders a reality of its own, impossible and
necessary, literally ab-surd.

"WATT"

Watt is Beckett's most wildly comic novel, perhaps because Watt himself is
Beckett's most obsessed logician, his most persistent searcher for meaning—
and so, inevitably, his most clownish character, with the exceptions of
Didi and Gogo. His very name suggests both a unit of energy and a
question: What? It is his questing spirit that runs the little mechanisms
that keep him moving onward through a landscape, both physical and
mental, that bewilders him. He is as much a principle as he is a character,
as we see in the very first scene of the novel.

In this hilarious and much-ignored scene, many of Beckett's central concerns are introduced before Watt appears. A humpback Mr. Hackett,
approaching his "seat" (a tram bench), finds it occupied and "did not
know whether he should go on, or whether he should turn back." This is
a small introduction to a major subject, the perpetual repetition and
uselessness and inevitability of motion. The text continues, "Space was
open on his right hand, and on his left hand, but he knew that he would
never take advantage of this. He knew also that he would not long remain
motionless. . . . The dilemma was thus of extreme simplicity: to go on, or
to turn, and return, round the corner, the way he had come. Was he, in
other words, to go home at once, or was he to remain out a little longer?"
One conjures Chaplin or Keaton or Stan Laurel, scratching his head over
the most minimal task. To "go on," for Mr. Hackett, is to advance to the
"seat," "the property very likely of the municipality, or of the public,"
which was not his but which he thought of as his. To turn back is to go
"home," back to one's room, one's solipsism. The dilemma, generally
stated, is to proceed along the line of History, calling yours things that are

not yours, seeking to join your voice with the choir of voices, *or* to turn back "home," toward the dark identity that pre-exists entrance into the outside world.

> Night is now falling fast, said Goff, soon it will be quite dark.
> Then we shall all go home, said Mr Hackett.

After some conversation about how Tetty's experience of giving birth is "one of riddance," Hackett says, "Tell me no more . . . it is useless." Clearly Hackett's experience of the world has made him identify with the child gotten rid of. He says he has always wondered "what it feels like to have the string cut." Later, he speaks of how he fell off a ladder at the age of one, with nobody around, and acquired, presumably, his present deformity. His father, it turns out, was "breaking stones on Prince William's Seat," and as he remembers the fall he hears the "distant clink of the hammers." Jacqueline Hoefer has offered a helpful elucidation of the meaning of Beckett's ladder. She proposes that Arsene's comment, much later in the novel, "What was changed was existence off the ladder. Do not come down the ladder, Ifor, I haf taken it away," is an allusion to the end of Wittgenstein's *Tractatus*, where he uses the ladder as an image of the process of logical reasoning. One climbs the ladder to a point where it is no longer needed; one uses words to approach silence. The ladder, then, is a symbol of the process of "going on," of taking rational steps toward the light. We are born at the bottom of the ladder, and it is our ancient, Sisyphean labor to climb it, rung by rung, word by word. Hackett has fallen off the ladder, and it is for this reason that motion is a dilemma to him. His rather pathetic situation off the ladder is contrasted, in the first of the many lyrical passages in the novel, with his father's toil, breaking stones on property not his own ("Seat" recalls Hackett's municipal "seat"). Hackett tells Nixon, "I am scarcely the outer world," a description applicable to Watt, for whom motion is always a problem, and who is and who is always, like Hackett, "a solitary figure," regarded as strange by others. Nixon, referring to Watt, tells Hackett, "The curious thing is, my dear fellow, I tell you quite frankly, that when I see him, or think of him, I think of you, and that when I see you, or think of you, I think of him." And later, the porter whom Watt knocks down cries, "The devil raise a hump on you."

Hackett and Watt, then, are set apart from the others. Nixon avers that Watt, who has just appeared on the far side of the street, is setting out on a journey, and how he is going about it is the subject of an hilariously mismanaged conversation among Hackett and the Goffs. Nixon says that Watt was on his way to the station, and wonders why he got off the tram across the street from them. The others suffer reasons, the reasons are logically rejected. The conversation becomes tedious as they attempt to determine, logically, why Watt got off, if he wished to go to the station, and why, having gotten off, he continued by foot *toward* the station, an action which rules out a possible desire to turn back.

> Perhaps, said Mr Hackett, he suddenly made up his mind not to leave town at all. Between the terminus and here he had time to reconsider the matter. Then, having made up his mind that it is better after all not to leave town just now, he stops the tram and gets down, for it is useless to go on.
>
> But he went on, said Mr Nixon, he did not go back the way he came, but went on, towards the station.
>
> Perhaps he is going home by a roundabout way, said Mrs Nixon.
>
> Where does he live? said Mr Hackett.
>
> He has no fixed address that I know of, said Mr Nixon.
>
> Then his going on towards the station proves nothing, said Mrs Nixon.

Mrs. Nixon is right, of course, their analysis is proving nothing, it is comically trying to understand the irrational by rational means. It is useless to go on, yet Watt is going on anyway, impossibly trying to go "home" by a "roundabout way." Perhaps, as Hackett suggests, he has removed his individual will from the act of going on, referring it to "the frigid machinery of a time-space relation." In a sense, Watt is not going on, because he has gotten off the tram, and yet he is not going back, because he continues to walk toward the station. Perhaps, as Hackett suggests, he has removed his individual will from the act of going on. Yet was it not a "decision" to take matters into his own hands in order to leave things up to chance? Watt's motives and direction are not resolved easily, indeed cannot be resolved at all. The triviality of the problem is precisely to the point: Watt is a figure who causes them (and us) to ask What? about the simplest things, to perceive dilemmas in the most ordinary affairs.

The conversation between Hackett and the Nixons derives its comedy from a clash between the realm of Habit, represented by the Nixons, and the "suffering" of life off the ladder, represented by Watt and Hackett. The relationship of these last two characters is clinched in the passage in which Hackett says he has been "intrigued" by Watt and burns with curiosity and "wonder," a sensation he doesn't think he could bear for more than a half hour. It is hard to bear the idea of Watt because it involves the breaking of Habit. The above passage occurs just after Watt appears, "motionless, a solitary figure," like a thought, a vaguely outlined and vaguely outlandish man, or more a principle than a man. Watt is someone or something ("Hackett was not sure that it was not a parcel . . .

wrapped up in dark paper and tied about the middle with a cord") that causes us to inquire into, say, the direction we travel in, the cause and effect of events like getting off a tram, that opens for us a whole world of comically futile speculation and endeavor.

> What does it matter who he is? said Mrs Nixon. She rose.
>
> Take my arm, my dear, said Mr Nixon.
>
> Or what he does, said Mrs Nixon. Or how he lives. Or where he comes from. Or where he is going to. Or what he looks like. What can it possibly matter, to us?
>
> I ask myself the same question, said Mr Hackett.
>
> How I met him, said Mr Nixon. I really do not remember, any more than I remember meeting my father.

Charter members of "the outer world," the Nixons regard such questions as so many houseflies. Watt is merely a topic of passing conversation for them, someone whom Goff knows, beyond his voluntary memory, and yet does not know at all. Watt appears and disappears, here and elsewhere in the novel, like a memory or thought. He is last seen, in this episode, standing on a bridge, "faintly outlined against the last wisps of day," and then, as an afterthought during their conversation, Mrs. Nixon says simply "he is gone," to which Mr. Nixon replies "is that so" and the conversation goes on. Watt is more alive in their discussion of his journey than he is an actual person. He fades away like the light of the dying day that is emphasized so often in this scene. It is appropriate that the light is "failing," the day "dying," "the last flowers" about to be "engulfed," because the passage of light to darkness is a motif of Watt's journey, or of all his journeys, for Watt is an "experienced traveller."

There is much in this first scene to prepare us for Watt's adventures. Beckett places us with spectators, considering Watt; we become, like Hackett, intrigued and wondering. Hackett serves as a kind of transition from the "outer world" of the Nixons to Watt's world, into which we abruptly plunge. Hackett is much affected by the enigma of Watt. At the end of the scene the Nixons stroll off, having settled things comfortably in their minds ("He is a university man, of course, said Mrs. Nixon. I should think it highly probable, said Mr. Nixon"), but Hackett remains, "crying, in the night." The scene concludes, "Mr. Hackett . . . looked towards the horizon that he had come out to see, of which he had seen so little. Now it was quite dark. Yes, now the western sky was as the eastern, which was as the southern, which was as the northern." All directions have become one in the dark. Beckett's world is one of the "failing light" of directions, questions, reasons, speculations, all fading hopefully but futilely into a dark that cannot last. We experience, in the opening pages of *Watt*, a comic irony directed at the tedium of the patterns of rational thinking and the discourse created by the normal functioning of words, to the point where it seems a conversation out of Carroll's Wonderland. At the same time we experience a sense of the reality that lies beyond these words, something which the presence of Watt suggests to us, an involuntary memory of something real, from which we have become estranged. Mr. Nixon "did not like the sun to go down on the least hint of estrangement," but we are left with Hackett crying in the night, and are about to enter Watt's world. "Estranged" is a good word for this tenebrous world; in it, we will become estranged both from the outer world, the habit of mind and behavior and language, *and* from the pure darkness to which we can no longer turn back.

It is never made clear why Watt gets off the tram across the street from Hackett. The point is made that the tram line, with its series of "stations," is a Beckettian image of the *via dolorosa* of human existence, the going on from birth to death, bearing the burden of consciousness. And the point is made that Watt gets off. When we come upon him directly, after the initial scene, he is at a station, about to get on a train. We assume, relying on the chronological conventions of the novel, and not given any signals to the contrary, that what takes place with Watt at the station is occurring some time after he got off the tram and spoke with Nixon. Only when the novel is over will this assumption be called into question, and the dilemma of direction raised again.

For those who get off trams and trains, and who fall off ladders, motion is a problem. We encounter Watt bumping into a porter and regarding as an "extravagant suggestion" the remark that he look where he's going. The porter's job is described in its tedium: "On the platform the porter continued to wheel cans, up and down. At one end of the platform there was one group of cans, and at the other end there was another. The porter chose with care a can in one group and wheeled it to the other. Then he chose with care a can from the other and wheeled it to the one. He is sorting the cans, said Watt. Or perhaps it is a punishment for disobedience, or some neglect of duty." It is, of course, both. Most human tasks could be described in the same manner, and would require the same linguistic tedium to be so described, a tedium that makes the use of language seem as Sisyphean a task as futilely sorting cans. It is useless to go on, as Hackett says, because to go on and to turn back are one and the same, neither final.

Once on the train Watt meets a Mr. Spiro, editor of *Crux*, a popular Catholic monthly. (It is weirdly prophetic that two characters named Nixon and Spiro appear in rapid succession.) Spiro "must speak to a fellow wanderer," and so describes to Watt some of the absurdly scholastic questions that *Crux* deals with, quoting obscure theologians, yammering along as the silent fields fly by and the voices, "singing, crying, stating, murmuring, things unintelligible," prevent Watt from hearing anything Spiro says. One gets on the track and hears language, the language of reason ludicrously applied to the theological study of trivia.

Watt gets off (though typically we don't see him get off) just as Mr. Spiro is pursing the question of whether or not a rat which has eaten a consecrated wafer has ingested the Real Body, and if he has, what is to be done about it. As a result of this congruence, we aren't sure whether, in the following passage, Watt or the rat is referred to: "Personally I would pursue him, said Mr Spiro, if I were sure it was he, with all the rigor of the canon laws. He took his legs off the seat. And pontifical decrees, he cried. A great rush of air drove him back." The momentary confusion here suggests Watt as a rat who has swallowed a consecrated wafer. Like Christ, he embodies the paradox of the spiritual inhabiting the physical, here become a comical paradox. What is to become of Watt? Will that part of him that is drawing him to Knott's house be fulfilled? Spiro's rational language removes him from what is, after all, a crux of human life. He flies on through the night, along the tracks, as Watt proceeds to Knott's in a "funambulistic stagger," his walk a fantastically unstable means of moving "in a straight line." Beckett's protagonists, like the Expelled in the story of that name, are compelled to journey in straight lines and have a good deal of trouble doing so, to their credit. Watt soon grows weak and falls in a ditch. The notion of proceeding in a straight line is, in a post-Euclidian world, an absurd notion in any case, yet our conceptions of progress, direction, process, are hopelessly and rigorously Euclidian, worthy of the Flat Earth Society.

Lying in the ditch, Watt knew it would be difficult to get up and move on, yet there is in him an imperative to go on, as well as an inner imperative to rest and listen "to the little nightsounds in the hedge behind him . . . the breath that is never quiet." What he hears is the sound of pure process, the million little changes that add up to no change, the leaves rotting and the flowers blooming, the wind blowing nowhere. Then the voices come to him again, "with great distinctness, from afar, from without, yes, really it seemed from without . . . indifferent in quality, of a mixed choir," singing to him a song about surds ("Fifty two point two eight five seven one four two eight five seven one four") and human process ("greatgranma Ma grew how do you do blooming thanks and you drooping thanks and you withered thanks and you forgotten thanks").

This is a drama of consciousness awaking from dark to light. What these voices do, singing what Beckett calls in his Addenda a "threne," is initiate a process of thought at the same time that they express the futility of thought, the fact that the process will go nowhere, except in an endless enumeration of decimals or generations. The threnodic quality of the song is derived from its speaking of no goals achieved, nothing finally encountered, only a round of bloom and decay. The comedy of the song, expressed in its repetitive and singsong quality, lies in its contradictory nature: *because* you seek you shall not find. This is the contradiction in enumerating the decimals of a surd, in approaching the irrational rationally. The choir of voices Watt hears rouses him from the ditch, disturbing his silence, setting him in motion, at the same time that it detains him there, briefly. The song expresses his dilemma, his necessity to seek what he cannot find in the seeking: a refuge from thought. Watt travels in order that he may rest at last. The sense of the irrational initiated a rational attempt to come to terms with it. In the ditch we hear the nightsong of being gradually become a song of seeking.

One problem that Beckett has with Watt as protagonist (and with Murphy before him) is that Watt is inarticulate. Beckett seems more ill at ease with the authority of his third-person voice in *Watt* than in *Murphy*. There are no sustained monologues in *Murphy*, but *Watt* has several, and the finest of these is Arsene's speech to Watt after Watt arrives at Knott's house, a speech in which Beckett creates, for the first time, the sardonic voice that will become the voice of the Trilogy and "Texts for Nothing." In *Watt*, as we shall later discover, Beckett sets up a third-person narrative only to undermine its authority entirely.

Arsene's "short statement" (!) prepares us for Watt's experience in Knott's house, and puts into clearer perspective some of the paradoxes I have been describing. The first part of his speech is about change. Arsene berates Watt for sitting in Knott's kitchen, waiting for the dawn.

> The man arrives! The dark ways all behind, all within, the long dark ways, in his head, in his side, in his hands and feet, and he sits in the red gloom, picking his nose, waiting for the dawn to break. The dawn! The sun! The light! Haw! . . . Then at night rest in the quiet house, there are no roads, no streets any more, you lie down by a window opening on refuge, the little sounds come that demand nothing, ordain nothing, explain nothing, propound nothing . . . the secret places never the same, but always simple and indifferent, always mere places, sites of a stirring beyond coming and going, of a being so light and free that it is as the being of nothing.

In this marvelous and tonally complex passage, the dark lyricism of the description of Watt's quest is salted with Arsene's ironical interpolations about its futility. Arsene laughs at Watt's thinking he is proceeding from darkness to light, toward refuge. The "dark ways" are described as Christ's wounds, suggesting that Watt's suffering is spiritual, or at least a-temporal, that what Watt seeks at Knott's house is a kind of redemption from mortal life, "all the soil and fear and weakness offered, to be sponged away and forgiven." What Arsene is commenting on here, and laughing at, is that redemption from life's dark ways is a loss of life—not, as Christians have traditionally imagined it, a life free of the physical in the abode of the eternal. According to Arsene, and he should know, having had his stay at Knott's, Watt wishes for process to continue (the dawns to break, the sounds to occur, the roads and gardens to remain) but to mean "nothing." The idea of going on, of bearing the burden of consciousness, will, to Watt, no longer be necessary at Knott's, it will be sponged away. At Knott's Watt hopes to exist beyond all that.

But what Arsene has come to realize is that this hope of redemption is impossible: "How I feel it again, after so long. . . . All forgiven and healed. For ever. In a moment. To-morrow. Six, five, four hours still, of the old dark, the old burden, lightening, lightening. For one has come, to stay. Haw!" It is impossible because we live in change, and cannot live outside it. Arsene goes on to a more abstract example, still using as his subject "the man," including thereby Watt and all who seek redemption. The man has arrived at Knott's house: "He is well pleased. For he knows he is in the right place at last . . . he being what he has become, and the place being what it was made, the fit is perfect. And he knows this. No. Let us remain calm. He feels it. The sensations, the premonitions of harmony are irrefragable, of imminent harmony, when all outside him will be he . . ." He is redeemed, and at one with his world, like Crispin at one with his soil, like the rabbit in Stevens' gently satiric "The Rabbit as King of the Ghosts," who feels at night that "everything is meant for [him] / And nothing need be explained." "What a feeling of security!" says Arsene, "nature is so exceedingly accommodating, on the one hand, and man, on the other." The life of forms is imagined behind him: "Having oscillated all his life between the torments of a superficial loitering and the horrors of disinterested endeavour, he finds himself at last in a situation where to do nothing exclusively would be an act of the highest value, and significance." Having described this state with some relish, Arsene brings his point home: "The fool! He has learnt nothing. Nothing." The man learns this in two senses, in the sense of not having learned anything, and in the sense of having learned nothingness. Because change occurs, as it must occur. The dark will become light, the light dark, turn and turn about.

To describe the change that inevitably occurs, Arsene switches to a personal incident. He was once in Knott's yard, peacefully regarding the light on the wall:

> I felt my breast swell, like a pelican's I think it is. For joy? Well, no, perhaps not exactly for joy. For the change of which I speak had not yet taken place. Hymeneal still it lay, the thing so soon to be changed, between me and all the forgotten horrors of joy. . . . The change. In what did it consist? It is hard to say. Something slipped. There I was, warm and bright, smoking my tobacco-pipe, watching the warm bright wall, when suddenly somewhere some little thing slipped, some tiny little thing. Gliss—iss—iss—STOP! . . . I felt, that Tuesday afternoon, millions of little things moving all together out of their old place, into a new one nearby. . . .

Arsene's is a radical sense of atomistic process. Susanne Langer's "pure sense of life." It is only when change occurs (or when it is perceived) that one feels the "joy" of what one had, for joy—and despair—are concomitant with change. The "only true Paradise," says Beckett in *Proust*, "is the Paradise that has been lost." Arsene elaborated on this idea when he says,

> But in what did the change *consist*? What was changed, and how? What was changed, if my information is correct, was a sentiment that a change, other than a change of degree, had taken place. . . . This I am happy to inform you is the reversed metamorphosis. The Laurel into Daphne. The old thing where it always was, back again. As when a man, having found at last what he sought, a woman, for example, or a friend, loses it, or realises what it is.

To lose it *is* to realize what it is. Only in this sense does the phrase "horrors of joy" seem anything but merely perverse. In Beckett's world joy and horror, hope and despair, are aspects of the same realization, that only in process of change can you realize at once the joy of what you had and the pain of losing it. Watt will only be able to experience Knott in the process of failing to find refuge with him.

Arsene describes the feeling that he had *prior* to the change, the feeling of harmony, as being "so sensuous that in comparison the impressions of a man buried alive in Lisbon on Lisbon's great day seems a frigid and artificial construction of the imagination." The comparison is telling, for to feel this static harmony, the harmony Arsene sought and Watt will seek at Knott's, is to experience "nothing," to be "transported . . . to some quite different yard, and to some quite different season, in an

unfamiliar country." It is what Murphy thinks that he realizes about what
Mr. Endon experiences: the annihilation of consciousness, as of one
buried in an earthquake or autistically unaware of the outside world. It
cannot be *known* (recall Arsene's emphasis on feeling instead of knowing);
in this state, the voices have ceased, language has yielded to silence. Such
a state does not, strictly speaking, exist, for change is constant; rather, it
is the "presence of what did not exist," not an "illusion." And we seek it,
we desire it, "it is useless not to seek, not to want, for when you cease to
seek you start to find, and when you cease to want, then life begins to ram
her fish and chips down your gullet until you puke . . ." The experience
of "the being of nothing" occurs, then, between the seeking and the
finding of it, since one only finds it when one has lost it. It is a presence.
To say that it is an instant is to falsify it, for it is timeless. Its analogy, in
mathematics, would be a surd: we can extend the decimals of, say, 2/7 (as
the voices do in their threne), but we cannot, through these decimals,
obtain the surd, because it *does not exist* in the domain of rational
decimals.

Thus Watt's situation is paradoxical. He seeks Knott, or Naught, a
refuge from change. If he did *not* seek him, then life as Habit would
absorb him. Yet if he seeks Knott, he cannot find him in the seeking—for
to seek is to engage oneself in the coming and going. As Richard Coe
states, in Beckett "the condition of man is a kind of Purgatory . . . the
ultimate realisation of the Self in a *Néant* beyond space and time, void
united with void; yet to desire such a Paradise is to be aware of a self
desiring, and a Self desiring is not a void, and therefore cannot enter."
Watt comes, seeking, and he will eventually have to go, as Arsene is
going: "And then another night fall and another man come and Watt go,
Watt who is now come, for the coming is in the shadow of the going and the
going is in the shadow of the coming, that is the annoying part about it,"
says Arsene. Watt will seek the "light"—that is, Knott, redemption—
which is to seek nought, nothing, an impossible end. There is only the
seeking, in change. There is no final light, nor final dark, only a movement from one to the other.

Changelessness can be perceived only in change, the irrational
only by means of the rational, silence only in words. In the world of
process, life and death, purpose and purposelessness, are one. In the
following passage, Arsene touches on these paradoxes; he has just spoken
of the servants coming and going around Knott, who neither comes nor
goes but "seems able to abide in his place":

> Or is there a coming that is not a coming to, a going that is not a going
> from, a shadow that is not the shadow of purpose, or not? For what is the

shadow of the going in which we come, this shadow of the coming in which we go, this shadow of the coming and the going in which we wait, if not the shadow of purpose, of the purpose that budding withers, that withering buds, whose blooming is a budding withering? . . . And what is this coming that is not our coming and this being that is not our being and this going that will not be our going but the coming and being and going in purposelessness?

Process is both purposeful and purposeless. To return to the paradox that Beckett describes in his essay on Joyce, if one is an individual coming and being and going, one has purpose; if one is a part of a universal coming and being and going ("this coming that is not our coming," etc.), then one is purposeless. Watt is both an individual and a term in a series of servants revolving around Knott. Arsene continues, "And though in purposelessness I may seem to go now, yet I do not, any more than in purposelessness then I came, for I go now with my purpose as with it then I came, the only difference being this, that then it was living and now it is dead, which is what you might call what I think the English call six of one and half a dozen of the other, do they not, might you not?" The distinction between being alive and being dead with purpose is the distinction between being complete and whole (six of one) and being part of a series (half a dozen of the other). Watt is Watt, and Watt is a servant ousting Arsene and moving Erskine upstairs, who is soon to be moved upstairs by Arthur, who in turn has ousted Erskine and will be moved upstairs by Micks, who in turn will oust Watt, and so on, "for ever about Mr Knott in tireless assiduity turning." It is dizzying to read the long passages in *Watt* in which these series are worked out. "For Vincent and Walter were not the first, ho no, but before them were Vincent and another whose name I forget, and before them that other whose name I forget and another whose name I also forget, and before them that other whose name I also forget . . ." These passages are sudden bogs that trap the reader in their relentless logic, making him painfully aware of the medium of language. They are parodies of rational discourse, language extended to fulfill its suddenly distorted utility, which is to analyze, to follow through to conclusions. The language both fulfills and undermines itself, and in that contradiction is the source of the comedy.

The drift of Arsene's speech is a subtle and intellectual develop-ment of the basic premise that the universe is as Heraclitus saw it, changeless change. In the first place, to realize truly that we live in change is to realize that change subverts all concepts of meaning and direction. Thus Arsene laughs—"Haw!"—at Watt's search, which was, and still is, his own. Second, to realize truly that we live in change is to be aware of the essential formalism of change. Motion always tends to pattern, what we might here call Form (to distinguish it from forms, or what Beckett calls in *Proust* "the haze of conception—preconception"), and pattern leads us, drives us to conceive of a Content, an essential meaning: God, Godot, whatever. The recurring patterns of existence are manifestations of a principle of order; they suggest a design and with that, a designer. And so we are back where we started, seeking changelessness in change, a final light or a final dark, mounting or descending the ladder, in a world that dawns and dies continuously.

In this context, Arsene's intrusive explanation of his rude laugh becomes more clear, and helps us to relate his Heraclitean vision to comedy. Arsene speaks of three laughs: the bitter, the hollow and the mirthless:

> The bitter laugh laughs at that which is not good, it is the ethical laugh.
> The hollow laugh laughs at that which is not true, it is the intellectual
> laugh. . . . But the mirthless laugh is the dianoetic laugh, down the
> snout—Haw!—so. It is the laugh of laughs, the *risus purus*, the laugh
> laughing at the laugh, the beholding, the saluting of the highest joke,
> in a word the laugh that laughs—silence please—at that which is
> unhappy.

This final laugh is the greatest, the highest, the finest, the most inner and the most *formal* of the three. *Dianoetic* means relating to the thought process, particularly that of logical thought. Arsene's dianoetic laugh is, ultimately, a laugh at the human condition ("the highest joke"), a condition involving him as well as Watt. It is beyond the laughter of a man detached from the futile pursuit of meaning. It is laughter which includes as its target both subject and object. It is the laughter of a man who realizes that his own thought is an inextricable part of the process he is laughing at, the laugh of the Cretan who has just observed that all Cretans are liars. It is laughter that comes from the realization that, as Richard Coe remarks in reference to Arsene's entire speech, "man can *never* escape his own rationality." The dianoetic laugh is both ironic and accepting; its acceptance is dependent on the operation of its irony, at the same time that it sets the irony in motion. It is the laughter of Darl on the way to Jackson, the laughter of the comedy of language. It debunks matter and relegates itself to form, is intimately connected to what Beckett calls the "Idea" in *Proust*, the essence of things revealed when all conceptions and preconceptions have been cleared away—in this case, by the action of a scornful irony.

Arsene's laugh derives from the consciousness of consciousness, the impossible situation of commenting, with one's mind (one cannot avoid it) on the futility of the mind's operations. Arsene's speech is a superb strategy for establishing the heightened narrative perspective on Watt which is to follow in the relation of Watt's adventures.

Watt's desire is to experience Naught, to come to rest. Arsene says, "And yet there is one who neither comes nor goes, I refer I need hardly say to my late employer, but seems to abide in his place . . ." The dilemma is that what does not change (Knott) can only be experienced in change, and so Watt will take his place in the servant rotation, the inexorable coming and going. For Knott / Naught is, literally, Nothing, a void. As a haven and a refuge from change, he exists only as Idea. Knott may be described, as Sam will describe him later in the novel, as that which a circle encloses, a void which can only be described by the line that moves around it in dynamic directionlessness (relative to linearity). Knott is then, both Form and Idea.

Before Arsene's speech, as Watt is sitting in the kitchen, the following image occurs:

> Watt saw, in the grate, of the range, the ashes grey. But they turned pale red, when he covered the lamp, with his hat. The range was almost out, but not quite . . . So Watt busied himself a little while, covering the lamp, less and less, more and more, with his hat, watching the ashes greyen, redden, greyen, redden, in the grate, of the range.

This is an image of Watt's mind, fading into rest and stirring from rest. Near the end of his speech Arsene says that he thinks he has said enough to light a fire in Watt's mind that can only be snuffed with difficulty, just as Vincent did for him, and so on. He has, then, at once dimmed and fanned Watt's desires with his laughter. After Arsene leaves, Watt can't be sure if the day has yet dawned or not, despite his holding his hat before the lamp. The certainties of day and night are gone. The first section of *Watt* ends with a premonition of dawn:

> For if it was really day again already, in some low distant quarter of the sky, it was not yet day again already in the kitchen. But that would come, Watt knew that would come, with patience it would come, little by little, whether he liked it or not, over the yard wall, and through the window, first the grey, then the brighter colours one by one, until getting on to nine a.m. all the gold and white and blue would fill the kitchen, all the unsoiled light of the new day, of the new day at last, the day without precedent at last.

This passage is delicately poised between joy at the dawn of an entirely new day, the unprecedented nature of which fires the quest growing within Watt, the individual—and irony at the day's being only one day in a series, and Watt only one servant in a series, extending to infinity. It is a passage poised between Watt's nostalgia and Arsene's "Haw!" Although Arsene's speech has its effect on our experience of this coming dawn, Beckett allows Watt the lyricism of waiting, the strength of his desire. Watt knows the day will come because (1) it always *does* come, in a universal round, and because (2) the fire within him wills it, or so he feels. It is a fine and typical moment of Beckettian comedy, the beauty of the passage deriving from the very irony that calls it into question. The dawn is both Watt's hope and his despair—that is to say, it is neither one, and both. As Arsene says, "Erskine is here still, sleeping and dreaming what the new day holds in store, I mean premonition and a new face and the end in sight. But another evening shall come and the light die away out of the sky and the colour from the earth— . . . haw!" This too is inevitable, and this too is not final. Watt yearns for the light, and will see it fade to darkness; he will yearn for darkness, and see it fade into light. There are no ends in sight in this comic round.

Watt enters Mr. Knott's service. Knott's establishment is a peculiar mixture of the real and unreal, like Kafka's castle. Some aspects of it, like Knott's confidence-man disguises, are impossible; some aspects, like Knott's eating habits and the servant arrangement, are bizarre; and some, like the phone and the postman and the occasional callers, are commonplace. These outside "acknowledgements" of Knott's establishment keep it going. The inner world of Knott's depends on the outer; as Arsene says, Knott is "quite incapable of looking after himself." What is considered by the mind to be beyond the mind exists by the mind's good graces. Unless words enclose it, nothingness cannot exist, and, enclosed by words, it becomes something. It is not only Knott's house that is kept going by the outer world, but Watt as well. The incident of the Galls makes this clear, and introduces the subject of language to some of Arsene's ideas.

Two men, one old and one middle-aged, knock at Knott's door and announce they have come to tune the piano, after introducing themselves as the Galls. After tuning it, they mysteriously pronounce to one another as "doomed" the piano, the piano-tuner, and the pianist. Then they leave. This incident is the first of many that Watt experiences at Knott's, in that it is "of great formal beauty and indeterminable purport." It continues to "unfold" in his head, over and over again, passing from light to shadow and back, sound to silence and back, in "the irrevocable caprice of its taking place." It "gradually lost, in the nice processes of its light, its sound, its impacts and its rhythm, all meaning, even the most literal." In the outer world Watt had been content with the outer meaning of events. He would have said, before entering Knott's, that the Galls came, pronounced as doomed the piano, etc., and left. "That is what happened then." But at Knott's the event becomes unintelligible, and "this fragility of the outer meaning had a bad effect on Watt, for it caused him to seek for another, for some meaning of what had passed, in the image of how it had passed." Watt cannot accept that the incident has broken up into "the farce of its properties," into a Bergsonian shimmer of vibrations, movements, changes. He runs the incident again and again through his mind, brooding on its properties, pursuing its meaning so that he can put it out of his mind, for "to explain had always been to exorcize, for Watt." He is like Bergson's Intellect, brooding on what eludes it, forced to confront that "nothing had happened, that a thing that was nothing had happened, with the utmost formal distinctness." In its clarity it *seems* to mean, and that seeming is the fuel for Watt's logical machine.

Watt has no choice, he is "forced to submit" to the pursuit of meaning; "to elicit something from nothing" is his inheritance. The more meaning dissolves, the more he seeks it, so that he may "extract" something "in self-defence" from the suffering of having a radically unique event elude his Habit of thought. There are no words to describe or explain an event in which nothing occurs, yet Watt desires words to be applied to his situation, to Mr Knott, and "in a general way to the conditions of being in which he found himself." Although he seeks rest from the outer world, he still needs "semantic succour," is compelled to suffer the pain of going on in his mind, as if his mind were a motor that could not stop. Though occasionally satisfied by his "dereliction" from the outer world, he "often found himself longing for a voice, for Erskine's, since he was alone with Erskine, to speak of the little world of Mr Knott's establishment, with the old words, the old credentials." This is his comic dilemma. He is Hugh Kenner's "The Man of Sense as Buster Keaton," processing a chaos of new information with archaic habits of mind, trapped by mechanism. Or, to make another comic analogy, when Watt undergoes at Knott's the painful experience of not quite being able to *name* things, such as a pot, he is like Lewis Carroll's Alice stepping into the wood of no names: "Well, at any rate it's a great comfort . . . after being so hot, to get into the—into the—into *what*?" she says, driven by questions as the familiar is left behind.

The comedy of Watt's stay at Knott's derives from the unnerving contradiction between what Watt experiences and what he can say about it (since, as we later learn, he is relating his story to someone else). He is the servant of two masters: of his desire to escape meaning and of his need to search for it, if only in self-defence. The comedy of his situation is cogently expressed in the phrase, "to elicit something from nothing requires a certain skill," and in this hilarious passage: "For the only way one can speak of nothing is to speak of it as though it were something, just as the only way one can speak of God is to speak of him as though he were a man, which to be sure he was, in a sense, for a time, and as the only way one can speak of man, even our anthropologists have realised that, is to speak of him as though he were a termite." More than any other modern writer, Beckett is aware of how mysterious and unspeakable the subjects of our discourse are, and with what comical confidence we marshal our language units to express them.

The Galls incident allows Beckett to meditate on the theory of the problem. But that incident is only prelude to the other problems that absorb Watt, problems that will elicit from his mental processes the wild strings of reasoning that are Beckett's comic hallmarks. The problem of disposing of the food that Knott does not eat results in Beckett's first extended use of "the comedy of an exhaustive enumeration." The problem occurs, given Mr. Knott's garbage, and given the idea that a dog is to come and dispose of it when and if there is any, in determining by what means the dog and the food were to be brought together. This banal problem had already been solved long before Watt arrived, but he considers it in a parody of ratiocination. "But was there any guarantee that the messenger would indeed give the food to the dog, or dogs, in accordance with his instructions? What was to prevent the messenger from eating the food himself, or from selling all or part of the food to some other party, or from giving it away, or from emptying it away into the nearest ditch or hole, to save time, and trouble?" Examples of this reasoning proliferate. In its attempt to make sense of what is, after all, "irrevocable caprice," language takes on a comic life of its own, floating free from whatever reality it was meant to explain. As Watt seeks to cover every logical possibility, his language comes to seem, after pages, irrational. We are reminded, as we laugh, of how much normal reasoning takes for granted, how much it operates only in habitual channels. As Watt reasons, we enter a world of Rube Goldbergian logic, extending itself to what we fear is infinity, madly pursuing its own processes, operating from the principle that the world itself is a machine, and so making us realize how much the world is *not* a machine. In exposing the mechanisms of language, the comedy implies what lies beyond language.

Watt's thinking is continually undermined. In detailing the makeup of the Lynch family (the "disease" of mankind breeding itself on and on) Watt concludes, at one point, "Five generations, twenty-eight souls, nine hundred and eighty years, such was the proud record of the Lynch family, when Watt entered Mr. Knott's service," to which a footnote is appended: "The figures given here are incorrect. The consequent calculations are therefore doubly erroneous." This blow is immediately followed by this paragraph: "Then a moment passed and all was changed. Not that there was death, for there was not. Not that there was birth, for there was not either. But puff puff breath again they breathed, in and out, the twenty-eight, and all was changed." The mechanism involved in a rational grasp of things is defeated by change. When Kate Lynch is mentioned as a "bleeder," this footnote appears: "Haemophilia is, like enlargement of the prostate, an exclusively male disorder. But not in this work." This work is a lie, an invention, a fiction, something spun out of the mind. When considering the bell that sounds in the night from Erskine's room, Watt, in his mania for exploring every possibility in an attempt to account for the event, even entertains the notion that he himself might have rung the bell: "And if he had got up and gone down, to where the bell was, and he did not know where the bell was, and pressed it there, could he have got back into his room, and into his bed, and sometimes even fallen into a light sleep, in time to hear, from where he lay, in his bed, the bell sound?" The very syntax of this is funny, and the comedy is as much a function of the familiarity of the reasoning as it is of its absurdity. Sense dissolves into nonsense; nonsense is expressed sensically.

It is not as if Watt could say, I know nothing, and rest in that knowledge. Nor can he be content, like the people in the outer world, that he does know something. Watt simply (Haw!) can't be sure, and is driven by that uncertainty. The "old words" don't work at Knott's, and those are all he has. In reference to the dog-feeding:

> Not that for a moment Watt supposed that he had penetrated the forces at play, in this particular instance, or even perceived the forms that they upheaved, or obtained the least useful information concerning himself, or Mr Knott, for he did not. But he had turned, little by little, a disturbance into words, he had made a pillow of old words, for a head. Little by little, and not without labour. Kate eating from her dish, for example, with the dwarfs standing by, how he had laboured to know what that was, to know which the doer, and what the doer, and what the doing, and which the sufferer, and what the sufferer, and what the suffering, and what those shapes, that were not rooted to the ground, like the veronica, but melted away, into the dark, after a while.

The melting shapes recall Faulkner's disembodied imagery in As I Lay Dying; the "pillow of old words," our mean comfort in the face of reality, is a phrase that Addie Bundren would have appreciated. The "veronica" is

both a rooted shrub and a "true" image (*verus* + *iconicus*)—more specifically, the image of Godhead: Jesus, and by extension, Knott. Veronica,
beholding the bloody handkerchief, *knew* what the sufferer and what the
suffering, the image she beheld was both essential and presentational.
Watt, on the other hand, is only presented with shapes that never take
form, about which he can know nothing. Perhaps the most interesting
thing about the above passage is that its rhythm and movement defeat its
point: the inherited words *are* a pillow of sorts, a momentary contentment, an illusion of stasis and order. But the passage does not end with
the image of the pillow. It picks up again. "Little by little . . . ," and
continues its rumination, ending in futility. Words are at once a comfort
and a burden.

  "Saying is inventing," says Molloy, and then, "Wrong, very rightly
wrong. You invent nothing, you think you are inventing, you think you
are escaping, and all you do is stammer out your lesson, the remnants of a
pensum . . ." His first pronouncement is that words are false, the critique
that follows is that words are assumed. We are not even privileged to lie in
any pure sense. The very word "inventing" implies both truth and falsehood. "Saying is inventing" is a vicious-circle paradox, hence "wrong,
very rightly wrong." The epistemological problem must be reflexive; we
can't know that we can't know. This extends to the narrator, whom we
later learn is Sam: "And so always, when the impossibility of my knowing,
of Watt's having known, what I know, what Watt knew, seems absolute,
and insurmountable, and undeniable, and incoercible, it could be shown
that I know, because Watt told me, and that Watt knew, because someone
told him, or because he found out for himself. At this point, truth and
falsehood clearly merge, and we perceive this not just as Watt's problem,
but as Sam's and ours—we who so blithely confront words on a page and
think *them* a fiction.

  Seeking to solve the mystery of the bell, Watt rather magically
enters Erskine's locked room and beholds there a picture of a circle,
broken at its lowest point, and a dot, outside the circle and seemingly on
a different and shifting plane of perspective. Watt considers the possibilities of what the picture might mean, and concludes with "the thought
that it was perhaps this, a circle and a centre not its centre in search of a
centre and a circle respectively, in boundless space, in endless time. . . .
Watt's eyes filled with tears that he could not stem . . ." Watt's crying
leads us to consider that perhaps the meaning of the picture is this: that
Watt (the dot) is unable to attain the same plane as, much less enter into,
the circle that surrounds the nothingness that is Knott. Watt wishes the
dot to slip into the circle from below, "home at last." To achieve "home,"

Watt has gotten off the tram and come to Knott's house. But he does not think he has entered the circle, because he does not *know* Knott, has not achieved rest or refuge. Words are still with him. Yet if that which is Not cannot be known, it can at least be formally defined, delimited in some way. Hence the circle, the defining circumference, and its damnable breach, leading Watt "on." The circumference of the circle is an image, specifically, of the revolving of the servants around the fixity of Knott, as well as an image, generally, of the coming and going around an essential nothingness, which could not be experienced or sensed except by the coming and going. The nothing which is contained in the circumference is made something by that circumference, even though it remains nothing. Form is all. About to depart from the ground floor, Watt considers, "What had he learnt? Nothing. What did he know of Mr Knott? Nothing. Of his anxiety to prove, of his anxiety to understand, of his anxiety to get well, what remained? Nothing. But was not that something?" The circle is an image of, among other things, the labor of consciousness, endlessly revolving, achieving nothing but the perfection of its own shape. And yet it achieves nothing by making the "presence" of nothingness felt. Thus in the futility of Watt's words is his strange success.

If the circle were completely self-contained and whole, then Watt could despair, but the circle is broken, and at best Watt can only cry and achieve a temporary refreshment in crying. The breach keeps Watt hoping, going on. Yet is this representation a mere fiction? Watt considers whether the picture is indeed a stable part of Knott's or, like him and Erskine, a "term in a series." Watt concludes that it is such a term, and nothing is resolved.

Two passages near the end of section II establish Mr. Knott as a Godhead of sorts. The first is a liturgical, the second a Biblical allusion:

> Watt had more and more the impression, as time passed, that nothing could be added to Mr Knott's establishment, and from it nothing taken away, but that as it was now, so it had been in the beginning, and so it would remain to the end, in all essential respects.

> Add to this that the few glimpses caught of Mr Knott, by Watt, were not clearly caught, but as it were in a glass, a plain glass, an eastern window at morning, a western window at evening.

That is, Watt sees Knott through a glass darkly. But not only that. Watt also glimpses Knott in the sunrise and sunset, as the "significant presence" behind process. Mr. Knott is a "harbour" and a "haven" from change, yet can only be glimpsed in and through change. Knott represents a principle that is alive, yet beyond the world of forms. As such he is an Idea of God, or the shape of an Idea of God. Like a circle, he is a perfect form, not one to be found in nature. Molloy says that the experience of hearing "pure sounds, free of all meaning" is analogous to seeing something "inordinately formal." "Inordinately" I take to mean in excess of the forms we normally experience—that is, presentational forms. All Knott's presentational forms, the costumes he wears about the house, are disguises. From Knott's voice "nothing was to be learnt," the words of his low, rapid songs "were either without meaning, or derived from an idiom with which Watt, a fair linguist, had no acquaintance." Knott's voice, like the voices murmuring in Watt's head, is a kind of pre-verbal chatter, sounds that are not yet words, suggesting both words and silence. Knott is the principle that makes one embark on the impossible task of attaining silence in words. There is no other way; we can't go "home" again. Near the end of section II, Watt remembers a quiet and lovely and brief pastoral experience he had with Knott in the garden:

> So there for a short time they stood together, the master and the servant, the bowed heads almost touching . . . until the worm was gone and only the flower remained. One day the flower would be gone and only the worm remain, but on this particular day it was the flower that remained, and the worm that went. And then Watt, looking up, saw that Mr Knott's eyes were closed, and heard his breathing soft and shallow, like the breathing of a child asleep.

This is a brief moment of stillness, the worm of process momentarily arrested, the Garden returned to. The sleeping child sound takes us back to the lost Paradise of the womb, the silence before words. In the next section, we behold the disintegration of Watt's language.

Section III seems to be, chronologically, the last one of Watt's story (on the novel's structure, more later). As such, it takes place at "the end of the line," the point to which Watt buys his ticket after leaving Knott's house. Since the "line" in Beckett describes the Habit of living in both a personal and historical sense, then the "mansions" and their grounds and pavilions in section III would seem to be a kind of afterlife. It is common in the criticism of *Watt* to refer to the strange setting of III as a mental asylum, a viewpoint which limits the resonance of this section. The word "mansions" suggests a heaven-haven: "Let not your heart be troubled: yet believe in God, believe also in me. In my Father's house are many mansions; if it were not so, I would have told you: I go and prepare a place for you" (A.V. John 14:1–2). As the section unfolds we come to see this setting—the distant and imperious mansions, the little gardens, the barbed wire, the windy and lucid weather—both as a real and a mock Paradise.

Certainly there are suggestions of a mental asylum, what with the institutional overtones: attendants, cells, loud patients playing at ball, "rescuers" ready to help out should someone cut himself on the barbed wire. But these make up Beckett's reticent joke rather than the salient reality of the scene; they convey the hope of heaven as a hope of ultimate "asylum," of being *cared for.* It is as ironic a vision of Paradise as Arsene's. Watt and the narrator ("me" becomes "Sam," addressed as a third person) remain, most of the time, in their separate mansions, "in our windowlessness, in our bloodheat, in our hush" or "in a vacuum" or "in deepest night": isolate and wordless. But section III is a record of their rare conversations in the gardens when the weather suited both of them. They find holes in the barbed wire, they touch, they talk. It is the most intensely darkly lyrical part of the novel, the least ironically described vision of human communication.

Knott was not a haven or a refuge for Watt, and neither are the mansions. Although one can be "in his separate soundless unlit warmth," there is nothing Paradisical in this womb-like silence. Rather, Watt and Sam are "peers in peace" only in their infrequent meetings, although "the disappointment of one of us at least was almost certain, and the regret, the bitter regret, at ever having left his mansion at all, and the vow, the hollow vow, never to leave his mansion again, on any account." The painful burden of consciousness is shouldered again, the "ancient labour" of communicating meaning, of seeking to understand, is begun once more. There is no rest, no death: Watt, like the protagonists of the Trilogy, must go on.

This further passage from the Gospel of John illuminates the relationship between Watt and Sam: "I go and prepare a place for you. And if I go and prepare a place for you, I will come again, and receive you unto myself, that where I am, there ye may be also. And whither I go ye know, and the way ye know. Thomas saith unto him, Lord, we know not whither thou goest: and how can we know the way? Jesus saith unto him, I am the Way, the Truth, and the Life: no man cometh unto the Father but by me" (A.V. John 14:2–6). Watt and Sam are related much as are Molloy and Moran. The former in each case has lived off the track, or apart from the Organization (the life of forms), and the latter sees himself mirrored in the former and seeks to recount what he has experienced. Moran discovers the Molloy within himself; Sam embraces Watt symbiotically, and tries to catch his rapidly murmured, Knott-like speech concerning his tenure at Knott's. Watt comes from Knott. That he is a Christ figure in this respect is made clear when Sam first sees him advancing backwards, falling in the briars, then resting on the barbed wire and turning to face Sam:

> His face was bloody, his hands also, and the thorns were in his scalp. (His resemblance, at that moment, to the Christ believed by Bosch, then hanging in Trafalgar Square, was so striking, that I remarked it.) And at the same instant suddenly I felt as though I were standing before a great mirror, in which my garden was reflected, and my fence, and I, and the very birds tossing in the wind, so that I looked at my hands, and felt my face, and glossy skull, with an anxiety as real as unfounded.

Sam sees himself in Watt. Their symbiosis is expressed in their embrace across the bridge and in their strange walks along the "couloir" between their respective barbed-wire fences: Sam forwards, Watt backwards, together, simultaneously coming and going, as a unit.

What can or does Sam learn from this suffering servant? The Way, the Truth, and the Life? In the first place, we can't know. Sam's information is, to put it mildly, unreliable: "Of this impetuous murmur much fell in vain upon my imperfect hearing and understanding, and much by the rushing wind was carried away, and lost forever. And it takes time for Sam to adapt to each stage of the successive inversions of Watt's discourse, and so much is not understood by him. Nor could Watt understand Sam. And Sam's hearing begins to fail him. And so on. As an instance of human communication, their dialogue is farcical. And yet, the much quoted and much translated examples of Watt's discourse are, as Michael Robinson says, "the nonsense of a rational mind. It is not pure irrationality but the inversion of words or letters according to an inflexible logic that adopts its own consistent form of expression rather than the equally arbitrary common form." Watt's discourse *means*. It can be translated into common English—though to do so is to falsify its import. Watt's languages exist as languages in their own right to the extent that they can be pronounced and have some sort of logical structure, however inverted or inconsistent. Sam says that with Watt "euphony was a preoccupation," and so it is: Watt's discourse is always musical and rhythmical. Language approaches music, approaches the purely formal, as did the voices that sang to Watt in the ditch: "Lit yad mac, ot og. Ton taw, ton tonk. Ton dob, ton trips. Ton vila, ton deda," etc. The world of forms has, for Watt, collapsed (he cannot understand Sam, for example), all his former habits have been unlearned or inverted. And yet something lives on, something touches, talks, however strangely, something goes on, bringing Watt out of his solipsism. A euphony, a communication—as Stevens would say, "a queer assertion of humanity"—is established. Sam says, "To be together again, after so long, who love the sunny wind, the windy sun, in the sun, in the wind, that is perhaps something, perhaps something." It is the "something" that has come out of the "nothing" at Knott's, something that lives in the very music of that passage, the lyrical rhythms of its word-dance. Watt experienced Naught, in ineffable sadness and resignation, and this *is* a Way, a Truth, and a Life, though it has nothing to do with the Habit of living.

Watt, like Christ, is of two worlds. The "divine" world in *Watt* is as complex as the idea of the kingdom of God in the Gospels. In the first place, "the kingdom of God is within you" (Luke 17:21). Watt is never seen as a functioning part of the "outer" world, even before journeying to Knott's. He is something different, as is clearly established in the opening scene. He reminds us of something ancient, something in our fathers and in ourselves, what Molloy represented to Moran. "Or was it not perhaps something that was not Watt, nor of Watt, but behind Watt, or beside Watt, or before Watt, or beneath Watt, or above Watt, or about Watt, a shade uncast, a light unshed, or the grey air aswirl with vain entelechies." It is this "something" that Fitzwein sees in Mr. Nackybal, as we shall see. Whatever it is, it has nothing to do with the world of reason, direction, meaning, purpose. It makes Watt seem strangely more than human.

The kingdom of God is more realized in Knott's house, where Watt journeys in order that he might fulfill what is inside him, and be cleansed of all else. He fails because of his humanity, his *need to know*, when Knott cannot be known. And so he journeys to the end of the line, disappearing in what must be considered, in the light of the setting of section III, a kind of death, though ultimately a temporary one. In III, we discover Watt in another metaphor of the kingdom of God, the mansions in which one can abide, like Knott in his room, "in empty hush, in airless gloom." But Watt can't and does not wish to abide there. He continues, rather, to crucify himself on the cross of his humanity by painfully journeying to the gardens to keep alive his verbal quest. Watt is Kierkegaard's subjective thinker, who strives for the infinite because it moves within him, yet is not "able to discover it through anything appearing outwardly," and so involves himself in the self-contradiction that Kierkegaard felt to be "the true form of the comic." Watt is a comic Christ.

"The only Paradise is the Paradise that is lost." So Watt never frees himself of the burden of his human consciousness. But he is not a parody of Christ; if that were true, *Watt* would be only ironic, and there would be little need for nightsongs, and meetings in the gardens, and Knott's child's breathing—all the dark lyricism in the novel, the small joys. Watt represents a Way, a Truth, a Life, even if he does not embody or fulfill them—just as Christ was both a fulfillment of prophecies and a sign that fulfillment would come: "Truly, truly, I say to you, the hour is coming, and now is, when the dead will hear the voice of the Son of God, and those who hear will live" (R.S.V. John 5:25).

Sam offers the following words as a bridge between the examples of Watt's own discourse and the substance of what Watt told him: "To these conversations we are indebted for the following information." But the narrative that follows—absurdly rational, as we shall see—could not possibly have been conveyed in the inverted simplicities of Watt's discourse. Within a paragraph the word *obnubilated* turns up. It would seem that Sam had "translated" Watt's conversation into his own style. But such a translation would have to be, for the most part, invention. Is it Watt who is still laboring at the ancient labor? The previous examples of his speech— fragmented, sensory, simple, passive—indicate that he is not. So is it *Sam* who is endeavouring to make rational sense of what Watt says? Where does Watt leave off and Sam begin? The answer can only be, in Watt's language, "Ton wonk."

This casts a new light on the third-person narrative of the first two sections, which seem to be a reflection of Watt's thoughts (and indeed, for purposes of convenience, I have so identified them in my discussion of these sections). Watt never speaks within the narrative, so we identify the voice of the narrative with his voice. Yet it remains a third-person narrative, with occasional intrusions of a first person. Whose voice, then, is it? The problem becomes more pronounced and complex in the first-person narratives of the Trilogy and the "Texts for Nothing." In the fourth of the "Texts," the first person, railing at his creator, says, "He protests he doesn't reason and does nothing but reason, crooked, as if that could improve matters. He thinks words fail him, he thinks that because words fail him he's on his way to my speechlessness, to being speechless with my speechlessness . . ." This illuminates Beckett's narrative technique in *Watt*. Beckett makes rational discourse out of Watt's irrational adventures. Beckett makes words out of words failing Watt. Beckett yearns for speechlessness and so invents an almost speechless protagonist and then talks about him. Wordlessness is contained within words, but of course it can't be, and so a comedy of language results.

The narrative paradox is made clearer with the introduction of Sam in section III. Beckett invents himself as a fictional character, throwing the whole narrative into question. In the main text of III— Sam's story of Watt's story of Arthur's story of Ernest Louit, Mr. Nackybal, and the Grants Committee—rational discourse is, again, reduced to a comic absurdity. In the only direct record of Watt's speech, Watt seems to be approaching speechlessness, though he fails. Then we read the product of his and Sam's conversations, expressed by Sam in the same voice of much of the first two sections, and we note the distinction between Watt's experience and the record of it. It becomes clear that reason, in its innate and hectic absurdity, is the product, not only of an individual sensibility, but of words themselves, of the whole idea of *telling a story*. Using words, one becomes a term in a universal series, each term using the same language, laboring at the ancient and futile labor.

John Mood has demonstrated that out of thirty-seven combinations, permutations, series and lists in *Watt*, twelve have errors. He concludes from this that an inner and personal system of certainty, founded on reason, is as "hopelessly flawed" a project as "the quest for the reality of meaning of whatever structure or significance . . . is out there." Reason only creates an *illusion* of order. In Arthur's story, told to Mr. Graves, we experience the linguistic manifestations of a rationalist mentality, creating a vision of chaos. For example,

> So Mr Magershon turns to Mr O'Meldon, to find Mr O'Meldon looking, not at him, as he had hoped (for if he had not hoped to find Mr O'Meldon looking at him when he turned to look at Mr O'Meldon, then he would not have turned to look at Mr O'Meldon, but would have craned forward, or perhaps backward, to look at Mr MacStern, or perhaps at Mr de Baker, but more likely the former, as one less lately looked at than the latter), but at Mr MacStern, in the hope of finding Mr MacStern looking at him.

As Poe might put it, such language does not hold "the solemn sea / To the sands upon the shore." It is only an extension, however, of "Dick and Jane saw the wet grass and decided it had rained." In the recounting of the actions and divagations of the Grants Committee, the strictures on language that reason imposes are carried to absurd lengths, and we experience the obverse of reason. We simply find it difficult to figure things out. It is said that five members of the Committee looked at one another, and a kind of time-lapse occurs as Arthur attempts to convey rationally such an action in its entirety. The result, rather than being analytically clear, is a kind of hallucination. As in time-lapse photography, one experiences a radical and unreal sense of *change*, beautiful perhaps in its own right but hardly comforting in its vision of order.

Reasoning things through leads, not to order or fixity, but to a chaos of detail. Arthur says, "If I tell you all this in such detail, Mr Graves, the reason is, believe me, that I cannot, much as I should like, and for reasons that I shall not go into, do otherwise." One simply goes on, laboring, helpless to stop. Reason cannot produce a reason for its own being, except that it is an involuntary escape from nothingness. "Watt learned later, from Arthur, that the telling of this story, while it lasted, before Arthur grew tired, had transported Arthur far from Mr Knott's premises, of which, of the mysteries of which, of the fixity of which, Arthur had sometimes more, than he could bear." The story, in its incomplete form, does not accomplish its original intention—that is, to illustrate how the aphrodisiac Bando has to be smuggled into England. We learn, as a kind of afterthought, that had Arthur finished his story, we would have discovered that Mr. Louit wound up running Bando *after* his academic demise. But Arthur's intention is not really to reach that point, but to work out, in a rationalist fantasy, a story to transport himself from Knott's. But one tires of the words, too. Watt says that although he understood the story with more clarity than anything else at Knott's— being himself a rationalist *par excellence*—and that he enjoyed it, he grew tired of it, as did Arthur. And why? Because Arthur desired to leave Louit and *return* to the mysteries and fixity of Knott's, "For he had been absent longer from them, than he could bear." So the circle continues, in change.

There is a counterpoint to the rational craziness of Arthur's story which leads us into the last part of section III, the part concerning Knott himself. It first occurs when Arthur interrupts his story to remark to Mr. Graves how much he despises details, and yet is compelled to relate them. He says that when Mr. Graves sows his vegetables he doesn't do so "with punctilio," but quickly opens a rough trench line and absently and fatalistically lets the seeds fall. Mr. Graves, whose occupation brings him close to natural process, is passive and casual and humble before Chance. Arthur says that as a younger man Mr. Graves no doubt "used a line, a measure, a plumb, a level" to place his vegetables in careful order, and wonders at what age Mr. Graves ceased to use these "mechanical aids" and arrived at his present freedom, when all he needs "is earth, excrement, water and a stick . . ." In his tediously detailed wondering about all this, Arthur makes us glad for the simplicity of these elemental words, with which he ends his long sentences. In this way, the brooding about punctiliousness and freedom is made relevant to the use of language, to Arthur's very narrative. The point of this brief address to Mr. Graves, in the context of the entire story of Louit, is to counterpoint the idea of freedom from reason's tedium in a kind of surrender to natural process, over and against the rational, manic disorder of Louit's and Neckybal's confrontation with the Grants Committee.

Beyond the formal atmosphere of the Grants Committee and their and Louit's obsession with cubes and cube roots (along with their clear avoidance of surds such as the cube root of three, with the exception of O'Meldon's alarming introduction of a false cube—beyond these lies the Formality of natural process, diurnal change. Some examples of this counterpoint, inserted as brief interludes in the ongoing chaos, are the following:

> Soon the room, empty now, was grey with shadows, of the evening. A porter came, turned on all the lights, straightened the chairs, saw that all was well and went away. Then the vast room was dark, for night had fallen, again.

> When the demonstration was over, then it was question-time. Through the western windows of the vast hall shone the low red winter sun, stirring the air, the chambered air, with its angry farewell shining, whilst via the opposite or oriental apertures or lights the murmur rose, appeasing, of the myriad faint clarions of night. It was question-time.

The western and eastern windows recall the times when Watt glimpsed Knott through a dark glass. Here are glimpses of what Stevens would call reality, changing to no purpose except to change, seen in a sudden change of focus from the hectic structures and speculations of the world of forms, parodically represented by the Grants Committee.

One member of the Committee, Mr. Fitzwein, seems to glimpse this world, not out the windows, but in the face of Mr. Nackybal, and it unnerves him. Fitzwein, Chairman of the Committee, is immediately struck by Nackybal's face: "Mr. Nackybal now, to the general surprise, transferred, from the sky, his eyes, docile, stupid, liquid, staring eyes, towards Mr Fitzwein, who after a moment exclaimed, to the further general surprise, A gazelle! A sheep! An old sheep!" As the Committee goes about its business of ascertaining information about the old man, Fitzwein interrupts again with "A goat! An old quinch!" and "His eyes coil into my very soul." The Chairman claims that Nackybal's face is familiar, and from then on is not able effectively to chair the questioning, which duty is taken over by others. Fitzwein, obviously obsessed with the face, only obstructs the Committee's questioning with irritating remarks that reveal he has not been paying attention to the proceedings. He has been transported. Finally, Fitzwein becomes impatient with the proceedings and begins to speak of going home to bed. "Raise your point for the love of God, said Mr Fitzwein, and let me get home to my wife. He added, And children." Again he says, "Where have I seen that face before." What Fitzwein sees in this bony hairy old Caliban, who scratches his crotch and falls asleep during the proceedings, and whose "mental existence" is supposedly "exhausted by the bare knowledge, emerging from a complete innocence of the rudiments, of what is necessary for his survival," is the face of Primal Man, the Form behind forms, the archetypal, pre-knowledge, pre-rational, free man. We survive, "every man his own fertiliser," we excrete, we plod, gross masses towards our graves in the ending light. It doesn't matter that Mr. Nackybal is a hoax, that "his real name was Tisler and he lived in a room on the canal." That fact only underscores the archetypal quality of his face; like Molloy, he lurks in all of us. It is what the face of Watt is to Mr. Hackett: passive, docile, and above all, free. And yet, and yet, the original sin of ratiocination is there: Nackybal has been taught to cube root easy figures.

Just so, Watt attempts to come to terms rationally with Knott. The rest of section III is taken up with Watt's random speculations about Knott. We move from the analytical chaos of Arthur's story to the mysterious "ataraxy" of Knott's world.

> Of the nature of Mr Knott himself Watt remained in particular ignorance.
> Of the many excellent reasons for this, two seemed to Watt to merit attention: on the one hand the exiguity of the material propounded to the senses, and on the other the decay of these.

Watt (and Sam and we) are in ignorance because our mode of thought is designed to grasp something, and Knott is Nothing. He is both a "fixity" and a continually changing presence, wearing various clothes, appearing in various guises, murmuring meaningless songs. Watt attempts, of course, to enumerate these changes, but only confronts the mystery of Knott's presence: "For there was no place, but only there where Mr Knott was." Knott is the constant presence, the unifying key, like Stevens' *noued vital*.

In the midst of Watt's ratiocination there appears, abruptly, a sort of interlude paragraph, which brings into focus what Arthur spoke of as "freedom." It is worth quoting in full:

> To think, when one is no longer young, when one is not yet old, that one is no longer young, that one is not yet old, that is perhaps something. To pause, towards the close of one's three hour day, and consider: the darkening ease, the brightening trouble; the pleasure pleasure because it was, the pain pain because it shall be; the glad acts grown proud, the proud acts growing stubborn; the panting the trembling towards a being gone, a being to come; and the true true no longer, and the false true not yet. And to decide not to smile after all, sitting in the shade, hearing the cicadas, wishing it were night, wishing it were morning, saying, No, it is not the heart, no, it is not the liver, no, it is not the prostate, no, it is not the ovaries, no, it is muscular, it is nervous. Then the gnashing ends, or it goes on, and one is in the pit, in the hollow, the

> longing for longing gone, the horror of horror, and one is in the hollow,
> at the foot of all the hills at last, the ways down, the ways up, and free,
> free at last, for an instant free at last, nothing at last.

In this freedom, desire is gone, direction is gone. One exists at once in change and out of change, as Arsene did looking at the light on the wall. One lives an instant in its integrity, in its lack of duration, in its nothingness. And yet that instant is in a series, and the series involves change. There is, in this moment of freedom, no cause and effect, no hope or despair. Antinomies disappear. One exists in the momentarily calm heart of Zeno's paradoxes. This paragraph bears no relation to the paragraphs surrounding it, it is interpolated, a sudden rest from thinking. In the next paragraph Watt returns to ruminating on Knott, but in the instant of this interlude we come as close to *experiencing* Knott / Naught as we can. Then we go on, because it is a muscular, a nervous, an involuntary impulse to do so. At the end of III we see, as Sam sees, Watt departing "over the deep threshing shadows backwards stumbling, towards his habitation," until we see him no more, "but only the aspens." Shadows and wind and quaking aspens, these are expressive of the formal beauty of change, seen with a kind of painful nostalgia. "And from the hidden pavilions, his and mine, where by this time dinner was preparing, the issuing smokes by the wind were blown, now far apart, but now together, mingled to vanish." Watt and Sam have come together and parted, like the smoke, in the wind of change, irrevocably a part of the endless round of change. This is the last we and Sam see of Watt, but it is not the end of his story, or, rather, the telling of his story.

"As Watt came, so he went, in the night." He came as dawn was about to break, and he leaves Knott's premises at night, and in his coming was his going, and as he goes Micks comes and Arthur mounts to the first floor, "and through the open door the light, from darkness slowly brightening, to darkness slowly darkening . . ." Circles, series. Watt, with an expression of such "vacancy" that Micks is astonished, and with an air about him "aswirl with vain entelechies," begins his journey to the railway station and thence to "the further end" of the line—a line that will end, presumably, at the mansions.

Watt has been changed by his experience at Knott's. He seems to be not so much concerned with the meaning of things as with their form. Micks, waiting in the kitchen to take Watt's place, delivers a speech about himself and "Watt listened for a time, for the voice was far from unmelodious. The fricatives in particular were pleasing. But as from the proscript an encountered nightsong, so it faded, the voice of Micks, the pleasant

voice of poor Micks, in the soundless tumult of the inner lamentation."
What matters to Watt is not the substance of what Micks relates, but that
all words are the music of a lamentation, a lament, perhaps, to the loss of
silence, a lament to futile labors. And so he makes no helpful parting
speech to Micks, or so he realizes after finding himself on the road. And
having arrived at the station, and perceived an apparently human figure
advancing at a distance, Watt at first ruminates on what the figure might
be, but then realizes that it is not necessary to be precise about this. "For
Watt's concern . . . was not after all with what the figure was, in reality,
but with what the figure appeared to be, in reality. For since when were
Watt's concerns with what things were, in reality? But he was forever
falling into this error, this error of the old days when, lacerated with
curiosity, in the midst of substance shadowy he stumbled." The old error
is the error of reason, of trying to name what a thing is (a woman, a
priest, a nun, an "inverted chamberpot"). Though "logic was on his side,"
logic is not knowledge, or a road to knowledge, of reality. Watt assumes
the figure is approaching, and waits for it, in order to know it, but the
figure turns out, comically, to be moving away, and finally grows fainter
and disappears. Indeed, it might have been an "hallucination." With his
curiosity, with his logic, Watt comes to know nothing. Logic operates in a
world of forms, not "entelechies." And yet, ignoring substance and listening to the music of forms, to the formal changes of light and sound in
appearances, one can sense the Nothingness of Being, the silence that
words enclose, the form-giving cause rather than the existing forms. Once
having been admitted to the station waiting-room, Watt "lay on a seat,
without thought or sensation, except for a slight feeling of chill in one
foot. In his skull the voices whispering their canon were like a patter of
mice . . ." He hears, once again, the music of pre-thought, proto-words,
the nightsong soon to become the day labor.

The sensations and perceptions that Watt experiences in the waiting-
room, as dawn slowly comes, are those of thought emerging from pre-
thought, as the influence of Knott's wears off. The room, uniformly gray
and white, is an image of Watt's skull, smells and sounds and light
gradually entering, objects (the chair, the colored print) gradually outlined, defined and named, studied in detail. The process of coming into
the world, expelled from refuge, begins once again: a "merry whistling"
sounds far off and then, abruptly and violently, Mr. Nolan the signalman
unlocks the door and kicks it open, knocking Watt to the floor. "Now I
am at liberty, said Watt, I am free to come and go, and I please," just as
Mr. Nolan told him earlier he would be. The irony is savage. The
"freedom" of the outside world, with its insistence on coming and going as

meaningful and purposive movement, is well symbolized by the violent blow, like the blow infants receive as an introduction and awakening to the world of forms. From the moment of Watt's being knocked to the floor unconscious, the outside world takes over the novel, and we are treated, in the last pages, to its comical inanity, cruelty, vitality, and obsession with time ("The five fifty-five will be upon us").

Eventually Watt goes on: gets up, buys a ticket to the end of the line and, characteristically, disappears. The train entering "did not take up a single passenger"; as in the first scene of the novel, Watt seems to vanish. In that first scene he is last glimpsed "faintly outlined against the last wisps of day." At the end Watt rises from the floor just as the sun rises, and as he disappears, our attention is shifted from him to a goat rising from a ditch and moving away down the road, to the trembling sea and the quivering leaves. Watt, presumably, vanishes to the "mansions" of section III, but it is not so much an apotheosis as it is a going on, in the eternity of process, fading and reappearing like a shadow slipping through the world of forms.

Confronted with the exhilarating dawn of a summer day and forgetting the recent trouble with Watt, Mr. Gorman the station-master is moved to exclaim, "All the same . . . life isn't such a bad old bugger. He raised high his hands and spread them out, in a gesture of worship. He then replaced them in the pockets of his trousers. When all is said and done . . ." This is at once ironic and true. It is ironic because the outside world's idea of "life" is unthinking Habit. Mr. Gorman is worshipping himself. But it is also true because life isn't so bad "when all is said and done," when the silence is reached and labor completed, if that is possible, when life is Life: pure process, "nothing at last." In the balance of Beckett's irony and lyricism, here expressed in the reviving of a cliché, is Beckett's comedy.

I have discussed Beckett's comedy as involving a constant clash between the labors of rational consciousness and the "nightsong" of lyrical rest: how each gives rise to the other, in a sinking to silence and a rising to speech, a darkening and brightening of the mind as a language maker. It is appropriate to conclude with a brief discussion of the structure of *Watt*, since confusion over it has resulted from a failure to see it as a comic structure, full of contradiction.

Michael Robinson discusses it at some length, mentioning, among other things, that the entire book is Sam's narration, though this fact is only revealed in section III; that while III takes place *after* IV in terms of the chronology of the narration, the story that is narrated in III (Watt's stay on the first floor) fits right in chronologically, between Watt's stay on the ground floor (II) and his leaving Knott's (IV); that the shift in narrative time "adds force to the ironic ending" and results in a sandwich-like structure, "the two outside parts describing Watt's arrival and departure" creating "a satisfying unit," a closed circuit. A few holes begin to appear in this rational formulation. How can Watt be said to have related to Sam the very opening and closing scenes, in which he is not present? Sam is not present either, unless we identify Sam as Hackett, which is a clever play on sounds but gets us nowhere (Hackett does not know Watt, but Sam and Watt appear to have known each other for some time). Did Sam make up the opening scene, or the very last scene, after Watt vanishes? Putting the question of the Addenda aside (who wrote those? and the footnotes?), it can be assumed that the novel follows this basic chronology: (I) Watt leaves the tram, sees Nixon, goes to the railway terminus, travels to Knott's house; (II) Watt is Knott's servant on the ground floor; (III) Watt is Knott's servant on the first floor; (IV) Watt leaves Knott's, travels to the railway station, buys a ticket and vanishes. And it can be concluded that the placing of III at the end of the novel would disrupt this chronology while satisfying another, as well as depriving the novel of a certain circularity. But what about the opening sentences of section IV, in which Sam addresses himself to the problem of the narrative, and which Robinson avoids mentioning? "As Watt told the beginning of his story, not first, but second, so not fourth, but third, now he told its end. Two, one, four, three, that was the order in which Watt told his story. Heroic quatrains are not otherwise elaborated." The "four, three" order is clear, but what are we to make of "two, one"? Section II clearly comes after I, in a conventional narrative sequence. But that's Sam's sequence (presumably), and not Watt's. The more one tries to puzzle this out, the more one's thoughts take on the cast of Watt's own, and that, it seems to me, is the major and comic point.

The narrative is, rationally speaking, a bog. Section III indicates a radical distinction between the narrative *as story* (which seems to be chronologically sequential) and the narrative *as a story told* (which is certainly not chronological and, given the opening and closing scenes, not even clear). Section III accomplishes this by undermining our complacency about third-person narrations. Between event and rumination about event, there is no clear relation. Watt's reaction to the Galls incident is instructive. What we encounter, on reading this novel, is a sequence of events taking place with "formal distinctness," but the "purport" of the events has been filtered through untrustworthy minds (Watt's, Sam's, Arthur's, Beckett's) until—to paraphrase a passage on the Galls—the incident of Watt's journey ceased so rapidly to have even the paltry significance of one man, coming to serve at Knott's, serving a time, then going, that it seemed rather to belong to some story heard long before, an instant in the life of another, ill-told, ill-heard, and more than half-forgotten.

In other words, the formality of the story breaks down in the process of being told, and yields to a greater Formality, that of existence itself, the essential existence of men and smoke and aspens and goats and pots and stones—ancient and arresting, like the face of Mr. Nackybal. "I seem to have known him [Watt] all my life," says Mr. Nixon. Our experience of *Watt* is not an experience of a rationally sequential narration, but an experience of light and sound and change, the music of words like a nightsong in our heads, heard in a ceaselessly darkening and brightening light: Hackett crying as night comes, Watt in the kitchen as dawn comes, Arthur appearing "on a morning white and soft . . . the earth . . . dressed for the grave," Watt disappearing as Case, Nolan and Gorman stand "in the early morning light" with "the sky falling to the hills, and the hills falling to the plain," ready to begin "a day's march."

It does not matter so much that someone has come and gone, or that someone has organized words to tell about it, but rather that we have sensed through these events and words the changelessness and silence in which we cannot abide. Just as Watt, on leaving Knott's, appears to be vacant of expression and touched with something not-Watt, with "entelechies" perhaps—yet these "entelechies" are "vain," and inside the passive vacancy Watt's mind is "busy, busy wondering. . . ." The comedy establishes and undercuts both the rationalism and the something that exists beyond it, the world of forms and the unknowable energy that informs it—expresses them in a dynamic relationship, as the terms of a circular paradox. In so doing, Beckett's comedy of language discovers both the absurdity and the necessity of what keeps man going on, *through* the absurdity and the necessity of his language: "But he had hardly felt the absurdity of those things, on the one hand, and the necessity of those others, on the other (for it is rare that the feeling of absurdity is not followed by the feeling of necessity), when he felt the absurdity of those things of which he had just felt the necessity (for it is rare that the feeling of necessity is not followed by the feeling of absurdity)."

LINDA BEN-ZVI

Samuel Beckett, Fritz Mauthner, and the Limits of Language

In discussions of philosophical influences on the writing of Samuel Beckett, the name of Fritz Mauthner, an Austrian empiricist and philosopher of language, has been appearing with increasing frequency in the past several years. Richard Ellmann was the first to draw attention to the Mauthner-Beckett connection by revealing that in 1932 the nearly blind Joyce would "ask the young man to read to him passages from Mauthner's *Beiträge zu einer Kritik der Sprache* ['Contributions toward a Critique of Language'] in which the nominalist view of language seemed something Joyce was looking for." Mauthner's three-volume, 2,200–page work, written in 1902 and as yet untranslated from its original German, provided the young Beckett with a philosophical verification for his own skepticism about language, expressed a year earlier in his study of Proust: "There is no communication because there are no vehicles of communication." It also provided Beckett with a model. By placing language at the heart of the *Critique*, subsuming under it all knowledge, and then systematically denying its basic efficacy, Mauthner illustrates the possibility of using language to indict itself. The same linguistic centrality and nullity lie at the core of Beckett's work.

The position of linguistic idealism that Beckett posits—"the spirit of Mauthner," as Edith Kern calls it—has been noted by several critics. Kern attributes Beckett's "remove from traditional linguistic patterns" to Mauthner's influence. David Hesla, in an extended note at the end of his

From *PMLA* 2, vol. 95, (March 1980). Copyright © 1980 by Modern Language Association of America.

book, *The Shape of Chaos*, goes as far as to say that "One of the howlers of this study may well be the omission of Fritz Mauthner." More recently, both James Knowlson and John Pilling have commented on Mauthner's significance to Beckett studies. Pilling notes that "following Descartes and Schopenhauer as key figures in Beckett's thinking is Fritz Mauthner" and emphasizes that

> It would be difficult to overstate the relevance of [Mauthner's ideas of language] for students of Beckett. The premises are the same, the conclusions are the same; only the realm of discourse . . . is different. . . . Mauthner in fact provided Beckett with the necessary ammunition to destroy all systems of thought whatever, even "irrationalism."

Despite this increasing interest among Beckett scholars, Mauthner remains a shadowy figure; he is almost totally overlooked in philosophical circles, and only one of his eleven major works—a refutation of Aristotle—has been translated into English. The brief remarks about his theories of language that have appeared in Beckett studies are generally taken from the only book in English devoted to his *Critique*, Gershon Weiler's *Mauthner's Critique of Language*. Weiler, who also wrote the short biographical sketch of Mauthner that appears in the *Encyclopedia of Philosophy*, offers a clear summary of Mauthner's analysis of language but fails to convey Mauthner's spirit, which must have first impressed both Joyce and Beckett with its passionate, rambling vituperations, contradictions, and logorrhea. When returning to the original, however, one is immediately struck by similarities between the *Critique* and Beckett's writing, similarities explained in part by the authors' shared recognition of the limits of language.

I

Mauthner's skepticism about language can be traced to two interrelated sources: his personal biography and the biography of his time, the waning days of the Hapsburg dynasty. Fritz Mauthner was born in 1849, of German-speaking Jewish parents in Hořice, Bohemia, and moved with his family to Prague when he was seven. His early years in Prague—which along with Vienna and Budapest was a cultural center of Hapsburg society—bear a marked resemblance to those of Franz Kafka, born in the same city thirty-four years after Mauthner. Both men grew up speaking German in a Czech-speaking society; both were exposed, in varying degrees, to the Hebrew language as part of a perfunctory Jewish education, which they both found abhorrent; both attended German gymnasiums; both studied law at the University of Prague and participated, as students, in the

German-speaking Law Union; both had a love for Goethe that bordered on idolatry; and both carried away from their childhood education a deep hatred for the stultifying regimen and hollow forms under which they were educated. Kafka called his own education "sawdust—sawdust, too, which had already been chewed by thousands of jaws before me." Similarly, one of the recurring images that Mauthner uses in the Critique is of the rigid school system that he equates with the futile exercises of philosophy itself:

> Thus, one can conceive of the old question school [Frageschule] of mankind, of philosophy, as a school in which work is done always at one and the same question, in which this one task can never be solved because the work takes longer than one generation of teachers and students. After its labor pains, mankind sends in new students, and for each new student, work must begin anew. Death relieves the teachers, and each teacher must begin anew. But the question that generations labor to answer is written on the blackboard eternally. Each preceding generation believes that it works for the following, and each of the following must begin anew. For the question mark on the blackboard itself is not unchangeable: after all, it is a sign, it is language. And perhaps that which we call philosophy is nothing but the questioning glance of mankind, the question per se, a question without content.

Although he was greatly influenced by Kant's Critique of Pure Reason and Schopenhauer's The Fourfold Root of the Principle of Sufficient Reason, Mauthner believed that both works fell into the error common to all philosophical inquiry: they failed to question the very premises on which their metaphysical speculations were based, because they did not analyze language itself. This concern with the articulation and criticism of the methodologies of philosophy was part of a much wider movement at work during the period in which Mauthner wrote. As Allan Janik and Stephen Toulmin have chronicled in Wittgenstein's Vienna, a radical reassessment in all areas of intellectual endeavor characterized fin-de-siècle Vienna and Prague. Adolf Loos in architecture, Ernst Mach in physics, Gustav Klimt in painting, Schönberg and Mahler in music, and Freud in psychology—all were concerned with returning their investigations to the bases on which their individual disciplines had rested undisturbed for so long. "The proving ground for world destruction" was the term that Karl Kraus, leading polemicist and force in language reform, used to describe these years, the period in which the smug complacency of the Hapsburg society, with its sense of Hausmacht, was being eroded by probing investigations that would lead to twentieth-century revolutions in almost every area of society. Mauthner, as drama critic of the *Berliner Tageblatt*, was caught up in this general intellectual ferment, a ferment that helps explain the often apocalyptic-sounding phrases of the *Critique* and, even more, the audacity of a journalist in undertaking such an investigation.

The *Critique* met with relative success when it first appeared in 1901–02, and eventually, by 1923, it went to three editions; but its iconoclastic form and its author's maverick position outside established philosophical circles made it more a curiosity of a questioning age than a significant influence on the language philosophy of the period. Now, however, when many of the skeptical views of the *Critique* have become commonplaces, Mauthner is receiving belated attention. Since 1975 two books devoted to his ideas on language have been published in Germany.

Joachim Kühn's *Gescheiterte Sprachkritik: Fritz Mauthner, Leben und Werk* studies the part that Mauthner has played in twentieth-century German literature, particularly in the movement called *Sprachskepsisdichtung*. Kühn argues that many major trends in modern German literature take their point of departure from Mauthner's skepticism about language. Kühn also briefly mentions the connection of Joyce and Beckett to this skeptical school of writing. Beckett, he observes, "sought in Mauthner's writing for arguments [against language] and the philosopher offered them to him with his complaint about the lack of a relationship between language and reality as well as about the corruption of the language of his time." Kühn is wise enough to recognize that Beckett did not "write in this and no other way because he read to Joyce out of Mauthner's works; nevertheless, it appears as if he had received an important impetus from them."

Mauthner has also had an impact on another literary man. In his recent biography of Jorge Luis Borges, the Argentinian writer who shared the Formenter Prize with Beckett in 1961, Emir Rodriguez Monegal reports that Borges, early in his career, became acquainted with the work of Mauthner and found many of the ideas influential in his own writing. When interviewed about Mauthner, Borges said, "He published some very bad novels, but his philosophical papers are excellent. He is a wonderful writer, very ironic, whose style recalls that of the eighteenth century." Although Borges did not mention the *Critique*, he cited Mauthner's *Dictionary of Philosophy* as "*one* of the books I have consulted with great pleasure."

Finally, Beckett himself mentioned Mauthner's name in *Radio II*, published in the collection entitled *Ends and Odds* (1976) and presented on BBC in April 1976 with Harold Pinter, Patrick Magee, and Billie Whitelaw, under the direction of Martin Esslin. In the piece, an animator and a stenographer attempt to wrest secrets from a Mr. Fox, a prisoner tortured into making certain disclosures by a character referred to as Dick, who says nothing throughout the piece but wields a bull's pizzle when Fox lapses into silence. In a list of exhortations concerning their endeavor, the stenographer reads the following: "The least word let fall in solitude and thereby in danger, as Mauthner has shown, of being no longer needed, *may be it*—three words underlined." This reference, which reduces Mauthner's notion of language to virtual philosophical double-talk, may be Beckett's personal joke, directed at those scholars who might fix on Mauthner as a key to the Beckett treasure trove: that Mauthner "*may be it*—three words underlined." What supports this idea of critical parody is the inclusion in the radio play of another name, Laurence Sterne, also frequently mentioned as a source for Beckett's writing. But if Deirdre Bair is correct, Beckett has rejected the Sterne connection, and he may be pointing out a warning to those who want to ride philosophical hobby-horses. Unlocking the secrets of composition is what *Radio II* is all about; and as the work indicates, the secrets, like the secrets of self, are not reducible to any *one* thing, torture as one may with pizzle or pen.

Having said this, however, I should add that any light that may be shed on Beckett's works and on the development of his theories of language is useful, though one reference, or one influence, is never *it*. Beckett's mind has absorbed many ideas, none of which can claim ultimate sway in the creative process but all of which provide some degree of intellectual grist. As Ruby Cohn has pointed out, "Beckett's heroes not only deny that they are philosophers; they flaunt an inviolable ignorance. . . . But however vituperatively they may insist upon their ignorance, they, like their creator, reveal an impressive fund of knowledge garnered by a compulsively examining mind."

It is significant to note, moreover, that within Beckett's encyclopedic mind Mauthner was not merely a passing interest. Although Beckett read the *Critique* in 1932, he has admitted recently that he still finds Mauthner of importance and includes the rare volumes among his personal library today. More important than Beckett's present opinion, however, are his initial response to the *Critique* and the possible influence the work had on his own use of language when he first encountered it.

II

In 1932 Beckett was twenty-six years old; he had recently resigned from his academic career at Trinity College, Dublin, and had embarked on a literary career in Paris. Behind him were the published poem "Whor-

oscope," based on the life of Descartes, and two critical works: "Dante
. . . Bruno. Vico . . . Joyce" (1929), an essay in defense of Joyce's *Work in
Progress*, and a treatise on Proust, completed in 1931. In the first of these
studies, basically an apologia for the difficulties in Joyce's work, Beckett
had issued a strong call for a literature where "words are not the polite
contortions of 20th century printer's ink. They are alive." Noting the
difficulty of achieving this vitality—where "the words dance"—Beckett
indicated his awareness of the limitations that language, particularly English, imposes. Beckett sees Joyce as attempting to withstand the abstraction of English by resorting to "primitive economic directness," giving no
quarter to "the conventional language of cunning literary artificers."
Joyce, Beckett argues, is finally able to achieve "a quintessential extraction
of language and painting and gesture, with all the inevitable clarity of the
old inarticulation."

Beckett describes a different clarity of inarticulation in his next
critical work, *Proust*. Again he is concerned with the problem of finding a
language that will not distort and that will remain faithful to what Beckett
here calls the Proustian equation: "The unknown, choosing its weapons
from the hoard of values, is also the unknowable." Despite Proust's own
accomplishments, particularly his ability to capture past experience through
the workings of involuntary memory, "reality . . . remains a surface,
hermetic." Even should the experiences of the past pierce the habituated
nature of man in the present, the writer is still faced with the ultimate
failure of language to articulate this experience. What Proust has been able
to write is an "inspired perception" that may give form to the dilemma of
living but cannot explain or alter it: "We cannot know and we cannot be
known."

Similar ideas about the insufficiency of language and traditional
literary forms are also present in the unpublished novel "Dream of Fair to
Middling Women," which Beckett began soon after completing *Proust*, at
approximately the time he became acquainted with the writings of Mauthner.
Through the voice of his fictional persona in the work, Belacqua Shuah,
Beckett indicts the traditional novel:

> To read Balzac is to receive the impression of a chloroformed world. He
> is absolute master of his material, he can do what he likes with it, he can
> foresee and calculate its vicissitude, he can write the end of his book
> before he has finished the first paragraph, because he has turned all his
> creatures into clockwork cabbages and can rely on their staying put
> wherever needed or staying going at whatever speed in whatever direc-
> tion he chooses. The whole thing, from beginning to end, takes place in
> a spellbound backwash.

Belacqua commits himself to a quite different kind of literature, a type predicted in Beckett's earlier critical writing: "If I ever do drop a book, which God forbid, trade being what it is, it will be ramshackle, tumbledown, a boneshaker, held together with bits of twine. . . ." More specifically, Belacqua describes the form of language that such a book will employ:

> I shall write a book, he mused, tired of the harlots of earth and air . . . a book where the phrase is self-consciously smart and slick, but of a smartness and slickness other that [sic] of its neighbours on the page. . . . The experience of my reader shall be between the phrases, in the silence, communicated by the intervals, not the terms, of the statement, between the flowers that cannot coexist, at the antithetical (nothing so simple as antithetical) seasons of words, his experience shall be the menace, the miracle, the memory, of an unspeakable trajectory.

While the quotation indicates that Beckett, even at this early stage, had some notion of the form his writing would take, the rest of "Dream" indicates that he had not yet been able to put the theory into practice. There are examples of the strong Joycean influence—"Poppata, big breach, Botticelli thighs, knock-knees, ankles all fat nodules, wobbly mammose, slobbery-blubbery, bubbubbubbub, a real button-bursting weib, ripe"—that John Fletcher notes in a comment on the photocopy of the original corrected manuscript now held in the Beckett archives at the University of Reading.

Besides a recognition of the limits of language, a commitment to a new type of literature, and a tutelage that had not yet run its course, Beckett brought to his first reading of Mauthner in 1932 a solid background in philosophy. Trinity College was a center for studies of both John Locke and David Hume; Beckett's tutor, Arthur Aston Luce, was a leading authority on the works of Berkeley and Descartes; and Beckett himself, in the years just preceding his introduction to the *Critique*, had done research on both Descartes and the Belgian occasionalist Arnold Geulinex.

III

The avowed purpose of Mauthner's *Critique* is to plot what Beckett was to describe in the "Dream" as the "unspeakable trajectory." I quote at length from the first page of the *Critique* because many of the themes that Mauthner develops and that Beckett employs are stated at the very beginning of the study.

In the Beginning was the Word. With the word, men stand at the beginning of their insight into the world, and if they stay with the word they'll stop there. He who wishes to move on, even if it be only a tiny step that may serve to advance the thought efforts of an entire lifetime, *he must try to redeem the world from the tyranny of language.*

No insight is of any help, no language-critical atheism. There is no holding on in thin air. You have to advance step by step, and each step is a new illusion since it is not suspended freely in the air. If he who strives upward were to pause ever so slightly upon each step—be it ever so low—if he were to touch it only with the tips of his toes, then, at the moment of contact, he too would not be suspended freely; he too is chained to the language of this very moment, of this very step. And this would be true even if, for this moment, he had built language and step himself.

During years of work, therefore, it was self-deception all the time when he who wanted to take upon himself redemption from language hoped to accomplish his task in a regular step-by-step book. He who calls himself an atheist is not a free man, he is an opponent of the one he denies. He who sets out to write a book with a hunger for words, with a love of words, and with the vanity of words, in the language of yesterday or of today or of tomorrow, in the congealed language of a certain and firm step, he cannot undertake the task of liberation from language. I must destroy language within me, in front of me, and behind me step for step if I want to ascend in the critique of language, which is the most pressing task for thinking man; I must shatter each rung of the ladder by stepping upon it. He who wishes to follow me must reconstitute the rungs in order to shatter them once again.

The renunciation of self-delusion is contained in the insight: *I am writing a book against language in a rigid language.* Since language is alive it does not remain unchanged from the beginning of a sentence up to its end. "In the Beginning was the Word;" here, while I am uttering the sixth word, the initial phrase "in the beginning" has already changed its meaning.

Thus, I had to arrive at the decision either to publish these fragments as fragments or to deliver up the entire work to its most radical redeemer: fire. Fire would have brought peace. However, as long as he is alive, man is like living language and believes that he has something to say because he speaks.

(I, italics mine)

The reader of the *Critique* is initially struck by Mauthner's clear awareness that his endeavor is doomed and his equally clear commitment to go on. Just as Beckett, in "Three Dialogues," inexplicably continues to feel an "obligation to express" what cannot be expressed, Mauthner persists in regarding the "redemption of language" as a challenge despite the predictable failure of his efforts. All Beckett's characters stand at the beginning with the word; and, try as they may, they can never climb the ladder to linguistic freedom. Like Arsene in *Watt* (1959), who uses the same ladder image in his long monologue—an image for which Mauthner's text may have acted as source—they keep slipping and are condemned to "existence off the ladder." Mauthner would agree with Arsene that, in dealing with the unutterable or ineffable, "any attempt to utter or eff it is doomed to fail, doomed, doomed to fail."

Such certain failure did not deter Mauthner, as it did not deter Beckett: both place "the fidelity to failure" at the center of their works and see their major task as promoting recognition of the basic condition of human experience—"unknown and unknowable."

To indicate the similarities between the writings of the two men, I have isolated only those sections of the *Critique* that bear on Beckett's treatment of language, and I have arranged them in the order of importance that Mauthner accords them in his study, not necessarily in the order in which they appear in the three volumes.

1. Thinking and speaking are one activity.
2. Language and memory are synonymous.
3. All language is metaphor.
4. There are no absolutes.
5. The ego is contingent; it does not exist apart from language.
6. Communication between men is impossible.
7. The only language should be simple language.
8. The highest forms of a critique of language are laughter and silence.

Thinking and speaking are one activity (1).

The heart of Mauthner's critique is his insistence on the primacy of language—not merely as a tool of expression, a means to articulate metaphysical speculation, but as a central concern in its own right. He begins his study with the assertion that, in fact, there is *only* language. What we commonly refer to as thinking is merely language seen from a different vantage point; thinking and speaking are one and the same activity:

> One of the points of departure of this work is that there is no thinking outside speaking (i.e., outside language), that thinking is a dead symbol for an ostensible mistakenly seen attribute of language: its imaginary ability to promote insight [*Erkenntnis*].

Mauthner's most consistent theme is the inseparability of thinking and speaking and the mistaken notion of most men that they think independently of speaking:

What stands most clearly in the path of knowing truth is that men all believe they themselves think, when actually they only speak, and also that scholars and students of the mind all speak of thinking for which speaking should be at most the instrument or the clothing. But this is not true; there is no thinking without speaking, i.e., without words. There is no thinking, there is only speaking.

Having reduced knowledge to a form of speech, Mauthner is able to reduce thinking to demonstrable linguistic habits. What we consider to be knowledge is always the current usage of language. And what is gained from this language is ultimately very little. "To be sure, knowledge of language (knowledge of all languages in existence) if it were possible would be insight into the world as well." But Mauthner denies such a possibility. Language, instead of offering any insights, merely illustrates how different men in different societies use it; it becomes a reflection of a *Weltanschauung* 'a world view,' but not an insight into metaphysical questions. So Mauthner is left with the contention that all we know is what we say and that what we say only reflects who we are and in what society we live—nothing more. He even denies that languages have the same skeletal structure and indicates that one logic is therefore impossible. Mauthner seems to imply that human understanding would of necessity have to acknowledge that there are as many logics as there are languages with different structures.

How to write such a "literature of the unword" was Beckett's major concern in 1932. Mauthner provided an answer. By reducing knowledge to speaking, he suggested that the writer could merely allow characters to speak and their words would become signs, not of knowledge, but rather of the failure of knowledge. Instead of being about anything, words would indicate the very impossibility of moving beyond language. "The churn of stale words," as Beckett referred to communication in his poem "Cascando" (*Collected Poems in English and French* [1977]), becomes the observable concomitant to the inability to think, whether characters speak directly or use the guise of writing their words:

> I did not want to write, but I had to resign myself to it in the end. It is in order to know where I have got to, where he has got to. At first I did not write, I just said the thing. Then I forgot what I had said. A minimum of memory is indispensible [sic], if one is to live really.
>
> (*Malone Dies*)

Whatever form the "babble" took, the subject would always be the same—the inability to *say*, that is, to know. All Beckett's heroes are like the speaker in *The Unnamable*, who says of himself: "I'm a big talking ball, talking about things that do not exist, or that exist perhaps, impossible to know, beside the point." The impossibility does not keep the speaker from continuing to talk, however, for talking is the only form of thinking possible:

> This voice that speaks, knowing that it lies, indifferent to what it says, too old perhaps and too abased ever to succeed in saying the words that would be its last, knowing itself useless and its uselessness in vain, not listening to itself but to the silence. . . .
>
> (*The Unnamable*)

By equating words with thought and both with confusion, Beckett comes close to finding a form in which to create the kind of literature that he had described in "Dream" and in a letter to Axel Kaun written in 1937:

> Is there any reason why that terribly arbitrary materiality of the word's surface should not be dissolved, as, for example, the tonal surface, eaten into by large black pauses, in Beethoven's Seventh Symphony, so that for pages at a time we cannot perceive it other than, let us say, as a *vertiginous path of sounds* connecting unfathomable abysses of silence.
>
> (Harvey; italics mine)

Both Mauthner and Beckett talk about silence, but neither takes refuge in it; they graph instead the "vertiginous path of sounds." Both talk because for them talking is a necessary condition of living. Beckett repeatedly equates speaking with life itself: "To have done then at last with all that last scraps very last when the panting stops and this voice to have done with this voice namely this life," the speaker in *How It Is* (1964) proclaims. All Beckett's heroes desire "words to be applied to their situation" (*Watt*), but no surety ever follows, because the words never bring them any closer to knowledge. The most direct statement of this condition can be found in *Fizzles* (1976): "Closed place. All needed to be known for say is known. There is nothing but what is said. Beyond what is said there is nothing."

As Beckett indicated to Axel Kaun, and repeated in "Three Dialogues," an "art of impotence" is not only possible, it is the only art worth pursuing. Mauthner had said the same thing:

> Thus mankind can despair of ever knowing reality. All philosophizing was a mere up and down between wild despair and the happiness of quiet illusion. Quiet despair alone can—not without smiling about itself for doing so—dare the last attempt of modestly making clear to itself the relationship of man to world, through a denial of self-deception, through the confession that the world is no help, through a critique of language

and its history. That, of course, would be the redeeming deed: if critique could be done with the calmly despairing suicide of thinking and speaking, if critique would not have to be done with apparently living words.

Instead of concentrating on what cannot be known, on metaphysical speculations that have no possibility of confirmation, Beckett takes for his theme the Mauthnerian "denial of self-deception" and frames it in language.

Language and memory are synonymous (2).

Having made thinking and speaking synonymous, Mauthner goes on to indicate the source of this single process. Since he remains a strict empiricist throughout his work, even when this stance leads him to adopt untenable positions about the nature of communication and language, Mauthner maintains that all we know—all that our language consists of—are sense impressions. Unlike Jackson's parrot in *Malone Dies*, who could remember only the first words of the dictum *Nihil est in intellectu, quod non prius fuerit in sensu*, Mauthner believes that all that is in the mind was first in the senses:

> During these investigations we have learned again and again that the utterances of our souls cannot be anything that has not been in our senses first and that therefore there cannot be anything in our mental life except sensual impressions as memories of these same impressions, innumerably many recollections the existence of which one summarizes in the words force-of-memory or simply memory.

Mauthner rejects a reality that stands outside the expressions used to convey experiences, and as an empiricist he bases language on the memory of sensory experiences. For Mauthner, therefore, memory becomes the connection between sensory experience and language:

> In short, the entire life of our souls, the vegetative one as well as the animal and conceptual one, is *nothing but memory*; and especially the conceptual life of our souls, or reason, we recognize as nothing more and nothing less than the memory of our sensual impressions or—language.

The word "memory" in Mauthner's lexicon includes all experience, and language becomes "nothing but man's individual memory of his experience." Finally, he says, "We are so little capable of separating our memory of similar things from concepts or words that frequently we would be better off to say simply language instead of memory, and words instead of recollections." Words, for Mauthner, ultimately become "the sole index of memory."

In *Proust*, Beckett indicated that he, too, recognized the importance of memory in relation to the ability to express oneself. In most situations, human beings are trapped in a world of habit that keeps them from reclaiming images of the past, encapsulated in memories. Proust saw the possibility, however, that on rare occasions individuals could transcend the present and recapture "the ideal real" through the working of what he called "involuntary memory." Mauthner denies memory this power. All memory, he argues, distorts:

> That which we called all too humanly the basic fault of memory, that is its essence. It does not notice the difference between *sameness and similarity*. It notices faultily, it notices falsely. And without this essential mistake there would not be a development in the organic world, and in the world of the mind there would not be any concepts or words. But memory is also essentially unfaithful. Memory would be unbearable if we could not forget. And the words or concepts that only arose because of false memory would be unusable for everyday use were it not for the characteristic of memory that consists in being unfaithful. . . . We would neither live nor think if we could not *forget*.

> (I, italics mine)

After *Proust* Beckett apparently adopts this skeptical view of the veracity of memory. However hard his characters attempt to recapture "yesterday"—"that bloody awful day, long ago, before this bloody awful day" (*Endgame* [1958])—their memories are blurred, half-realized: "total object, complete with missing part" ("Three Dialogues"). When Molloy describes his bicycle, he comments that the passage should be rewritten in the pluperfect. Yet the past in Beckett's writing never remains totally finished; characters continually resurrect it, and their resurrections distort the present, on which memory is grafted.

All language is metaphor (3).

Since the memory, which is synonymous with language, is able to offer only an approximation of past sensory experience, Mauthner believes that language itself can be only an approximation, or what he calls a metaphor, of reality. He argues, "No word has ever any other but a metaphorical meaning" (II). What language does is to make an association between events experienced and events articulated. The word "metaphor" he uses interchangeably with association "in the sense of trope or figurative comparing, generally speaking" (II). Language is reduced to making "pictures of pictures of pictures" (I).

Mauthner coins a word to indicate the basis for this metaphorical condition of language; he calls the approximation caused by the memory *Zufallssinne*. The word translated literally means accidental or chance occurrences of the senses.

> We hold that our five senses are accidental and that our language, which came about from the memories of these *Zufallssinne* and was extended through metaphorical conquest of everything knowable, can never give us insight into reality.

What man remembers, then, is not the actual experience but an approximation of the original. The word *Zufall* is a very important one for Mauthner. The senses are accidental and everything is in flux. "*The world came about through our evolving senses, but the senses too come about through the evolving world.* Where can there be a detached picture of the world?" (I).

Nowhere, Mauthner replies. It is impossible to arrive at any idea of reality, for all knowledge of reality originates in the senses that are themselves a part of that reality. All man can hope to gain is a representation or an approximation of reality (see III). The heart of Mauthner's avowed skepticism comes from this impossibility of ever grasping more. He is finally brought to the conclusion that there is no certainty of anything. No matter how much man wishes to gain a certainty, he can never move beyond memory and the subsequent distortions that it imparts to language.

Mauthner does see at least two advantages to the functioning memory, even though they are associated with its tendency to distort. For one thing, Mauthner observes, memory frees man from the confines of time:

> According to the memory of the human race, an oak is this or that tree as it grew thousands of years ago and, according to the results of reason, as it will grow after thousands of years. This temporal element [*dieses Zeitmoment*] or—if you choose to say so—this independence from time is essential to the activity of reason; maybe this is due to the fact that there belongs to the production of the most simple concept or word a comparison of the present with a past perception, i.e., memory, i.e., an overcoming of time.

The metaphorical nature of memory and of language provides man with the possibility of drawing inferences and connections with other times, albeit imprecisely.

The second boon that memory provides is respite from pain. Memory may allow man to distance himself from sources of pain that were attached to particular temporal events:

> For insight is always cheerful since insight, knowledge, philosophy, thinking . . . always consist merely of language. But language is nothing but recollection, the sum of the recollections of the human race, because recollection is cheerful, even recollection of the most sorrowful events. . . .

But insight itself into this sorrow must take the shape of language—thus language is liberation from pain by means of memory.

Mauthner, however, qualifies the curative powers of memory by indicating that the distancing that memory allows—the ability to make a subject of one's life—is an objectification that few achieve:

> Here already language gains its magic as a means of art; or rather art intensifies itself in the extreme, it turns into a magic which lets the most exalted human being regard himself as a work of art in his most bitter hour—the most horrible pain is no longer felt since it is made the subject for thought.
>
> This is the calm cheerfulness of the very few great men; language created this cheerfulness for them. Confronted with their bitter hour language turned for them into angry laughter.

Of all Beckett's characters the only ones who ever escape from the contingencies of time are those who die, like several characters in *More Pricks than Kicks* and Murphy: ". . . the impression he received was of that self-immersed indifference to the contingencies of the contingent world which he had chosen for himself as the only felicity and achieved so seldom" (*Murphy*, 1957). Such indifference, Beckett may be saying, is won only at the expense of life itself. Murphy, remember, is able to climb the ladder—possibly the Mauthnerian ladder—but it leads to his death. "Do not come down the ladder," he is warned, "they have taken it away." Arsene's injunction about the inevitability of "life off the ladder" is overcome by Murphy in a surcease that Mauthner, too, saw as the only way out of the contingency of senses and the memory.

The two concessions that Mauthner makes to memory—the escape it provides from time and pain—are also treated by Beckett. While memory can liberate man from the temporal, Beckett realizes that memory also gets in the way of man's attempt to live in the present. This is the realization involved when Hamm says that his was always the life to come. Or when Unnamable laments:

> I who am here, who cannot speak, cannot think, and who must speak, and therefore perhaps think a little cannot in relation only to me who am here, to here where I am, but can a little, sufficiently, I don't know how, unimportant, in relation to me who was elsewhere, who shall be elsewhere, and to those places where I was, where I shall be.

And while the "few great men" may achieve a "calm cheerfulness." Beckett's heroes never do. There is much use of the word "calm" in Beckett's writing: the word reverberates throughout *Waiting for Godot* (1954), acts as a refrain in *Malone Dies* and *The Unnamable*, describes what is sought in *How It Is*. Yet for all the talk of calm, Beckett's characters never seem to reach the state they say they desire.

There are no absolutes (4).

Mauthner's skepticism is thoroughgoing. Moving beyond even Hume, he denies the possibility of knowing anything: God, nature, or even self. "Real truth is a metaphorical concept; men have reached the concept of truth, like the concept of God, without relying on experience. In this way it is possible to say that God is truth." The same rejection he applies to the laws of nature: "Thus what we call a law of nature is nothing but our own state of mind toward inductive concepts or words which came to be framed in us. Little enough but at the same time, everything we have." Even nature falls under language and is seen as an example of man's subjective reaction to his own experience, framed in words. Mauthner carefully builds to such a rejection by indicating that language could free man if, and only if, it were freed from the contingencies that memory and common usage place on it. He makes clear, however, that such freedom, articulated through words that are themselves distorted, is impossible.

Beckett probably found Mauthner's insistence on the connection between negation and language more interesting than his total denial of absolutes. There does not seem to be a commensurate assertion in all Beckett. The color of the Beckett world is not black but gray, indicating the impossibility of asserting even negation with any certainty; "perhaps" is the word that haunts Beckett's heroes. If they could only deny as Mauthner does, they would be free of waiting: for Godot, for the end, for salvation. Such surety is never forthcoming. Since they never reach the comfort that denial brings, they can never have done with "it all." So they are trapped in a stasis that precludes cessation: "All my life long I have dreamt of the moment when, edified at last, in so far as one can be before all is lost, I might draw the line and make the tot" (*Malone Dies*). In Beckett the bottom line is never reached. While he, unlike Mauthner, does not state the impossibility of "making the tot," his characters recognize that language is the major obstacle that makes their task virtually impossible. They keep trying to find words that will allow them to stop talking; but they continually fail, and their failure is the same failure that Mauthner describes: they cannot overcome the limitations of language.

The ego is contingent; it does not exist apart from language (5).

Mauthner's most radical extension of the theory of *Zufallssinne* is his assertion that the ego is also a myth: "when the ego wants to express itself from behind memory, then we no longer let ourselves be deceived. We know of no enduring ego, we only know of moments of the drive of living and the memory of each individual moment." In *Proust* Beckett recognizes the lack of continuum in selves held "victims and prisoners" of time and of the "unceasing modification of . . . personality, whose permanent reality, if any, can only be apprehended as a retrospective hypothesis." Mauthner, too, recognizes that the only corroboration of an ongoing self is what memory provides and that therefore, since memory is fallacious, the ego is impossible to verify. Man may *feel* a sense of self, but when he attempts to locate a *me* within himself, he can find nothing—no object—with which to identify this feeling:

> Mankind at present no longer supports the consciousness of its existence with Descartes' pedantic "I think" but much more humbly and in a childlike way with the feeling *I am.* I am conscious of myself, I feel that I am the center for so and so many perceptions of vision and hearing which simultaneously clamor for my attention.
>
> However, on the needle point of the moment I can impale only one impression, and so the ego in "I am" would be lost again if I did not have a memory of the fact that being remained in the flux of becoming, that *I was.* Thus, my ego plunges from the full of life of the present into the black nothing of the past in order to find itself. And he who wants to clarify to himself this most common process either stands unconscious and silent or must erect bogeys of words as if he were a philosopher.

The situation Mauthner describes, that of a self seeking in the "black nothing" of the past for verification of an ongoing self, becomes one of the major preoccupations of Beckettian heroes. They, too, can never totally reconstruct a past event, for the past seems to remain that elusive time which does not bear close scrutiny. Since the sense of the self is tied to the past, the self, too, becomes impossible to verify. Molloy expresses the common dilemma that follows so closely the Mauthnerian description of "bogeys of words" erected to describe the indescribable sense of being:

> Yes, even then, when already all was fading, waves and particles, there could be no things but nameless things, no names but thingless names. I say that now, but after all what do I know now about then, now when the icy words hail down upon me, the icy meanings, and the world dies too, foully named.

Mauthner provides Beckett not only with the theme of an ego trapped within the contingencies of time but also with the idea that an ego, even if it existed and could be found, would have no means of expressing itself: "Language is a 'tool for the understanding of the external world unsuited for judgments about the inner world.' " Language, Mauthner says, may be used to discuss the macrocosm but never to talk about the inner self. Since the ego has no way of articulating itself, it cannot be verbalized and thus can never be known. Mauthner expresses this dilemma in the following way: "We have bodily organs and senses for the observation of the movement of bodies; but we have no sense besides our organ of thinking for the observation of thinking. The so-called self-observation has no organ." This situation is exactly the situation familiar to all students of Beckett, and nowhere is the Mauthner influence clearer than in this idea of a self that cannot be known since it cannot be given voice:

> This rascal of an ego . . . just in the fact that it cannot project its feelings, cannot throw them outward, cannot utter them, in the fact that it has to keep them within itself—in this lies the admission that it is unable to include them in the world of reality.

Repeatedly, Beckett uses the same equation that Mauthner presents—a self with no organ of self-observation. Laura Barge has cited this impossible quest for self as one of the dominant themes of later Beckett prose: "But the subjective self never finds an objective self that can be defined as the true self. . . . That *I* never finds a *me*." The theme, however, is not of recent vintage; as far back as *Molloy* Beckett had his hero say, "And even my sense of identity was wrapped in a namelessness often hard to penetrate." As the novel itself indicates, in Moran's futile quest for his alter ego, Molloy, the self never can overtake itself, try as it may.

One function of the Beckett couple is verification of an ego through the testimony of an "other." If a character cannot remember yesterday, there is always a companion to act as witness to another time and another place. Even if the companions are "accursed progenitors," as Hamm calls his parents in *Endgame*, they point to a past and to a self that must have existed then. Didi's presence becomes testimony to a past that Gogo cannot remember; Willie's presence, even if not visible, becomes evidence of "the old style" and of the old self of a Winnie who must have lived then.

In other works, this acknowledgment of a past has been replaced by a sense of what Ruby Cohn has called the "antecedentless life." For example, in *Theatre I*, the crippled B, that most recent avatar of Hamm, asks for verification of self—"What does my soul look like?"—from a blind man, a character with whom he shares no past but only a present chance meeting on a public street. In two other works, *Theatre II* and *Radio II*, the verification also comes from strangers, who again have no common history with the self of the hero but, rather, act as recorders, objective compilers of the evidence of their being. In *Theatre II*, characters identified as A and B pore over evidence of a self within the "inner void" of a C. They finally find the task impossible, confronted as they are with "A black future, an unpardonable past—so far as he can remember." In a similar way the animator and the stenographer in *Radio II* seek evidence of an ego in Fox. The best that Fox can do is to speak of another, "my brother inside me, my old twin." This *me* inside the *I*, who can never be merged with an *I*, is also described in *Fizzles*. Here, however, the vantage point shifts; Beckett gives voice to the "twin" trapped in a self who gives him a voice that is not his voice: "It was he, I was inside." The problem for the *me* is to find words: "He is still, he seeks a voice for me, it's impossible I should have a voice and I have none, he'll find one for me, ill-beseeming me" (*Fizzles*). From this vantage point, the inarticulate *me* explains in the same work, "he will never say I, because of me." This refusal to say *I* because of a *me* that cannot be articulated explains the vehemence with which the speaker of *Not I* refuses to drop her third-person singular pronoun. This refusal is less a rejection of self—as it is often said to be—than an inability of the speaker ever to merge the inner and the outer parts of the ego.

In *Texts for Nothing* Beckett expresses the same idea: "Whose voice, no one's, there is no one, there's a voice without a mouth." If the inner self would simply exist inarticulate, the character might not suffer; as the character speaks, however, he is perpetually plagued by the sense that the words he uses do not give voice to the schismatic self he feels: "I don't speak to him any more, I don't speak to me any more, I have no one left to speak to, and I speak, a voice speaks that can be none but mine, since there is none but me." And yet the speaker knows that he lies because his words never cover the inner self: "It's the same old stranger as ever, for whom alone accusative I exist, in the pit of my existence, of his, or ours, there's a simple answer." The *I* is always *we*, whether admitted or not. Voice C in *That Time* echoes the same dilemma: "did you ever say I to yourself in your life come on now . . . could you ever say I to yourself in your life." At the very question, the eyes of the face, projected ten feet above the stage, close.

While Mauthner talks of the difficulty of capturing the inner self, he also indicates that our very sense of an outer reality is finally based on nothing beyond our subjective feeling that there must be a real world:

> I believe in the reality of the outer world since, within the limits of my skin, I believe myself to be determined sometimes from the inside sometimes from the outside. There is known within endless outer space and endless time this one case of a notion of inside and outside, and from this one case I conclude that there is a regularity that one could call the highest law of nature; namely, that there exists something like the real. Even the existence of unaccountable other organisms that feel like me is, again, simply an inductive conclusion derived from one single case.
>
> From the cradle to the grave my ego behaves as if the hypothesis of a world of reality were a proved fact. And all the unaccountable actions of my ego . . . have never yet given rise within me to the slightest doubt of the correctness of this most comprehensive hypothesis.

The duality between microcosm and macrocosm, often seen in Cartesian terms as the duality between mind and body, is reduced by Mauthner to a schism in language: "We cannot be, with our language, on both sides at the same time"; "Only in language do the terms 'mind' and 'body' exist. In reality they cannot be separated." What he implies is that the duality is not between mind and body as much as it is between what can be articulated and what cannot be put into words.

It is apparent that Beckett's presentation of the duality between the mind and the body, and between the self and the "not self," also places the dilemma clearly in the area of linguistics. His characters struggle, not with metaphysical ideas, but with language itself. They do not try to prove their existence or to delimit mind / body, microcosm / macrocosm; they talk because they too accept the existence of both reality and the self and because they seek substantiation of both. To admit that neither an outer world nor an inner reality exists is too terrifying for Beckett's heroes, as it was for Mauthner:

> As long as we live, the beautiful semblance of an ego feeling, of the unity of life, and the even more beautiful semblance of a unity between the ego and reality are a joy, the goading joy in the semblance of knowledge.

The very words that Mauthner uses conjure up the world that Beckett writes of: a world where the characters hold on to the "beautiful semblance" of both an inner and an outer world, a self and an external world of which the self is a part. Yet, as Mauthner indicates and as Beckett's characters experience, the joy is not a sufficient palliative to assuage uncertainty. Beckett's characters are too aware. They are closer to the philosopher than to the common man, whom Mauthner describes as basking in a false sense of being; their doubt is Mauthner's doubt.

Communication between men is impossible (6).

Having gone as far as he can go in the direction of individual language, Mauthner turns in the opposite direction and takes on the problem of language in its public function, as a vehicle of communication between individuals and in society. Here he faces the problem that all empiricists have faced: how to explain that language does exist as a shared means of communication between individuals when its source resides in individual experience. In order to explain a public function of language and still hold to his empirical basis, Mauthner makes some rather complicated assertions. First, he acknowledges that man needs someone with whom to share experience:

> Since there has to be always at least two for language, one could think that it should unite human beings like copulation and that at least it would represent the connection of two organisms, the act of intellectual begetting [*den Akt der geistigen Zeugung*].

Language, however, does not function in this way. Mauthner admits that it is impossible to have language without a listener. Yet, as he has already shown, no two persons can possibly have the same understanding of words since (1) words stem from individual experiences and (2) they are at best only metaphoric representations of prior sense experiences. Thus, though men think they communicate when they speak, they in fact do not: "We hand out words like banknotes and don't ask ourselves whether there are materially tangible funds in the treasury which correspond to them." Mauthner doubts whether two human beings ever conceive of the same idea when they hear or use the same words. They only assume a commonality of meaning.

What, then, is language? Mauthner answers as follows: "Language is only a convention—like a rule of a game: the more participants, the more compelling it will be. However, it will neither grasp not alter the real world." In his rejection of any absolute, Mauthner has in fact rejected the idea that there is even such a thing as communicative language; there are simply individuals talking, using certain linguistic conventions that, like all else, are subject to changes in time and that merely reflect a particular historical usage and a particular *Weltanschauung*.

In reflecting a particular time and habit of usage, however, language serves a useful function: it aids in common social intercourse. "Nobody," Mauthner agrees, "would deny the impure, common usefulness of language." "After all it is useful for the mundane alehouse, for the *need to communicate*, for the enjoyment of gossip on the part of the alehouse guests, and for the shouts to the waiter. That's the sort of thing language is good for." Since most persons, Mauthner believes, are satisfied to communicate on this level, they never feel the limitations of the language they use. "Human language suffices for practical purposes. . . . *Only those fools who understand and wish to be understood feel the insufficiency of language*" (italics mine). In Mauthner's view few such fools exist.

Beckett touched on the average person's use of language in his 1938 review of the poetry of Denis Devlin when he said, ". . . solution clapped on problem like a snuffer on a candle, the great crossword public on all its planes: 'He roasteth roast and is satisified. Yea, he warmeth himself and saith, Aha, I am warm' " (Harvey).

In his own writing, Beckett never presents such complacency. Although his characters talk of the most mundane things—food, clothing, the weather, sex—they are always aware that their words are used only to fill time, to ward off silence. Even the two tramps in *Waiting for Godot*, for all their resemblance to the average man, are fully aware of their inability to gain insights into the world through the words they use. "That wasn't such a bad little canter," Estragon says after a particularly long exchange. Mrs. Rooney in *All That Fall* (in *Krapp's Last Tape and Other Dramatic Pieces* [1960]), who calls herself "just a hysterical old hag," is raised to a tragic grandeur precisely because, as she painfully makes her way down the public road, stopping to talk with her neighbors, she is always aware of the failure of language: "I use none but the simplest words, I hope, and yet I sometimes find my way of speaking very . . . bizarre." As her husband comments on their way from the station, "sometimes one would think you were struggling with a dead language."

Yet despite their awareness that they are not being understood, most Beckett characters still desire a listener, someone with whom they can speak. They all share a fear of isolation and a desire to be heard: "Ah yes, if only I could bear to be alone, I mean prattle away with not a soul to hear," Winnie says in *Happy Days*. But she cannot bear this isolation; so she is comforted by the knowledge that somewhere behind her, barely visible and barely audible, is Willie—someone who keeps up the fiction of dialogue. In this play Beckett gives many examples of what Mauthner has described as the general misunderstandings that we choose not to notice in our desire to believe that we are understood. For instance, both Winnie and Willie laugh over the word "formication." But as James Knowlson points out in his notes to the bilingual edition, the word actually has two associations: a sensation like that of ants creeping on the skin, from the Latin noun *formica* 'ant' and the sexual connotation from the Latin noun *fornix* 'brothel.' Knowlson notes, "The laughter, although shared, arises from different things." This mere semblance of communication is what Mauthner believes all human discourse to be.

Although the failure of communication in Beckett's works may consist of such subtle wordplays as the one above, or what Nicholas Gessner has outlined in relation to *Godot*, usually the failures are more obvious. They are often the typical circumlocutions that are found in more naturalistic works. " 'Once a certain degree of insight has been reached,' said Wylie, 'all men talk, when talk they must, the same tripe' " (*Murphy*). And listen with the same indifference. Although many of the novels consist of one speaker in an extended monologue, in the rare places where they lapse into traditional realism—the scenes between Moran and his son in *Molloy* and the story of the Saposcats in *Malone Dies*, for instance—one finds familiar scenes of misunderstanding because of language. Of the Saposcats, Malone says, "They had no conversation properly speaking. They made use of the spoken word in much the same way as the guard of a train makes use of his flags, or of his lantern." The same might be said for all the Beckett couples, beginning with the paradigmatic Mercier and Camier: "They sleep side by side, the deep doze of the old. They will speak together yet, but only at haphazard as the saying is. But did they ever speak together otherwise?"

The only language should be simple language (7).

For all his skepticism about language, Mauthner holds to the notion that whatever words men use should be only of the simplest kind. One of his indictments against traditional philosophy and all intellectual pursuits is their tendency to reify words, to remove them from their usage in the vernacular. Mauthner continually argues for simple language. Such a concern from a man who has denied language any connection with reality may seem strange; but we must remember that Mauthner, though he denies that language can ever escape its limitations, is still bent on refining language. A simple language, divorced from abstractions, would be as close as man could come to ridding himself of "word-superstition" (*Wortaberglauben*).

> Language goes astray once it is no longer content to be among men, to accompany with a groan their pressing needs, once it wants to serve exalted [*überreizten*] spiritual needs which go beyond man and are disengaged from his pressing needs.

Mauthner makes clear, however, that man will never be able to rid language of ambiguity by using simple words. As Gershon Weiler points out, "The critique is not a programme of reforming language, but an activity which leads to a critical-sceptical attitude to language." Try as man may, he cannot get beyond the limits of his own words, and the task of the *Critique* is to disclose this fact. "I preferred everyday language [to a learned definition] in order to make clear how little a definition explains."

Like Mauthner, Beckett sees the use of simple language as an aid in communication, but as only a negligible one considering the larger problem of the inherent mystery of life. His own writing, in both English and French, shows an emphasis on direct statements and a rejection of what Mercier and Camier call "the stink of artifice." Malone, the writer spinning tales, comments on a particularly florid passage: "I know those little phrases that seem so innocuous and, once you let them in, pollute the whole of speech. *Nothing is more real than nothing.* They rise out of the pit and know no rest until they drag you down into its dark. But I am on my guard now." But no matter how simply characters speak, they are still not understood, because words can never be used to describe their condition. Beckett again demonstrates the same awareness that Mauthner has expressed: no matter how carefully chosen the words are, "The exalted notion of truth [is] human babble."

The highest forms of critique are laughter and silence (8).

Mauthner, on the first page of the *Critique*, predicted the ultimate failure of his endeavor: the impossibility of writing a critique in language that itself is subject to the contingencies of time and linguistic usage. The only true critique of language would be one that escaped the vicissitudes it described, one done without words—in laughter or silence. Words only distort, reflecting at best a particular *Weltanschauung*, which will soon be obsolete. Recognizing that "Our feelings, our life itself, our nature itself . . . remain inaccessible to language" and that "The essence of our being has nothing to do with language and thinking," Mauthner is left with what he himself calls a "godless mysticism [*gottlose Mystik*]" (Weiler).

The only human articulation of the mystical state, Mauthner says, is laughter: "Basically speaking, pure critique is merely articulated laughter. Each laughter is critique, the best critique . . . and the danger of this book, the daring aspect of this attempt, lies in merely having put an articulated text to this laughter, so that the result for the masses of people is like laughter in an opera." Carrying this theme of laughter further, Mauthner also wrote in his novel *Kraft*, published in 1894, "The first philosopher, the last redeemer of mankind, will laugh, and he will keep his trap shut; he will laugh infectiously, and he will teach his fellowmen to keep their traps shut like himself, and to open [them] only for laughter and eating" (quoted by Kühn).

The ideas of laughter and silence as the final answers to the limitations of language are found over and over in Beckett, and the parallels with Mauthner are striking. The "silent howl" over the human condition and the despair over the inability to articulate this condition are shared by many Beckettian characters. So is the laugh over jokes no longer funny and life no longer tolerable. The dream for so many of these characters is finally to reach a point where they will be free of the "tyranny of words," where they will have only silence. "My speech-parched voice at rest would fill with spittle, I'd let it flow over and over, happy at last, dribbling with life, my pensum ended, in the silence" (*The Unnamable*). Yet like the speaker in *The Unnamable*, they realize that such a state of silence is impossible as long as man lives and is caught up in the net of language:

> I know no more questions and they keep on pouring out of my mouth. I think I know what it is, it's to prevent the discourse from coming to an end, this futile discourse which is not credited to me and brings me not a syllable nearer silence.

Silence for Beckett, as for Mauthner, becomes a goal that is never attained as long as man holds on to the futile medium of language.

Nowhere is Mauthner's influence on Beckett clearer than in their shared recognition of the limits of language, their yearning for a "godless mysticism" that would transcend the limits imposed by words, and their equally tenacious—human—desire to go on speaking, knowing it is in vain. I quote at length from that section of the *Critique* where Mauthner for a moment steps in front of the philosophical curtain and reveals the human being trying to do what cannot be done: talk his way to silence. The similarity to what Beckett scholars have come to recognize as a recurrent refrain in Beckett's writing is clear:

> During the long years during which the basic idea of this attempt took hold of me and forced me to do the really hard work of testing their truth constantly against life and the achievements of science, during those years there were plenty of desperate hours and days on which it appeared to me more valuable to fertilize the field I till or to plant cherry trees or to choose the first dog I encounter as a reasonable teacher for my conduct in life. Nothing appeared more foolish than *the last attempt of speaking endlessly—with words which can never have a firm content—of nothing but of one's own ignorance.* But just as such dark hours and days frequently ended with the spurring feeling: *yes, it is the last attempt, it is the last word,* and, because it cannot be the solution to the riddle of the sphinx, it is at least the redeeming deed which forces the sphinx to remain silent, since it destroys the sphinx. Sadly I look back upon such

moods of heightened self-confidence. *What can we think or say in the language of tomorrow? . . . What appeared to be a last answer today will be a new question tomorrow;* and the question in turn will become an answer in the language of us foolish human beings.

(italics mine)

Several critics who have taken Mauthner quotations from Weiler's translations have stopped at the point that Mauthner seems to claim victory for his attempt. On the contrary, Mauthner, like Beckett's characters, recognizes the circularity of his actions; there can be no deed that forces the sphinx into silence. For Mauthner must use words to write his critique of language, just as Beckett must employ words to illustrate their own bankruptcy. Both are caught in the same net of language.

Mauthner's monumental outrage against these limits of language is so vivid and pervasive that when Beckett, sixteen years after he had read the *Critique*, sought one visual image for the human condition of being caught in a net of words, he created Lucky in *Waiting for Godot*, a figure whose antecedents can be traced with striking exactness back to Mauthner:

The philosopher who wants to gain insights by way of language, a way which ever turns upon itself, does not merely resemble the *common donkey on the treadmill, who, lured by food and driven by a whip, sets foot before foot;* he rather resembles *the learned donkey of the circus, who has come to the point of human freedom and who then has chosen the treadmill as the stage of his art* and who works vainly and elegantly like a tightrope walker—apparently ever upward, in reality ever in the same place and with fewer results than the common donkey; for the treadmill of language has no millstones.

(italics mine)

MARTHA FEHSENFELD

Beckett's Late Works: An Appraisal

This victim of more words than ever before inflicted on any other living subject has recently been castigated by both wordsmen and -women for "scraping the bottom of [his] . . . barrel" in offering recent plays and prose: "brief exercises," "*tableaux vivants,*" "having ceased to be comic," "intensity at the cost of . . . depth," and the inevitable "nothing remains to say," are some of the accusations—always carefully hedged by "the beginnings of critical wisdom" or some such safety clause. The implication is that these late works are either empty echoes of what was or benign sputterings replacing what can no longer be.

Even a brief examination of Beckett's late works from 1977 to 1981 yields evidence of continuing evolutionary development in each case. There are no less than five separate areas of excavation—and since this piece was begun, the list has already stretched to six, with probably more to come. The first is poetry written in French. According to a telephone conversation with Avigdor Arikha in the summer of 1980, Beckett is continuing the word-sound-shaped verse he wound into a conical spiral in *mirlitonades*—a selection of thirty-five short poems named for the paper-trumpet "mirliton" sold at fairs and carnivals, decorated with curling lines of doggerel verse. "My work is a matter of fundamental sounds . . . and I accept responsibility for nothing else," he wrote to Alan Schneider in 1957. He continues to submit himself to this discipline and this responsi-

From *Modern Drama* 3, vol. 25 (September 1982). Copyright © 1982 by *Modern Drama.*

bility by working within the strict boundaries of poetry, the most tightly economic of all the word arts—exercising his honed sensitivity to music in the realm of sound with intense energy and consummate delicacy.

In *Company*, published first in 1980 as *Compagnie* in Paris, and later in 1980 in English (retranslated by Beckett into the original language of the text), the importance of the Voice and its omnipresence and lack of fixity is essential to the nature of the work. "A voice . . . in the dark," unfixed in space . . . closing in, relentless, monotonous, like a drip that erodes . . ., that "will not cease till hearing cease." The early Reading manuscript in English is more specific about the location of the voice: in the paragraph following the incident of the hedgehog, the narrator confides:

> he receives it [the voice] more or less clear or faint from different points in space and discontinuously. It is bad enough bluntly to be told, *You took pity on a hedgehog out in the cold and put it in an old hatbox with some worms.* But how much worse when softly, *you.* Then clearer from another quarter, *took pity on a*—Pause—murmured in his ear—*hedgehog.* Faint from afar, *out in the cold.* Crescendo towards him, *and put it in an old*—Pause—to his face with strong articulation—*HAT-BOX.* Cavernous from above, *with some*—Long Pause—murmured in the other ear. *Worms.* For example. How infinitely worse. . . .

This section, which clearly demonstrates the eye and ear of Beckett the theatre director, is entirely omitted from the printed text of *Company*, although there are vestiges retained in the three paragraphs after the account of the hedgehog. "[A] clue is given by the voice afar. Receding afar or there with abrupt saltation or resuming there after pause. From above and from all sides and levels with equal remoteness at its most remote. At no time from below. . . . Given faintness of voice at its least faint . . ."; and two sections later: "Same flat tone . . . same repetitiousness. . . . But less mobility. Less variety of faintness. . . . Neither offending the ear with loudness nor through converse excess constraining it to strain. . . ." It is that voice—those voices that have been and are always with him, those catalysts—that forced him to "say it as I hear it" in words that he has felt obligated to set down from the beginning. Those voices continue to prod him into hearing and responding in kind, setting up a series of infinite cyclical patterns—a "Devised deviser devising it all for company."

A *Piece of Monologue*—considered by Beckett as "a text for the stage"—was written for the English actor David Warrilow and first performed at the Theatre LaMama in December 1979. It is a meeting of the seen and the unseen, earlier described by Beckett as a moment of achieving a visualized goal by Mr. Kelly, Celia's grandfather, in the 1938 novel

Murphy, and specifically referred to and characterized in *Film*, *Eh Joe*, *Not I*, *Footfalls* and *That Time*. In the printed text by Grove Press, 1981, there is a series of explicit stage directions for setting, lighting, and visual appearance of the Speaker, but there are no directions of any kind within the body of the text itself. It reads as if it were prose. Beckett made several suggestions to the actor regarding pace and pauses, and these were strictly observed. The Speaker stands motionless, describing a character in the third person—"he"— who moves in a setting that we do not see, but can only imagine with the eye of the mind.

The one-act stage play *Rockaby*, which received its première in Buffalo, New York in April 1981, was directed by Alan Schneider with Billie Whitelaw in the solo role. The narrowed focus is on the disembodied voice "V" and the listener "W". In this work there are not two separate characters—such as Willie and Winnie in *Happy Days*, Joe and Voice in *Eh Joe*, Mouth and Auditor in *Not I*, or Amy-May and Mother in *Footfalls*— but one and the same character, as in *That Time* and in the prose text of *Company*. Whereas he designated the location of the voices in the stage directions of *That Time* and *Footfalls*, Beckett does not specify placement in *Rockaby*; he simply lists W as *"Woman in chair"* and V as *"Her recorded voice."* The symmetrical action of the rocking chair that appeared in *Film* (and in the early manuscripts of *Eh Joe*) sets the vocal rhythm of *Rockaby*. Beckett specifies the technical elements: lighting is dual, "Subdued on chair[,] . . . spot on face constant throughout, unaffected by successive fades"; "Rock / Slight. Slow. Controlled mechanically without assistance from W"; "Chair / Pale wood highly polished to gleam when rocking. Footrest. Vertical back. Rounded inward curving arms to suggest embrace." He also notes in detail the costume, opening and closing of the eyes, and the attitude of the Woman. The costume description is carefully delineated: "Black lacy high-necked. . . . Jet sequins to glitter when rocking. Incongruous frivolous head-dress set askew with extravagant trimmings to catch light when rocking." Beckett even notes the desired volume of W's voice: "Lines in italics . . . [and] W's 'More' a little softer each time."

Like *Footfalls* and *A Piece of Monologue*, *Ohio Impromptu*, written by Beckett for the Samuel Beckett Symposium in Columbus, Ohio in May 1981, uses the device of narrator-and-audience in the persons of the two characters of Reader and Listener. The doppelgänger figure suggested in *Krapp* and *Footfalls* is here realized as the silent separate figure of the Listener by the Reader and as the vocal separate figure of the Reader by the Listener. Beckett stipulates that the Reader and the Listener are *"As alike in appearance as possible."* The Reader reads from a printed text, "an old quarto-type thing," "calmly, soothingly, like a bedtime story." The Listener does not speak but does communicate by knocking on the *"white deal table"* with his left hand: the first knock signals the Reader to stop speaking, to go back and to repeat a sentence in the narrative of the spoken text; the second knock, after the Listener pauses, signals the Reader to resume reading the text. The knock, like the goad of *Act Without Words I* and *II*, the bell of *Happy Days*, and the light in *Play*, is the technical impetus that stimulates instant response. In *Ohio Impromptu*, as in *Footfalls*, the narrative of literary fiction is juxtaposed with the immediacy of theatre. Like Amy-May in *Footfalls*, the Reader wheels between selective passages, stopping and starting on signal. And as in the text of *Footfalls*, there are the three levels of narrator-audience, reader-listener, participant-observer, that tell the story of the story of the story, which also leads back to before the beginning. Beckett suggested to the director Alan Schneider that the table be angled slightly so that the audience could see the Reader's face.

Since 1977, Beckett's work has shown a particular impetus towards the exploration of the possibilities of the visual image—both fixed and moving—within the framework of television, film and videotape. In the 1977 television plays *Ghost Trio* and . . . *but the clouds* . . . , limited movement within strictly prescribed boundaries produces an intensely concentrated focus not unlike the "very closed box" *Godot* needs in Beckett's description to Alan Schneider in 1956. The room in *Ghost Trio* is a box with three rectangular outlets all closed to the figure "F", who (like Joe in *Eh Joe* in a similar claustrophobic environment) goes first to the door, the way out and in—then to the window with limited access—and finally to the mirror, the most inward and introspective of all the avenues. A quote referring to the 1966 production from the BBC set designer of *Eh Joe*, Peter Seddon, is pertinent here: "We were concerned with . . . finding a room which contained *a* door, *a* window, *a* cupboard and *a* bed . . . Beckett was very concerned about the size of the openings. The cupboard being the smallest, then the window, then the door. The intention was to provide three different means of egress from the physical constraint of the room, each with a varying degree of apparent escape determined by a combination of the size of each opening and the space beyond it." During production conferences of *Film* in 1964, Beckett himself described the cinematographic action: "moving from the maximum of exposed exterior or man completely exposed and . . . at the other extreme the maximum of protected interior, enclosure, seclusion . . . a maximum of exterior quality, a transitional quality and a maximum of interior quality." In . . . *but the clouds* . . . , there are again three specific areas: "W", West—the way out to and in from the back roads; "E", East—the way to the closet where *transition* is visibly underscored by the *change* of outdoor to indoor dress; and "N", North—the location of "the sanctum," the holy place "where only God sees me," "the place where the poetry comes," the protected refuge of what is paradoxically and ironically the area of greatest vulnerability.

Ruby Cohn in her book *Just Play: Beckett's Theater* refers to the movement in . . . *but the clouds* . . . and suggests a pattern that effects a cruciform image, "since the fixed camera traces the protagonist moving along the arms and vertical of a cross." This intersection of horizontal and vertical movement is clearly visible in the diagrams from the 1975 Berlin production notebook for *Warten auf Godot* (at the Reading University Library), where it is an integral part of the overall stage plan. In . . . *but the clouds* . . . , the word "horizon" appears in the text, quoting from W. B. Yeats's poem "The Tower":

> . . . The death of friends, or death
> Of every brilliant eye
> That made a catch in the breath—
> Seem but the clouds of the sky
> When the horizon fades. . . .

Possibly Beckett has determined this line of movement, the horizontal in relation to the vertical, to provide a stage locus for the abstract idea—a picture for the word, so to speak, to externalize and underscore it.

With particular reference to F's movement in *Ghost Trio*, James Knowlson, coauthor with John Pilling of *Frescoes of the Skull*, has called attention to Beckett's keen interest in the early nineteenth-century essay "Uber das Marionettentheater" by Heinrich von Kleist, pointing "above all to the advent of self-consciousness and loss of harmony in man . . . yet to the value of economy and grace of movement." In this connection it is perhaps valuable to note Beckett's description of F's walk in "NOTES ON TRYST" (the earlier title for *Ghost Trio*): "Feet in any case not to be seen. He moves bowed through space with no visible propulsion." As well the Kleist essay makes reference to self-conscious fallen man having eaten from the Tree of Knowledge and therefore unable to attain the unaffected grace of the inanimate puppet; item No. 4 in the printed text of F's actions and reactions is "*F relapses into opening pose, bowed over cassette.*" (Relapse: to slip back as into illness *or* to fall into sin or error.) Undoubtedly, the range from fully collapsed to stiffly extended positions of the puppetlike figure (as well as the graceful weightless movement) has appealed to Beckett at least from the time of *Godot*, as this section from that text confirms:

ESTRAGON: We've lost our rights?
VLADIMIR: *(distinctly)* We got rid of them.
Silence. They remain MOTIONLESS, ARMS DANGLING, HEADS SUNK, SAGGING
    AT THE KNEES.
ESTRAGON: *(feebly)* We're not *tied? (Pause.)*
We're not— — —
VLADIMIR: Listen!
THEY LISTEN, GROTESQUELY RIGID.

The Figure in *Ghost Trio*, like Joe, moves from the area of greatest
security—the stool, embracing music-cassette; investigates possible intrud-
ers and intrusions from without; and finally goes to the mirror where,
according to Kleist, grace dissolves in the confrontation of the image with
itself. All pretenses gone.

Quad, the latest work for television, was announced by Beckett in
the early part of the summer of 1980 as a mime for four players, with
"colored lights, percussion instruments, the sound of footsteps and no
text"; it was written for the Stuttgart Preparatory Ballet School and
produced in June of 1981. There is much evidence, of course, that mime
has keenly attracted Beckett from the beginning: his total absorption in
the physical requirements of Clov's walks and looks, and Willie's climbs to
Winnic; his extensive notebook lists in the Beckett Archive at Reading of
the changing postures of Krapp, with his journeys to and from the cagibi;
the diagrams of Estragon and Vladimir's strict movement patterns; the
interlacing structures of the trio in *Come and Go*; and the stylized veilings
and unveilings by Joe in *Eh Joe* and O in *Film*. But the harmonious
chamber orchestration of sound and echo, light and darkness, and measured movement with its accompanying sound, evolves most specifically
from their previous syntheses in *Footfalls*, *Ghost Trio* and . . . *but the
clouds*. . . . And the picture of a square ABCD enclosing two diagonals
crossing at a central point E is a continuation of the same picture and
pattern that defined the circuits of movement included in the notes for
J. M. Mime, conceived about 1963 and now in the Beckett Collection in
the Trinity College manuscript room in Dublin.

Beckett related that the actual filming of *Quad* at the Suddeutcher
Rundfunk in Stuttgart as it evolved from the first rough text required
alteration resulting in several innovations. The colored lights simply "did
not work" so that the color was only in the costumes. Beckett's camera-
man, Jim Lewis, who had worked with him since 1966 on *Eh Joe*, *Ghost
Trio* and . . . *but the clouds* . . . , gave this account: "We couldn't use the
colored lights. First the combination of white plus blue plus red plus
yellow produced an effect of an indefinite shade of orange. I worked on it

and got a closer delineation but then the frequency of light going on and off with the entrance and exit of each player proved too distracting and had to be abandoned." The original idea for the placement of the percussionists on a raised platform behind the players was altered—they were placed at the point of each right angle outside the square and were hardly visible. The instruments used were two Javanese gongs (Beckett himself had played the gong during the recording of *MacGowran Speaking Beckett* made for Claddaugh Records in 1966), an African wood block and an African talking drum, and "a wonderful wastebasket—from Rathmines" (Beckett added whimsically). The players—"mimes not dancers"—were young, slight, all the same size, and wore floor-length colored gowns with cowls which covered headphones by means of which they could hear the percussion sounds and time their movements. They held themselves in the same position Billie Whitelaw had used for *Footfalls*, "crossing their arms tightly against themselves" under the loose gowns, "in a bent shape which they kept throughout," as if, Lewis said, "they were resisting a cold wind." The running time originally envisioned by Beckett as "approximately twenty-five minutes" became "about a quarter of an hour. They did it twice." The first time included the original complete cycle of four series without interruption, but the timing was "164 beats a minute," according to Lewis, "about nine minutes" according to Beckett's calculation. "It was feverish. Feverish monotony." The second time they played at "about 160 beats a minute—about four minutes, in black and white, white costumes, same grey square, no percussion, just a metronome and shuffling footsteps." The problem of "the negotiation of E without rupture of rhythm when three or four players cross paths at this point . . ." was resolved inventively. As each player arrived at a point close to the center, he made a "jerky turn to his left as a diversion away from it." At first it seemed "they were merely avoiding one another, but gradually one realised they were avoiding the center. There was something terrifying about it . . . it was danger."

The overall effect of this most recent Beckett dramatic work is unbearable and unrelieved tension strained almost to the breaking point. He has painted a picture, deliberately choosing color for the first time in using film. One sees through the eye of the camera fixed above, a group of figures moving in a tightly prescribed pattern in relation to one another but not necessarily aware (or unaware) of one another as individuals (as the distinct colors of costumes, sounds of footsteps, and instruments establish them). Beckett has exchanged the sound of the word for other sounds—the percussion instruments and the footsteps—which are the extensions of the movement. One hears something very close to a musical composition. Or perhaps that is precisely what one hears. Each figure comes out of darkness into dim neutral light, goes through its "course," returns to darkness. Darkness is the only relief, and like all relief in Beckett it is only temporary. The only cessation perhaps lurks in the black center that is to be avoided at any cost, even at the risk of perpetual motion. This pattern is clearly infernal; the players, like Dante's damned, are committed to an endless unyielding punishment—continuous movement of excruciating sameness.

A symmetrical accident ends this paper as I began it. In 1976 there was an exhibition of works by Avigdor Arikha held at the Victoria and Albert Museum in London: "A Tribute to Samuel Beckett." Beckett titled the group of illustrative interpretations of his works "Adumbrations"; and Mordechai Omer in the "Foreword" referred to this title and to additional words of Beckett's when discussing the "general relationship between literature and the visual arts: *like fire and water they are separated by a zone of evaporation.*" Perhaps this is the border area that Beckett is exploring now, the mysterious climate inhabited by the shadows, the ghosts, the "Spirit[s] made light," "All the dead voices," those "as much as . . . being seen," "living soul[s] . . . living soul[s]," "The semblance[s]" whose trembling air, like Dante's "airy bodies," is visible evidence of simultaneous being and nonbeing. The light and sounds are dim, dimmer, barely heard, just this side of silence and total darkness. But still just this side. Perhaps Beckett, unlike most of his contemporaries who *are* reduced to shadows of what *was* in their work, is instead reducing what *has been* in his work, distilling it to shadows of what *is* and *is to come*. A continuing beginning towards transparency.

S. E. GONTARSKI

The Intent of Undoing in Samuel Beckett's Art

Beckett's is an aesthetics of com-
promise, a reconciliation of principle and practice. Despite a series of
youthful polemical essays, Beckett's own creative output is marked by a
synthesis of that polemic and praxis. Repelled by mimesis from his earliest
years, Beckett is yet unwilling to abandon representation wholly. Repelled
by the thought of revealing the unconscious and opposed generally to
autobiography in art and biography in letters, Beckett is nonetheless
drawn to Freud and especially to Jung and develops an art that stands as
testimony to the centrality of the unconscious in the creative process.
Repelled by the artificiality and externality of the literary forms he inherited, he has, especially in the later, formalist works, tended to impose
patterns of music and mathematics as ordering principles, almost as if they
reflected pure or universal forms. Repelled by the conventions of the
omniscient and omnipotent artist, he was, nonetheless, attracted to them
in the psychologically and intellectually awesome figure of Joyce. In fact,
like Joyce, Beckett has been preoccupied with form (occasionally the form
that denies form), and although he has rejected overt mythic structuring,
he has, in the drama and later fiction, returned to formalist patterns,
accepting the *corso/ricorso* implicit in the early work. Beckett has also
travelled the Vico Road. It is among such dialectics that Beckett's art
makes its way, and what synthesis occurs does so only in the art work.

Beckett's aesthetics, however, is not offered to us unobstructed.

From *Modern Fiction Studies* 1, vol. 29, (Spring, 1983). Copyright © 1983 by Purdue
Research Foundation.

Although he began his career as a university instructor and literary critic—rejecting the former because he could not bear to teach others what he himself did not understand—that is, began as a teacher and critic and so developed an aesthetic sensibility long before a literature to embody it, Beckett never evolved into a theorist like Brecht or Artaud; he actively shunned the role, in fact. What aesthetic theory can be got from Beckett is usually culled from his early fiction and critical writing, the latter done to advance his academic career, to defend Joyce, or to earn survival money. But that writing is only one term in the dialectic; the second needs to be distilled textually as the precipitate from reconstructing, through manuscript notes and typescript stages, the biographies of his works, from coming as close as the critic can, *ex post facto*, to watching Beckett make aesthetic judgments. That practical aesthetics is often surprising as well as revealing, partly because Beckett is much less theoretically consistent than one might expect (the later work especially running against earlier theory) and partly because, despite the iconoclastic, dislocated nature of Beckett's art in general and the drama in particular (a pattern that Beckett works diligently to achieve), the plays most often emerge from and rest on a realistic, traditional, and even sentimental substructure, against which the final work develops dialectically. That traditional structure and realistic content are, moreover, never wholly erased in the creative process so that the final work is virtually a palimpsest.

The most salient characteristic to emerge from tracing the biographies of Samuel Beckett's texts is, perhaps, the lack of a single or a consistent pattern in their composition. The closer one gets to Beckett's mind during creation, the more one is struck by the fact that each new work, each new confrontation with pen and paper, each new confrontation with self, poses problems for the artist that cannot be solved with previous solutions. The problems of composition, the problems, to use Beckett's phrase, of "shaping the mess," are new each time he sits down to the writing table. If one play begins with the free flow of memories, like *Not I* or *That Time*, another begins with a strong if not rigid philosophical principle, like the Berkeleyan "esse est percipi" of *Film*. If some plays develop a rather clear dramatic line, like the threatened departure of Clov in *Fin de partie*, others are organized by the repetition of motifs and images, like *Eh Joe* and *Not I*, and still others like *That Time* are patterned by abstract musical structures. Such patterning undermines the emphasis on what we have traditionally called meaning or content, the work's appeal lying more with the interplay of signifiers than with their decoding, than with the signified. (This emphasis should not be surprising once we consider Beckett's musical heritage; an accomplished pianist himself, with a taste for the Romantics, he married a woman preparing for a career as a concert pianist.) In each case, writing is an existential activity, where shape and hence meaning emerge from and are delineated through the writing. Essence rarely precedes existence in Beckett's work, and his creative efforts could stand as confirmation of the theory of language and writing proferred by Jacques Derrida:

> To write is not only to know that through writing, through the extremities of style, the best will not necessarily transpire, as Leibniz thought it did in divine creation, nor will that transition to what transpires always be willful, nor will that which is noted down always infinitely express the universe, resembling and reassembling it. It is also to be incapable of making meaning absolutely precede writing. . . . Meaning must await being said or written in order to inhabit itself, and in order to become, by differing from itself, what it is, meaning.

Despite the variety of solutions to the problems of creation, fundamental patterns are discernible. At least some sense of a coherent, consistent aesthetics emerges. The most discernible pattern is, predictably, the deliberate undoing of the work's origins. It is a tendency toward abstraction, which is finally, as it was in Picasso's late work, reductive or essentialist. One invariably finds in Beckett's revisions a movement toward simplicity, toward the essential, toward the universal, and with such universalizing Beckett achieves many of the antiemotional effects Brecht achieved with his Alienation-effect and historicizing. Such an artistic preoccupation in Beckett's work is hardly surprising given the sparse, often minimalist nature of the drama and late prose especially. What is surprising is how rooted that work is in its more traditional and realistic sources. Often the early drafts of Beckett's work are more realistic, the action more traditionally motivated, the world more familiar and recognizable, the work as a whole more conventional than the final. Revision is often toward a patterned disconnection as motifs are organized not by causality but by some application of near symmetry. This process often entails the conscious destruction of logical relations, the fracturing of consistent narrative, the abandonment of linear argument, and the substitution of more abstract patterns of numbers, music, and so forth to shape a work. The work's evolution is finally almost a devolution, the doing an undoing, the movement, toward higher and higher levels of abstraction, not so much to obscure, although one suspects some of this, as to deempathize—not so much to disguise autobiography as to displace or to discount it. Such rejection even becomes the subject of at least one play, *Not I*, whose very title denies at least the autobiographical impulse, if not ego psychology itself. The result is almost paradoxical, at least

dialectical. We see in both Mouth and Beckett an autobiographical ambivalence as they struggle not to talk about self (or mind, or self-consciousness)
when the reality of self is all there is to talk about. Yet the origins of all
this dislocation are so grounded in the socially and psychologically realistic early drafts that the work depends on at least traces of a world more
ontologically coherent, more philosophically essentialist, than the final.
Such traces, moreover, create one of the undercurrents of nostalgia that
run through Beckett's work.

The dislocations and displacement of *Fin de partie* and *Happy Days*,
for example, are more plausible and definite in early versions. In a
typescript Beckett called "avant *Fin de partie*," Hamm and Clov (X and F
at this point) are clearly survivors of a World War I battle: "Détruite
progressivement dans l'automne de 1914, le printemps de 1918 et l'automne
suivant, dans des circonstances mystèrieuses." The locale is set specifically
in the Picardy region of France, "et plus precisément dans le Boulonnais
. . . alentour de Wissant." Beckett was familiar with the destruction in
that region, particularly the bombed-out city of St. Lô where he worked as
an ambulance driver for the Irish hospital, and many of the play's details—
the absence of pain killers, the depletion of food supplies, the prevalence
of rats as well as the condition of the protagonists—suggest strong connections with the St. Lô hospital experience. Further, in a notebook version
of *Happy Days* Willie and Winnie are obviously victims of technological
insanity. Willie, called B at this point, reads from his yellowed newspaper:
" 'Rocket strikes Pomona, seven hundred thousand missing' . . . 'Rocket
strikes Man, one female lavatory attendant spared' . . . 'Aberrant rocket
strikes Erin, eighty three priests survive.' " These original images are
clearly rooted in the nightmare of V-2 rockets churning England into
desert. In an early version of Beckett's dramaticule "Come and Go,"
called "Good Heavens," the inaudibly whispered secrets of the final
version are distinctly audible in the early draft and are all about failing
health: "Three months . . . At the outside . . . Not a suspicion. She
thinks it is heartburn." In the early version of *Film*, O is certainly going to
his mother's home—the way made tenuous by his failing sight—to care for
her pets while she is at hospital. The crisis of being, precipitated by his
being in her room, is at least in part generated by her impending death.
And if the very existence of Godot is in question in the completed
version, it is not in the earlier drafts, for Vladimir and Estragon have a
note from him, and in his (or His) own hand, no less. Beckett's own
creative thinking seems to issue from such realistic sources, recollections
of wartime horrors, and family illnesses.

In composition those origins recede to the vanishing point, but like Mr. Kelley's kite in *Murphy*, without ever quite vanishing. Revision moves toward undoing those origins, toward the abstract, toward simplicity, toward a universal that is almost Platonic and as such suggests an essentialism that belies many of Beckett's philosophical premises. One of Plato's objections to art (and hence to the artist) is that art is an imitation of an imitation. As Beckett noted in *Proust* (and this may be Beckett's own most Platonic aesthetic comment), Proust rejects the artist who is "content to describe the surface, the façade, behind which the Idea is prisoner." Beckett here is certainly not accepting Platonic idealism but rejecting the art of surfaces, mimesis, imitation (at least in part), realistic art, and philosophically empiricism, especially the materialism of Locke. Much of Beckett's artistic struggle in *Film*, for instance, is against the medium's inherent tendency to represent, to imitate the surface of reality so accurately. In fact, it takes Beckett at least another work in film, the television play *Eh Joe*, before he can approach the level of abstraction and detachment he was striving for in *Film*. And that quality is not fully achieved until *Ghost Trio* and perhaps ". . . but the clouds . . . ." Beckett's "Ideas" are less Platonic ideal forms than something closer to Jungian archetypes, if we could somehow modify the closure that system suggests. Beckett is simply trying to avoid presenting the shadows in the cave. His most fundamental impulse is thus the very opposite of obscurity; he is most often telling us as simply and as straightforwardly as he can what he sees beyond the shadows. And so one can find in Beckett's revisions a fundamental ambivalence to the great modernist standards of intricacy and complication. But the artist himself is constrained. He is not, after all, omniscient. Beckett's narrators (and the author himself) are often ignorant about their characters. They are epistemologically skeptical, Pyrrhonians. During rehearsals of *Endgame* at Riverside Studios in London, May 1980, the actor Rick Cluchey asked Beckett if the little boy in the story that Hamm tells about the beggar is actually the young Clov. "Don't know if it's the story of the young Clov or not," was Beckett's response; "Simply don't know." Beckett has given us all that he knows in the play, and that is, as he wrote to Alan Schneider, "all that I can manage, more than I could." Beckett's response is not simply a perversity, but a statement which devalues authority, which shifts emphasis from author to text. There are no privileged meanings to his work, he insists. Jung put the matter in slightly different but analogous terms: "Being essentially the instrument of his work, [the artist] is subordinate to it, and we have no right to expect him to interpret it for us. He has done his utmost by *giving it form*, and he must leave the interpretation to others and to the future" (italics mine).

From his earliest artistic years, Beckett rejected mimesis, relying as it does on a fundamental empiricism, on surfaces. The perfection of the illusion of reality interested him little. A flirtation with naturalistic film in the 1930s notwithstanding, his most strongly and frequently expressed aesthetics was antinaturalistic, *anti* any system that makes of art finally another set of conventions by imposing an artificial order (a phrase that, for the early Beckett at least, is redundant) on the life of man. Beckett's continuing artistic struggles are to discover or to develop accurate, pleasing, formal substitutes for the logic and causality that he rejected by repudiating naturalism or psychological realism. The aesthetic danger, however, is simply finding another external form, a danger to which Beckett may have at least partly yielded in his more formalist drama and prose.

Much of Beckett's sensibility was shaped early in his career, a good part of it during the Joyce years (from 1928 until Joyce's death in 1941). Although Beckett spent considerable energy imitating and defending Joyce, his own aesthetics was shaped mostly in recoil. But the aesthetic relationship was always ambivalent. One of the few comprehensive statements that Beckett has made about his relationship with Joyce appears in an account (actually a composite interview) pieced together by *New York Times* correspondent Israel Shenker. Because of its unidentified and unverified sources and because Beckett considers the material misleading, the Shenker interview needs to be approached with some caution. Still, much of the composite Shenker assembles is strongly corroborated by other evidence, principally the artistic struggle Beckett was having in his early years with the dominant aesthetics and psychological influence of Joyce. This psychological and aesthetic struggle manifests itself in Beckett's poetic tribute (of sorts) to Joyce, "Home Olga," and his first, but still unpublished, novel, *Dream of Fair to Middling Women*. Shenker reports Beckett's saying:

> . . . the difference is that Joyce was a superb manipulator of material, perhaps the greatest. He was making words do the absolute maximum of work. There isn't a syllable that's superfluous. The kind of work I do is one in which I am not master of my material. The more Joyce knew the more he could. His tendency is toward omniscience and omnipotence as an artist. I'm working with impotence, ignorance. I don't think that impotence has been exploited in the past. There seems to be a kind of aesthetic axiom that expression is an achievement—must be an achievement. My little exploration is that whole zone of being that has always been set aside by artists as something unuseable—as something by definition incompatible with art.

Beckett echoed these sentiments to John Gruen in 1969: "If my work has any meaning at all, it is due more to ignorance, inability and intuitive despair than to any individual strength. I think that I have perhaps freed myself from certain formal concepts." Beckett then went on to compare himself to such aesthetic revolutionaries as Schönberg and Kandinsky.

Two points need to be made about Beckett's observations. First, Beckett had indeed freed himself from "certain formal concepts," although he has often substituted another set. Second, Beckett was not always willing to contrast his work, even his method, with Joyce's. For Samuel Putnam's anthology, *The European Caravan* (1931), Beckett wrote of himself, he "has adapted the Joyce method to his poetry with original results." Beckett's description of his own creative process bears a notable similarity to Artaud's: "I made my debut in literature by writing books in order to say that I could write nothing at all. My thoughts, when I had something to say or write, were that which was furthest from me. I never had any ideas, and two short books [*l'Ombilic des limbes* and *le Pèse-nerfs*] . . . are about this profound, inveterate, endemic absence of any idea."

The inability, ignorance, and impotence Beckett speaks of are more than matters of creating helpless characters. The problem is more formal, a fundamental aesthetic problem with which Beckett struggled for years, the essential inability of the author to control his art, that is, the actions of his characters, the shape of his expression, and even the work's presentation to the public. Beckett's aesthetics here approaches Sartre's, offered in such essays as "François Mauriac and Freedom," that one measures the quality of literature by the degree of freedom characters enjoy independent of their creators; this is far from Joycean control. And yet, the evidence of composition so often suggests an undercurrent, a counter-culture to this freedom, a struggle to control as much of the artistic process as language and the limitations of the ego allow. The "formal concepts" from which Beckett has freed himself are the convention of the omniscient narrator (and author), a consistent voice, and the causality of psychological fiction, including the assumptions of a unified ego. Beckett has consistently tried to deny the obligation of the narrator (or author) to explain, to make sense, to posit causes for observed effects simply because what we have traditionally called meaning, or privileged meaning, is not Beckett's principal concern. Yet the counter impulse, a vestige of Joycean control, persists in the pattern of fastidious revision, which suggests a desire to control his expression and to "say something" precisely, and even in his becoming a theatrical director to try to control as much as he can of the theatrical performance. Beckett's predominantly developing aesthetics as early as 1928 anticipates much of the phenomenological emphasis of the writers of the *nouveau roman* and much of poststructural criticism. But early in his career Beckett himself was evidently torn between his own developing sensibility and the sort of literary omniscience Joyce preached. Beckett's analysis may describe his relationship to Joyce after Beckett was able to make his break, after he began writing in French. During the late Twenties and early Thirties, however, Beckett was still at times trying to be the word-man, still trying to model himself after Shem the Penman.

With *Dream of Fair to Middling Women* (1932) Beckett attempted to plot an artistic course away from Joyce, but even here he retains those flourishes of Joycean linguistic virtuosity that he exhibited in his poetic tribute to Joyce, "Home Olga," and that continue through *Murphy* and *Watt*. Although his narrator in *Dream* suggests that "the only unity in this story is, please God, an involuntary unity," the novel contains passages that imitate (albeit with some parody) "Work in Progress." In *Dream* Beckett begins his "Work in Regress," begins his examination of the problem of how to contain the chaos of life, of reality within the forms of art, and much of what is rejected here is a Joycean artistic control in favor of a more aleatoric aesthetics. The novel fails finally not so much for its lack of unity or structure but because it is more exposition than dramatization. Further, the formal problems, the problem of freedom and order, of life and art, are never solved in *Dream*, nor are they in the collection of short stories derived from it, *More Pricks Than Kicks*. As an aesthetic statement, however, *Dream* is as important as the study of *Proust*, which Beckett completed the previous year. Speaking to the Mandarin, Belacqua, Beckett's protagonist in *Dream*, expostulates: "The reality of the individual . . . is an incoherent reality and must be expressed incoherently . . ." Although Beckett is in the psychological avant-garde here, he will eventually grow away from a solution that approaches the imitative fallacy, but he does not find a substitute until the formal, symmetrical patterning of *Waiting for Godot* (a structure which is admittedly anticipated in *Molloy*). In *Dream*, however, Belacqua posits succinctly the aesthetic problem that Beckett faced at the time. Further, Beckett's technically omniscient narrator lapses into impotence: "What she meant by that," he admits, "and what pleasure she hoped to get out of that, cannot be made clear." Here are the impotence and ignorance that Beckett will spend his life expressing and shaping. In *Dream* Beckett, at least intellectually, rejects the sort of artistic omniscience that he associates with Joyce in later years and with Balzac at the time:

> To read Balzac is to receive the impression of a chloroformed world. *He is absolute master of his material,* he can do what he likes with it, he can

foresee and calculate its least vicissitude, he can write the end of his book before he has finished the first paragraph, because he has turned all his creatures into clockwork cabbages and can rely on their *staying put wherever needed or staying going at whatever speed in whatever direction he chooses.* The whole thing, from beginning to end takes place in a spellbound backwash. We all love and lick up Balzac, we lap it up and say it is wonderful, but why call this distillation of Euclid and Perrault *Scenes from Life?*

What Beckett rejects here is what Derrida calls "preformationism," "according to which the totality of hereditary characteristics is enveloped in the germ, and is already in action in reduced dimensions that nevertheless respect the forms and proportions of the future adult." Derrida's example here is Beckett's beloved Proust, who, Derrida objects, wrote the final chapter of the final volume immediately after the opening chapter of the first volume. In June of 1934, when Beckett reviewed for *The Spectator* a study by Albert Feuillerat, *Comment Proust a composé son roman*, he objected to Professor Feuillerat's reconstructing the three-volume *A la recherche du temps perdu* of the prewar years:

> Uniformity, homogeneity, cohesion, selection, scavenging for verisimilitude (the stock-in-trade of the naturalism that Proust abominated), these are the Professor's tastes, and they are distressed by the passage of intuition and intellection hand in hand. . . . And out of their distress they cry for the sweet reasonableness of plane psychology à la Balzac, for the narrational trajectory that is more like a respectable parabola and less like the chart of an ague, and for Time, proclaiming its day of the month and the state of its weather, to elapse in an orderly manner.

For Beckett, however, Proust is not a "preformationist" because of the aleatory quality of involuntary memory. He is a writer whose narrative line is much like that of Beckett's first novel, *Dream of Fair to Middling Women*, "like the chart of an ague"; he is a writer who "communicates as he can, in drips and drabs."

Beckett's own drips and drabs proclaim his narrator's, and finally the author's, impotence. And it is part of the paradoxical nature of Beckett's work that it can so powerfully proclaim its own impotence. Within the work, the narrator is powerless to do anything for Belacqua. Of him the narrator can say: "He remembers the pleasant gracious bountiful tunnel [that is, womb], and cannot get back." "And we cannot do anything for him," announces the narrator; "how can you help people, unless it be on with their corsets or to a second or third helping." The aesthetics Beckett is developing in these early years is diametrically opposed to the one Joyce expresses through Stephen Dedalus, where the artist is "like the God of creation," and which Joyce develops in the structure of both *Ulysses* and *Finnegans Wake*. As Joyce had said to Beckett, "I can justify every line of my book." And sometime later, "I have discovered I can do anything with language I want."

Further, the aesthetics that is gestating in *Dream* is not one in which art is viewed as a lasting monument, as an achievement, as the author's defense against Time or History, but is the opposite. Art is part of, not outside, the ephemeral, historical, transitory world. Early in *Dream* the narrator notes,

> Without going as far as Stendhal,—who said—or repeated after somebody— that the best music (what did he know about music anyway?) was the music that became inaudible after a few bars, we do declare and maintain stiffly (at least for the purposes of this paragraph) that the object that becomes invisible before our eyes is, so to speak, the brightest and best.

When less is more, diminuendo becomes crescendo. The quotation anticipates the paradoxical, self-cancelling nature of Beckett's middle prose and further anticipates the Beckettian aesthetic axiom on the impossibility of communication because "there is *nothing* to *express*, nothing with which to express, nothing from which to express, no power to express, no desire to express, together with the obligation to express." Beckett's oft-quoted statement deserves a gloss. "Nothing to express" is also an active phrase: what remains to be expressed is nothingness, even though that needs to be done with the faulty system of language. There is "nothing from which to express" because self is not a coherent unity but itself an absence. There is "no power to express" because author, narrator, and characters are impotent and language is faulty. The lack of "desire to express," however, does not necessarily suggest a lack of will to express. Derrida, for one, separates desire and Schopenhauerean will: "The will and the attempt to write are not the desire to write, for it is a question here not of affectivity but of freedom and duty," and "the obligation to express" is Beckett's most explicitly expressed duty.

Almost from the first, then, Samuel Beckett's literary sensibility has been consciously antimimetic and alogical, and that absence of logic, especially of causality, is for Beckett both an aesthetic principle and his fundamental subject matter as he shows man in an absurd, disconnected world, a world devoid of rational principle and order. Beckett distinguishes among abstract paintings on the basis of their internal arrangement and relation, praising the work of one painter, Bram Van Velde, because he is ". . . the first to submit wholly to the incoercible absence of relation." Like so many of Beckett's critical statements (the essay on Proust most conspicuously), the aesthetics Beckett articulates is as revealing about his own sensibility as his subject's. Certainly, Beckett sees life, internal and external, as chaotic, in flux, absurd, ungoverned by essential principles. What order exists is created, imposed by man, arbitrarily, artificially, to appease his soul and nerves. Man's faulty, artificial systems—language, mathematics, law, religion, of course, logic, and often art itself—create the veneer of order and as such distort reality, which for Beckett is simply chaos. Israel Shenker reports Beckett's saying, "I can't see any trace of system anywhere."

Beckett's antimechanistic and hence anti-Naturalistic aesthetics was prominent in his classroom lectures at Trinity College, Dublin, in 1931. What he objected to in the Naturalists was, "no complexity. Preconceived equation." One writer he praised was Flaubert, who is neither a "philosopher [n]or image monger" but something in between. He praises Rimbaud's "intuition" and the "necessity of artistic disorder" he finds there. In contrast to Balzac, Beckett enjoys Dostoevski because of his "rejection of motive" and Gide because of his emphasis on the *acte gratuit*. For Beckett, Gide denies "the importance of consciously useful gestures, concentrates action devoid of outer motive." Gide was "tortured by the need of action & can't choose or commit himself to an action, . . . acts without choosing" (which act, Sartre will tell us after World War II, *is the choosing*). Beckett believed that Gide preserved the "integrity of incoherence." Balzac, on the other hand, used the "symbolic act typical of character. [The] Act represents him. . . . No free will or conflict." Gide, however, is "obsessed by the unsatisfactory nature of options. Turns to impulse . . . can't bear artist depriving action of free will." Gide is interested in "liminal consciousness [that] imparts [the] quality of inconclusiveness." "Naturalistic and traditional novel," for the young Beckett, "seems like nature but is only surface." The great Greek drama "doesn't pretend to be real—remains a work of art—is human beneath." In Balzac's work, Beckett argues, "characters can't change their minds or [the] artistic structure crashes—must be consistent. This is [the] traditional artistic statement broken by Gide."

Beckett's classroom opinions were wide ranging and personal, if not eccentric. He detested sentiment and called it a "curve subject to psychological and mathematical laws (given a temperament, [a] life can be drawn)." And at this stage of his career, Beckett insists on a fundamental critical responsibility of the artist: "When [the] French artist abdicates as a critic, everything goes wrong." He found that Corneille and Balzac abdicated, but "Racine is always present as a critic." Beckett finds "apparent cases of criticism in Balzac, but he doesn't criticise his own mind, [only] the representation of it." In Thomas Hardy, Beckett finds "psychology and tragedy as fabricated as Balzac." Beckett's interests are in the "*claire/obscure*" he finds in Racine. "Balzac," he complains, "paints like David, Dostoevski like Rembrandt." When he complains about Racine, he faults him for a problem Beckett himself must struggle to avoid. Racine is often didactic when he lifts his "personal impressions to the level of absolute value."

The resolution or reconciliation of this paradox of opening art fully to the chaos of life is one that dominates Beckett's artistic life. The treatment of a chaotic universe in art suggests paradox. The fundamental principles of reality are chaos and flux, whereas the essence of art is form and order. One resolution, of course, is Artaud's—the elimination of representation, of the distinctions between art and life. As an artist, however, Beckett seems unwilling to abandon the separation of the world from representation, to embrace finally the aesthetics proposed by Belacqua. Beckett's search is for a new form of representation, a form to imitate or to reflect or to contain the chaos of reality. Such an enterprise may finally be doomed to failure, but Beckett has experimented with several solutions to the paradox. A number of critics like H. Porter Abbot have argued that Beckett's forms, at least in the post-World War II trilogy of novels, are essentially imitative of that natural chaos. And this solution to Beckett's aesthetic problems seemed especially suited to the material Beckett was dealing with in his trilogy of novels and *Textes pour rien*, but it was never quite suitable for the drama. (The unpublished, unproduced *Eleutheria* may be Beckett's only attempt at such.) One danger of a wholly imitative form is to lose that traditional distinction between life and art. Even Derrida sees art as autonomous, separate from nature, while residing firmly within our world, and he quotes Kant on the matter: "Imagination is the freedom that reveals itself only in its works. These works do not exist *within* nature, but neither do they inhabit a world *other* than ours. 'The imagination (as a productive faculty of cognition) is a powerful agent for creating, as it were, a second nature out of the material supplied to it by actual nature.' " Beckett's "imitative" fictions are attempts at this "second nature." They retain their representative level and are ordered by the sort of repetition and pattern one finds conspicuously in Beckett's first produced play, *Godot*, and by their self-referential quality. The shift from *Watt* to the trilogy is from a mannerist (never wholly mimetic) work to a diagenetic one, where *action* is lodged within discourse. The trilogy is less an imitation of the world (and its chaos) than its own closed world. The danger of imitative form would be merely creating another level of "realistic" representation, creating a sign that accurately signifies or represents life's chaos. Such an aesthetics can simply become another order of Realism, one set of conventions substituted for another. Beckett's aesthetic problem is to develop signs and forms that maintain an internal relationship but do not grow into conventions or into signifiers of "true reality."

The imitative impulse occasionally surfaces in Beckett's art, as when he breaks down *some* of the work of art. In "Lessness" Beckett has accepted chaos or randomness or chance directly as cocreator. "Lessness" is a 120-sentence piece of narrative fiction, the second sixty sentences of which repeat the first, but in a different order. For this composition Beckett developed six families of images which he variously combined into sixty sentences:

> He wrote each of these sixty sentences on a separate piece of paper, mixed them all in a container, then drew them out in random order twice. This then became the order of the hundred and twenty sentences in ["Lessness"]. Beckett then wrote the number 3 on four separate pieces of paper, the number 4 on six pieces of paper, the number 5 on four pieces, the number 6 on six pieces, and the number 7 on four pieces. Again drawing randomly, he ordered the sentences into paragraphs according to the number drawn, finally totalling one hundred and twenty.

In "Lessness" Beckett has written only two versions of a mathematical progression that could go on, if we don't count duplications, to a potential number of 8.32×10^{81}. Beckett's two versions, like the two acts of *Godot* and *Happy Days*, suggest an (almost) endless series. And this number is still only partial. We have calculated neither the probabilities for paragraphing nor for the images within a sentence. In "Lessness" we have a form suggestive of, but not imitative of, natural chaos, for a man, Beckett, has selected the words, the arrangement of words and phrases in the sentence, the number of sentences, and the possibilities of paragraph structure. Beckett may theoretically embrace an aleatory aesthetics, but he remains too much the Joycean and Schopenhauerean to abandon human will. "Lessness" suggests a union between principles of symmetry and natural chaos, but its composition is the exception.

The danger of a wholly imitative form is that art loses its representational level, becomes essentially formless, and consequently something other than art, indistinguishable from nature. Beckett is more concerned with reconciling these contraries of form and chaos, art and reality, than with surrendering to either. His is not an antiart. He is certainly not intent on destroying form *per se*; quite the contrary:

> What I am saying does not mean that there will henceforth be *no form in art*. It only means that there will be *a new form*, and this form will be of such a type that it admits the chaos and does not try to say that the chaos is really something else. . . . *To find a form that accommodates* the mess that is the task of the artist now.

Beckett has even objected to Franz Kafka's work because of its essential coherence and failure to detail disintegration fully. "The Kafka hero has a coherence of purpose," Beckett argues. "He's lost but he's not spiritually precarious, he's not falling to bits. My people seem to be falling to bits." The artistic dangers are first in remaking the chaos into something rational and orderly, that is, conventional, and thus changing the chaos, applying some convenient system to the "mess"—logic, say—or pretending to understand and to explain it; and second, losing representation altogether. The function of the artist, for Beckett, is not to fit his material into a preconceived form, for, as he notes, art is always in danger of distorting reality: "the order and exactitude of their [the artists'] perception," he notes, are too often "distorted into intelligibility in order to be forced into a chain of cause and effect" (*Proust*). In Proust's work the aleatory element was involuntary memory contained within design. Beckett has striven for something similar. If imitation of chaos, that is, bringing art as close as possible to life, provides what shape there is to Beckett's middle fiction, the drama and later fiction seem to be shaped more formally. But as formalist aesthetics solves Beckett's problems, the undercurrent of artistic control grows increasingly dominant.

Such preoccupation with form suggests its separability from content, despite the fact that Beckett's most fundamental and consistently stated axiom has been the union of the two. And the problems of form have increasingly preoccupied Beckett. Early in his career his formal interest was two-fold. First, much of the early work was an assault on traditional, inherited literary forms, which were simply inadequate for his purposes. How does one write about chance, caprice, chaos, disconnection (psychological and metaphysical) in a style of form that is predictable or logical? And second, in an extension of a Hegelian argument, Beckett has decried the form / content dichotomy as early as his 1929 defence of Joyce's *Work in Progress* in "Dante . . . Bruno. Vico . . . Joyce," where he noted, "Here form *is* content[;] content *is* form. . . . His writing is not *about* something; *it is* that something *itself*." Shortly thereafter Beckett praised Proust because "he makes no attempt to dissociate form from content" (*Proust*). Yet Beckett's own work repeatedly demonstrates that matters of form and content can be treated separately—in the act of creation, at any rate. In works like *Eh Joe*, *Not I*, and *That Time*, the fundamental content is worked out rather easily in early drafts, yet the history of the work's composition is marked by repeated struggles to shape, to reform that initial material. Interestingly, when Beckett reaches a formal impasse he, as he did twice in the *Eh Joe* typescripts, often retypes his material into its original, coherent form, into what he calls a "continuity manuscript," and begins the process of fragmentation and reshaping afresh.

Beckett's primary artistic struggles, at least in the later work, have been to develop patterns, shapes, rhythms, cadences that "accommodate" the mess. His means are to assault the reader's expectations, to break down the mimetic notion of art, to move his art to higher and higher levels of abstraction, and to shape his fragments harmoniously. Such a thrust is fundamentally a blow against content itself or at least is a devaluation of, if not meaning, at least fixed meaning. Beckett is most postmodern when he creates signs (visual and linguistic) which suggest a variety of meanings. And what solution develops to the form/content problem is often brought about through abstraction, which is Beckett's most persistent means of transcending the form/content dichotomy, by subsuming both under the rubric we, along with Roland Barthes, might call "écriture" or Form. Barthes's concern in *Writing Degree Zero* is "to affirm the existence of a *formal* reality independent of language and style; to try to show that this third dimension [is] Form." And it is on this element, Form, that the later Beckett spends much of his artistic energy, and that affords the synthesis to the form/content dialectic. Form is the point at which a receding or vanishing eccentricity meets an emerging universality.

In his struggle against representation, Beckett is in the critical and creative avant-garde, and these critical positions as well as the literature that follows from them have had such a fundamental impact on twentieth-century art that, writing about modernism in general, Susan Sontag has essentially paraphrased much of Beckett's aesthetics: "Art is not about something," Sontag writes in 1966; "it is something. A work of art is a thing in the world, not just a text or commentary on the world." Such a work of art, then, is not necessarily a representation, not a shadow in the cave. It is virtually, as Sontag describes it, pure signifier. Aesthetics (and so criticism) for Beckett is less a matter of signifier/signified, of meaning, than of the interrelationships of signifiers, on the model, for Beckett, of music and mathematics. Sontag further echoes Beckett's aesthetic interest in silence: "The most potent elements in a work of art are often its silences." Speaking of the book *he* would write, Belacqua put it thus in *Dream* in 1932: "The experience of my reader shall be between the phrases, in the silences, communicated by the intervals, not the terms of the statement . . ."

The central compositional problem for Beckett is to create, to develop, to discover intrinsic forms (or at least some intrinsic clues to form), some alternative pattern or internal relation to replace logic, causality, and verisimilitude. Theoretically, at any rate, Beckett is searching for a form not imposed on the writing from without but one which grows out of the writing process. Beckett's search is for patterns to express the absence of relationship, to replace the conventions of realistic fiction or the formal use of mythic patterns (which he himself has tried in the "Actes sans paroles I & II"), or even to replace that other favorite unifying element, the coherent ego. Even the personal unity of the stream-of-consciousness novel is rejected, as is perspectivism, because both entail a unified ego. Beckett's process of composition usually follows the following lines, often simultaneously: after the initial image or incident is recorded (often straight from memory or the unconscious), what follows is a shaping process that includes: (1) deleting detail, explanation, and often connection; (2) rejecting, consciously destroying those artificial, manmade, extrinsic systems of chronology and causality; and (3) creating an alternative arrangement or internal relationship that will emphasize *pattern* if not *order*. This view of Beckett's creative process accounts for one of the peculiarities one notices examining his manuscripts: the core material (central situation and dominant images) is often present from the earliest draft, culled from memory or nightmare, and yet meticulous revision follows meticulous revision. The phenomenon reveals a number of Beckett's aesthetic principles. For one, Beckett shares with Artaud and Brecht a suspicion of the unconscious, at least the unmediated flow of the unconscious, even as it is his primary source and inspiration, and so Beckett further shares with Artaud a distrust of Surrealism and its method, automatic writing.

And yet Beckett's art is constantly circling back on itself, into its own wake: "The Vico road goes round and round to meet where terms begin" (*Finnegans Wake*). The abstracted, undone final version is dialectically dependent on the work's realistic, psychological origins, the being on the nothingness, the presence on the absence, on what is excised. Beckett's subject matter is indeed primarily autobiographical—images of early childhood, family deaths, loves, war horrors—its source fundamentally the id or, in Lacan's terms, the subject, but the primary artistic struggle (as opposed to the psychological or personal one) is with undermining or undoing this matter. Beckett's understanding of his own creative process is evident as early as his essay on Proust, where he draws distinctions between the artist and the writer and makes a somewhat Jungian and decidedly Derridean argument for the artist's being a conduit. "The work of art is neither created nor chosen," Beckett suggests, "but discovered, uncovered, excavated, pre-existing within the artist, a law of nature" (*Proust*). Moran can say of Molloy, for example, "Perhaps I invented him. I mean found him ready-made in my head." The echo of Jung here is strong. "The artist is not a person endowed with free will who seeks his own ends," Jung notes, "but one who allows art to realize its purpose through him." Yet Beckett insists on some level of artistic control. Both the Surrealist and Jungian explanations of creativity are incomplete for Beckett. Quoting Proust, he points out that after initial inspiration, the writer takes over the creative process. "The artist has acquired his text: the artisan translates it. 'The duty and task of the writer (not an artist, a writer) are those of a translator' " (*Proust*). And translation for Beckett is a search for form and distance, because, as Beckett told Harold Hobson, "it is shape that matters." Herein lies the Beckettian compromise: the writer shapes, forms, the artist's subconscious inspiration. And the compromise suggests that in composition at any rate form and content are separate problems, the union of whch may occur only in the Pineal gland of art.

If the Beckettian aesthetics is consistent with much of the modernist and even postmodernist sensibility, it also runs counter to at least part of that sensibility. For one, although we can find some affinities between the theaters of Brecht and Beckett, Beckett's is not a theater that leads to overt action, is never at least an overtly political theater, although formal innovation can, in its own way, contain political import. Moreover, if, as I have suggested, the bulk of Beckett's developing aesthetics is anti-Joycean, a rejection of the omnipotent artist (with undercurrents of artistic control), it is equally against the mainstream of twentieth-century Romanticism. Despite its sources in the unconscious, Beckett's art is not confessional. Using Antonin Artaud as her model, Susan Sontag distinguishes (a bit overly generally) modern and premodern writing thus: "All premodern literature evolves from the classical conception of writing as an impersonal, self sufficient achievement. Modern literature projects quite a different idea: that romantic conception of writing as a medium in which a singular personality heroically exposes itself."

Although in many ways Samuel Beckett is an exemplary twentieth-century romantic artist (he has all the bohemian credentials) and although his art is built on strongly autobiographical elements and is finally an art of failure, not achievement, much of Beckett's creative struggle is against those personal elements, and Beckett's means are, in part, to devalue content in favor of form. When Jessica Tandy, who played Mouth in the Lincoln Center production in 1973, complained that Beckett's specified time for *Not I*, eighteen minutes, made the play unintelligible, Beckett answered: "I am not unduly concerned with intelligibility. I hope the piece may work on the nerves of the audience, not its intellect." One reason for second acts in *Happy Days* and *Waiting for Godot* and for the *da capo* ending of *Play* is not only to destroy logical continuity, cause and effect, and to emphasize theatricality and performance, but, more important, to strengthen pattern, symmetry (or near symmetry), and, finally, form through repetition. In *Godot*, for example, the author tells us, "Next day. Same time." But the author's information seems to be a non sequitur. The tree sprouts leaves overnight? Pozzo and Lucky go blind and deaf, respectively, overnight? Logical continuity is destroyed while symmetrical structure offers a pleasing shape. Brecht suggested that the Epic Theatre should develop in curves. Beckett's repetitions often loop back on themselves, but like a helix or a gyre. The image is often the tightening sinistro spiral of Dante's Hell.

And not only in Beckett's primary aesthetic struggle with form, but with form made palpable, and this has in itself an alienating or distancing effect. In much of the drama the fact that we are watching a play (or a film in *Film*) is indispensable to the work's effect, as is the metafictional nature of the prose narratives. Abstraction itself is a formal element, a means of emphasizing the fact that we are watching a work of art, a representation. This is the very opposite of that literature which denies its own fictionality, of psychological realism, whose intent is involvement and which leads to Brecht's dreaded empathy. The consciousness of form in the abstract, "dehumanized" protagonists, and the patterning of repetition afford emotional detachment and are means of creating a reflective art and of countering the essentially realistic and even melodramatic nature of the subject matter. The commitment of Beckett's writing is not to the outside, to the world, but to the inside, to itself. It is not, for Beckett, the artist's function to explain anything, especially the outside world. Beckett's artistic aim is not to explain the mess, not to posit causes: "the only chance of renovation," Beckett tells us, "is to open our eyes and see the mess. It is not a mess you can make sense of." In a review for *transition* in 1938, Beckett stated this position with his characteristic youthful dogmatism: "art has nothing to do with clarity, does not dabble in the clear and does not make clear."

Beckett's thematic commitment is to the fundamental questions of reality, being, and knowing, to universal images of man's predicament, and not overtly with their social manifestations or their rational explanations, even as his own artistic methods reveal that his work is rooted in typical experiences, or, as Jung called them, "personal idiosyncrasies." Jung argues,

> The essence of a work of art is not to be found in the personal idiosyncrasies that creep into it—indeed, the more there are of them, the less it is a work of art—but in its rising above the personal and speaking from the mind and heart of the artist to the mind and heart of mankind.

For Beckett these "personal idiosyncrasies" are the originating impulse, and it is against these "personal idiosyncrasies" that he struggles in composition. Advocating artistic impotence, arguing against the bourgeois artistic value of clarity (*la clarté*), rejecting a realistic art, an art of emotional involvement, Beckett's art is yet tied to these elements, if only by negation. And so with the other contraries. The dialectics of form/content, realism/antirealism, Joyce/anti-Joyce are resolved or synthesized only in Beckett's art. Childhood memories, adolescent unhappiness, fears of mortality, wasted opportunities, familial and cultural alienation, memories of suicidal sweethearts: these are the elements Beckett's art needs and needs to undo as he struggles to make universal art out of personal neurosis. It is an aesthetics surprisingly close to Schopenhauer's: "[Art] repeats or reproduces the external Ideas, grasped through pure contemplation, the essential and abiding in all the phenomena of the world." It is a sentence likely to bring an approving nod from Beckett.

ALDO TAGLIAFERRI

Beckett and Joyce

In Aristotle's poetics the text takes the existence of reality for granted, whereas in Joyce the text *is* that reality. Here the text substitutes the world, albeit standing partially in opposition to it. Its explicit relationship with the world is that of a microcosm to a cosm, a microchaos to chaos (the relationship does not change). The contents which Aristotle selected to identify art are turned upside down: details traditionally considered trivial become central, and yet the irony of the inversion produces not so much a negation of the cosm but a recording—no less mimetic—of the objective transformation the cosm has undergone. In Joyce the word is at once mirrored reality and reality, which is the world itself; it becomes an object and acquires density of things, a life of its own. Joyce can play with words like Jahveh with stones and animals, in a medieval spirit which still implies a direct connection with reality—most direct, in fact, since it is a connection that turns into an identification. In 1929 Beckett hit the mark when he wrote of Joyce that: "His writing is not about something; *it is that something itself*" (*Dante . . . Bruno. Vico . . . Joyce*). And Umberto Eco, who deals with the same opposition in *Opera aperta*, makes a distinction between Mallarmé's *oeuvre pure*, which "tends to be an impersonal suggestive device which leads beyond itself" and Joyce's work, which "on the contrary appears to be an object centered on itself, looking inward, a mimesis of life, where references and associations come from within the aesthetic object." Joyce's strong mimetic disposition ambiguously retains the value of self-identification, and its opposite. By merely overturning

Translated by the author and Daphne Hughes. From *Beckett e l'iperdeterminazione letteraria*. Translation copyright © 1985 by Aldo Tagliaferri.

these contents, an objective framework of historical and mythical facts is brought to light through an epiphany of private experience, and the reader feels he must deal with those facts as if they were the reality that has helped to shape the work of art itself: even when it is the work which determines the contents selected, Joyce uses these to build a world, though a completely verbal one, objective and positive, trusting the indisputable value of the representation as such. In Joyce the "disparition élocutoire du poète, qui cède l'initiative aux mots" becomes a suspension of the subject similar to the suspension which takes place in the overdetermination of "scientific" psychoanalysis. In other words, Joyce is essentially mimetic, hypercausative and objective.

Let us now consider the word according to Beckett: one of his prevailing themes is a mistrust for words, the fear (a programmed fear, of course) that words may cease moving and acquire density, consistence, a fixed life of their own. Beckett differs from Joyce because he does not aim at mimesis, nor at language for its own sake. The Beckettian word hastens to point to something beyond itself, but this pointing has nothing in common with Aristotle's mimesis: the world is denied, and words are suspected of becoming a world when they cease moving, when they are not sufficiently taken over and rejected by successive words. No neologism, no verbal blend, no sound tempts Beckett's Ulysses with its siren song. The mimetic textures that in Joyce's work are superimposed on one another in synchronic verbal constellations, are dispersed in Beckett's trilogy by a stylistic fluency so transparent that one is tempted to consider it a non-style; and, as a matter of fact, Beckett's style could be defined as a lack of style aiming to bring about a feverish and endless motion from one word to another, from one *persona* to another, though none of these represents a truth speaking for an eternal omnipresent and implacable Subject.

This is a far cry from the predominantly mimetic course still taken by Joyce, with his love of the pun and medieval objectification of the word. Here, on the contrary, the word is seen as an objective non-correlative of an inexpressible, show-defying subject. Quite unexpectedly the representative ritual is again disturbed, simply by being accepted, then rejected as a new liturgical form, just when it seemed that Joyce's inversion of the content, his black mass as it were, had enabled us to break away from Aristotelianism once and for all. Beckett shows us not only how much still remained to be done (which would not involve any radical change), but how necessary it is to persevere in this direction, since the subject only has to stand still, the logos pause, for another objectification to be born, another lie, another flight from man's real predicament towards false images of the *persona* and God.

In the trilogy, for example, there is a progressive, programmed transition from imitation to negation of the world, and to the meta-critical instrumentation of the word-world. The logos communicates by its very absence: the subjectively existential irreducible coincides with silence. In *Molloy*, and again in *Malone Dies* to a certain extent, the Aristotelian cosmos, the hypercaused, is negated by means of a more or less Aristotelian representation. But, in the third volume of the trilogy, it is by representing the negation of the cosmos that Beckett shows that representation is impossible, the word a lie, and that it is necessary to make use of this lie (a fact that should be borne in mind lest it hypostatize) in order to achieve continual self-liberation—a liberation that gains meaning from its very inexorability. So the value of the representation is shifted outside the representation itself: its artistic validity is proportionate with the success of the attempt and amount of wager won. It refuses to become a world and at the same time refers back to no selected reality except nothingness, silence and perfect adherence to the subjective individual conscience. The dramatic nature of this referring back is also represented as an overdeterminate, but only in the sense of oversubjectivity: subjects follow hard on one another's heels, are named, erased, ephemeral and essential like an act of self-consciousness, are irreplaceable and at once extinct. Beckett's "progress" does not aim for the product, the art form, but departs from an art form so as to make any return to it impossible. Like Hamlet, Beckett's *persona* has "that within which passes show", and derives its appeal from its refusal to be shown, from a harking back to a concrete subject which includes both the being of the work and its non-being as equally constituent parts. Hamlet's artistic mirror actually shows man his own image, but this does not mean that the reader may see a likeness of himself in the work, or that the work is so construed as to be a potential imitation of his own likeness, but rather that work and reader together, mutually involved, restore man to himself.

The result, however, is on an even more rigorously horizontal plane than in Kafka. Nothing is static or dense, not gesture but ceaseless motion, as transparent as when it was the confident conveyor of an accepted reality, letting through not the world but the world-negating conscience.

In Beckett's work we can recognize the revelation of a void-filled gap, a putting off, a self-negation that cannot be reduced to a number of valences to be balanced, to a simple question of unfinishedness, but which imply a question, a proposal, an act of refusal as art now aims at denying rather than imitating, not an invitation to a free game of possibilities, but the obligation, the commitment to continue directed by the precise metacritical function of negation of all hypostatic values, the blanket that a thousand years of western tradition has woven to cover the untenable exposure of naked human subjectivity. What is essentially different about the beginning of this dissolution, compared with Joyce's, is the awareness that it cannot be concluded, the moral conscience that it should not be concluded.

There are two final images, one in *Finnegans Wake*, the other in *The Unnamable*, which can be considered symbolic of that radical divergence we have tried to clarify: *Finnegans Wake* could be cosily locked up like a casket, albeit with a thousand locks, enclosing an upturned but no less mimetic "aleph," nothing more of the external cosmos: absence, void, not seriously taken into consideration as such, cosily locked up with his own keys ("The keys to. Given").

Beckett's trilogy throws away the keys of mimetic self-identification as useless. After Moran, the doors and gates are without locks. And the image that opens rather than closes *The Unnamable* is that of a door: A door like the one that introduces Goethe's Mothers to there "where there are neither locks nor chains to remove", a door through which the work dissolves to nothingness before the hope of a new and historically existent subject: "in the silence you don't know, perhaps it's the door, perhaps I'm at the door, that would surprise me, perhaps it's I."

The work is progressively drawn inwards, fascinated by the hypothesis of its own absence, of a time and place when it did not exist, and at the same time instrumentalizes this potentially numinous hypothesis, using it as a springboard to take off into nothingness.

This hope, potentially just as numinous, can be kept alive as long as it is thwarted, and the critical moment of this condition is at the core of Beckett's poetics. Only partially expressed by the subject, it yearns for its complement, aiming not at self-fulfillment or completion but at total annihilation. A work in regress, then? Even if one may be tempted to accept and resolve the two-headed antinomy of mimesis-negation into a couple of identical opposites, Bruno-Cusano style, we prefer to consider negation as a fundamental and at the same time derivative tendency, thus downgrading Beckett's mimesis from an end to a means: Joyce's resulting self-assertion is turned to self-negation. Negation, in fact, has no part in a mimetic calling, being an intentional, additional act, while mimesis consists of inert or pre-existing, and therefore usable, material.

The conception of a mimesis meant as imitation of the dialectics of these two identical opposites disguises as polarizing the breaking of the circular motion of the mechanism in that it proves a divergence that can be neither reduced nor reversed.

II

By now, it should be clear that it would indeed be rash to use an undialectical concept of influence to gauge the relationship between Joyce and Beckett. No doubt readers of both will detect in Beckett's trilogy traces of ideas or themes already embodied in Joyce's work—such as Giordano Bruno's identical opposites, Vico's cycles, fragments of myths, and the overlapping figures of the Author and the Redeemer. The very concept of the Unnamable can be considered an offshoot of *Ulysses'* Nameless One, and the enigmatic use of the letter M comes straight from Joyce. On the other hand, far from practicing the mimetic revival of a heritage, Beckett, unleashing his will to desecrate and corrosive sense of humour, deforms and rejects an all-embracing literary experience. In this perspective we find that Beckett has used Joyce, and many other authors, to perpetrate a deed of radical departure from Western literary tradition, compelling us by his strategy to acknowledge the precarious nature of Being and Knowledge, in an artistic project with its own subversive aims. But just as Beckett chafed under the increasing awareness that Joyce, his closest literary ancestor, tended to weigh him down like a yoke, so it is not surprising that the poetics of *Finnegans Wake* represented a target for this subversion.

About *Finnegans Wake* a most enterprising collection of studies has been undertaken that is worthy of the keenest interest, in that it has focused critics' attention on the methodological necessity to put textual analysis before evaluating synthesis, at least in order of time. Yet a certain, ritualistic stiffness in the approach and objectivistic self-satisfaction in tearing apart the text lead us to suspect that critical concern for the real work is playing second fiddle to an ideological urge to extend to the realm of knowledge a gloating celebration over the death of the subject and dialectics. Of course, if this were the case, they would be lighting the right candle. Joyce is a firm believer in the hypostatized logos and delights in travesties and the opaque word, which turns reductiveness into ambiguity. He rightfully belongs to that substantial band of thinkers and artists who operate on the subject so radical a removal that it can only be performed by the unconscious exercise of their most unbridled subjective selves, being as it is a kind of massive return of the removed.

Beckett is a completely different matter. Puns and lapses, inversions, associations and double meanings are not merely the solipsistic game of a capricious demigod, allowing psychoanalysis to sneak in and permeate the work. In Beckett the word cannot be reduced to a symptom.

On the contrary, it is through word play that self-analysis, self-vaccination and preventive de-colonization are able to pass. The interpreter's task is to show how Beckett, unlike Joyce, works self-critically, taking over the remainder, absorbing into the text the critico-analytical function (in a Freudian sense) and squeezing art out of every smallest detail, so that it becomes heightened awareness, and the Freudian Ego, through countless misadventures, nay because of them, gains ground.

The real sense of inexorability in Beckett's word (and there are many other senses that peacefully co-exist with it, as has been suggested in the course of this study) can be equated wth Freud's concept of the endlessness of analysis, which is complementary to practical terminableness. The paradoxically scrupulous, pedantic, semantically contradictory speech of Beckett's characters "finical to a fault" suggests, often with decidedly humorous effects, a constant need to overlook no detail, leave no dross through which an uncritical or uncreative interpretation might arise. The unconscious is never allowed to materialize through portmanteau-words, or at any rate objects; instead it is dissolved, mixed, woven into conscience. Even the apparently subdued style often seems to stress the same cautiousness as Freud, with its "perhapses," its proneness to contradictions and gradual approximations, its awareness of heterogeneous alternatives and rejection of premature final solutions. The "credible perplexity" which the author-character of The Unnamable relies on so much is not far removed from Freudian Unsicherheit.

The worst risk facing an exegesis of Beckett's work is not that of turning it into an endless analysis of an unending work, but of reducing it to the very things the word uses as a launching pad in order to demystify and expel: an ideology, rationalization and fetishism of the word itself. A textual criticism runs the risk of supplying reading or decoding keys, interpretations, in fact "setting down coldly the sign of equality" (Malone Dies), which would be all very well in Joyce's case, just to restore consistence and autonomy to what the work has dissolved and instrumentalized.

If, for the practical reason of producing an analysis that is terminable and determinable, we choose to reveal to the reader that the Satanic or Oceanic symbol of the trident, which Beckett's characters often bear, is a W, often upturned to an M, the initials of their names; or if, in hunting for his admitted "fundamental sounds", we track the Biblical Abraham or Freudian Ego down to Moran; or if, deciphering the name of Sapo (the character who, according to an enigmatic admission of Beckett's in reply to a hint that he showed a certain resemblance to Beckett as a child, somehow "got a bit out of hand"), we notice that it sounds like "sa peau"

(=himself), we do so because we think that the choice of those particular fundamental sounds, and those particular puns, cannot be considered fortuitous or interchangeable. In the workings of art images are not variables with respect to the constants in a message, but are co-structured with it. The basic sounds overflow with cultural harmonics, not coinciding with but partly determined by them. The ideological and autobiographical supply nothing more than images here, but this is their very raison d'être, and no exegete should ever forget that, in poetry, the image determines the message.

To claim that cultural references are interchangeable and that ironically used ideological messages can be chosen at random, would correspond to shifting the whole meaning of the work towards an abstraction of its own message, or its own stylistic method; in other words, of a content or form, ideology or system, tragedy or game. The synthesis of these terms, which links the expulsion process quite intentionally with what is being expelled, will no doubt be missed by any interpretation that fails to identify either one of the two complementary elements (deciphering of the ideological content and singling out of the means and sense of its instrumentalization) because in that case it fails to understand the texture of Beckett's work, which, in its determinateness, is woven out of both terms. In this sense the act of recognition, or "running to earth," yields indispensable exegetic values, in that their specificity links them to the text, and to the particular contextuality of values which is the artistic result.

Adorno, in his essay on *Endgame*, produces a first class exegesis, precisely because it concerns, together and dialectically, an assessment of Beckett's artistic operation and the recognition of the corresponding textual artifice in which it is embodied. And even if we do not share the particular slant that this philosopher's final conclusions tend to give to Beckett's achievement, we are left with extremely brilliant and useful interpretative devices.

The attempt to pinpoint in Beckett's work, either to exalt or to execrate it, as does happen, only the negative or destructive moment, reducing it to a kind of horrific literary Hiroshima, is no less mystifying than the attempt to pluck out of it a hidden but reassuring positivity (the search for God, the decay of capitalism = patrilinear I = subject, a vaguely protesting and purifying game) for the simple reason that both are anxious to hide the opposite—paradoxical inversion and crisis of every positivity— that thrusts itself forward in Beckett's every page.

It is especially evident in the expulsion process and humorous and paradoxical inversion that is one of the favourite tricks used by this last heir of Irish ironists. As with every great ironist, in Beckett the humorous-ludicrous and tragi-pessimistic are complementary and inseparable. In claiming that it is, after all, a game, we must remember that, through the intentional presence (functional to the text) of a specific, cultural, auto-biographical material for expulsion, are also represented the very origins of the game. And there is nothing playful about the origins of games, as we know from Freud.

As for the relationship between psychoanalysis and literature which is put forward in this study, some reflections of a general character are opportune at this point. Ever since the linguistics plague wreaked such havoc in the psychoanalytical camp, the object of analytical discourse has lost the substance of the psyche. From the reality of castration and seduction to the phantom of fact, from the psychic reality of this phantom to its linguistic structure, we have come to the reality of discourse and pronominal nature of the subject. Every plague has its victims and ghosts. Structuralism conjured up the phantom of the origin of language. But the real foundation of any phantom lies in a dead body, and silence is the corpse in this case. Beckett restores every ounce to this body. His discourse has the effect of rehabilitating the absence, nothingness and the silence that make up the substance of discourse itself. His word, then, is as light and transparent as a ghost, but what it covers and carries round in this guise is a corpse (that is, the unnamable, the ineffable, infancy, the irreducible, death).

The birth of language is its relationship with silence, constantly updated and renewed in an art of the word, which consists of bending it, at every turn, to restore what it retracts. Infancy, like silence, thus turns out to be the substance of the subject. And even if this subject, as in Benveniste, is purely pronominal, it is not merely a question of the reduction of the I to language, but on the contrary a restitution (which, if we can see beyond, through the phantom, happens by means of the reduction itself) of the subject to a reality not simply of speech, to a non-linguistic substance, which is limited by the word and in turn limits it. The two functions of symbolizing, that is the evocative and the exorcistic, merge in this case.

If Lacan's unconscious is structured like a kind of language, Beckett's language can be said to be structured like a kind of unconscious. But this is true in that the structure of the unconscious is not reducible to any form of language. If it does not cultivate within itself that silence-cum-infancy of which the pronominal subject is both negation and manifestion, artistic language risks sliding paradoxically from simple evocation to the other side of the symbolic, that is pure exorcism. Just as the unconscious must be evoked in order to be exorcised, so artistic language must first be exorcised before being able to evoke.

Trust in the evocative value of the symbolic, in the substitutive magic of the word, is ill-based if, as happens in Joyce, it does not give enough importance to the implications of this power, that is to the subtraction of reality, and violence against the silence of being. Lacan, in a seminar in 1954, was right when he claimed that, if he uttered the word "elephant," an elephant would actually be conjured up in the room where he was speaking. What he omitted to stress is that, just because the concept comes to substitute the thing, if the elephant had been in the room before being conjured up, by pronouncing the same magic word he would have made it disappear. Evoking what is not and making a world out of it, language can hide the fact that it is made up of nothingness and silence.

This does not happen in Beckett, for he talks explicitly, with ironic detachment, about this outdated phase, which has given way to a much subtler interplay of exorcism and evocation: "If I said, Now I need a hunchback, one came running proud as punch of his fine hunch that was going to perform. It did not occur to him that I might have to ask him to undress" (*Malone Dies*). The nothingness under the hunch, the emptiness under the ghost's sheet, the failure of the evocation, are restored by Beckett to their basic role as the foundation of artistic language.

III

Adorno's essay on *Endgame*, as well as taking its place among the most brilliant interpretations of this well-known play, tackles the complex question of Beckett's underlying ideology and, in its conclusions, concerns his entire output. It starts with the observation that Beckett, instead of setting one philosophy against another, drives to their extreme consequences the implications of systems that suppose that some given tenet is unquestionable (whether that be the world, a hypostatized subject or an immanent dialectic) and, from within the systems themselves, undermines the potential to communicate of any language that claims "with most sound deductions and concepts the thesis of sufficient reason," a language defined by Beckett as "merely a simian vulgarity" (*Proust*). In a perspective where "signifying nothing" is the only thing that matters Beckett would retrieve, but only to empty it of sense, even the concept of absurd in the objectivistic acceptances diffused by a certain kind of existentialism.

The "absurdity" of the situations in Beckett lends itself to various considerations. We notice that the kind of absurd Beckett satirizes in

Molloy, with obvious reference to Camus' myth of Sisyphus, is character-ized by the fact that it always occurs in the self-same places and conse-quently within foreseen limits, albeit in an ideological proposition that claims to be historical, not fatalistic. Beckett's ironic attitude to Camus seems to be amply justified: the latter, having begun his essay declaring that he was taking the absurd as a "starting point" and not as a conclusion, contradictorily claimed that "the sense of the absurd is not the same thing as the notion of the absurd." Likening his Sisyphus to the stone to which his tragic destiny was bound, he was in fact objectifying the absurd, making it an acceptance of the so-called human condition and as such an objectively identifiable notion. In other words, Camus was reconciled to an abstract absurd that had become at once the starting point for a vision of life that finds a way of consoling itself in the awareness of its own acceptance of the absurd, and Beckett has revealed the contradiction. According to Adorno, Beckett, on the contrary, brings absurdity to life, even revels in it, not only to sidestep the contradiction Camus had fallen into, but as an end in itself, since Beckett's absurd seems to reflect a failed reconciliation between subject and object, which is expressive of a totally alienated culture: "unreconciled reality does not tolerate in art reconcilia-tion with the object." If Adorno fails to give a sense to the inversion operation carried out by Beckett, if he first denies and then declares that Beckett makes a positive statement in representing negation negatively, this depends on the fact that for Adorno, in an historical situation in which sense is impossible, both sense and non-sense prove absurd. So non-identity, whose coming is heralded by Adorno, really triumphs, but as an objectivized absurd, in the sense that no subject survives to grasp the absurdity. At which point the stalemate situation Beckett rightly attrib-uted to Camus is dramatically repeated, and Adorno's accusation holding existentialism reponsible for a process of abstraction lacking self-awareness loses its legitimacy: Adorno's underlying identification of subjectivity, his very linking of subject and identity, robs conscience of the process of abstraction of the subject (since this abstraction is inevitably sneaked in), and above all robs it of its power to become subject, each time taking shape in different choices of itself. And it is from this conception of the absurd that Adorno's interpretation of humour derives: he sharply reveals Beckett's tendency to make use of inversion situations with a view to parody, but hastens to add that by now even humour "has made itself ridiculous" and is, in short, impossible. Denying subjectivity, Adorno admits that Beckett's characters do have some precise functional existence of their own (which is obviously the characters' way of being), but "because dissocation as such is possible only in contrast with identity."

But Adorno is careful not to reveal the whys and wherefores of this phantomatic identity. If he recognized that humour, just like the absurd, exists for someone, the would-be power he tries to exert over the reader would reveal itself in all its inconsistency: in humour a subject refuses the absurd by objectifying it, making it alien to himself; humour cannot be challenged, since it is itself challenging someone, and Adorno cannot decide who this someone is, this subject neo-Hegelians often treat as an insignificant nothing, as an appendix of the System. The truth is that Beckett creates characters, and therefore subjects, because a sense of humour can only be given where there is a subject, and the reader himself, together with the author, is called upon to take part. Well and truly alienated from the world, subjectivity returns in Adorno's essay taking on the pseudo-divine role characteristic of the monologizing voice in Beckett, as if there were no such person as a certain German philosopher called Wiesengrund to establish relationships between a definite culture and a definite author (by means of the text, despite the fact he has asserted that one cannot "follow the illusion of grasping the sense philosophically"), and to argue with Lukács and Jaspers, but as if there were only a W who mysteriously comes and goes like a Worm or a Molloy. Beckett's use of inversion is far more shrewdly calculated.

Beckett always imagines there is a subject-innocence polarity in the reader able to sense the absurd and turn the humour into a refusal of the absurd, or rather sense paradox as awareness of the co-existence of refusal and co-responsibility in the essence of refusal itself, just where there is an attempt to pass off as objective contemporary man's impossibility to envisage victory over the absurd. There is some method in Moran's being unable to reach the absurd (originally alien to him) he has been sent to track down, except by fighting it: he belongs to a celebration cum parody of the absurd as the experience of a subjectivity challenged, or rather challenging itself, as we think we have shown. Adorno, on the contrary, claims that Beckett "does not oppose a vision of the world" to the ambiguous concept of absurd wielded by existential philosophy, but "takes it at its word," and this assumes (like the "conclusion," the arrival point of the absurd Camus refers to regarding the myth of Sisyphus) the need of an absurd as a given fact, as a "continuum" the manufacture of which cannot feasibly be delegated to anyone. Beckett's absurd is demoted by Adorno to the rank of object denied the need to become a product, since it is taken for granted. Adorno, wanting to challenge subjectivity more radically than Beckett does, at the same time rescues it from its predicament.

In Beckett the objectivised absurd is expressed as mutilation, decadence, senility, bodily paralysis. In Moran we witness the passage of the absurd as alienation from the world to the subject, in what presents itself as a pain in the knee, the symbolic start of the subject's alienation from himself. But both poles always exist in Beckett's following work, too. If, as in Camus and the post-Sartre novelists, subjectivity is made more and more implicit in the objectivation, it is because this is the direction of both the concrete and the absurd. Denying this directional trend from Moran to Worm still belongs to the tendency of the absurd to diverge from subjectivity which, asserting itself, may assert it too. The crisis of subjectivity occurs in that subjectivity is always challenging itself, in a definite, irreducible, ungeneralizable way. In other words, subjectivity is taken as diversity in its actual diverging, like a divergence that does not identify with itself: the sense of the absurd cannot be equated with a preconstituted notion of the absurd and "taken at its word." Identity always belongs to the objective, not subjective case: it stems from the self-objectifying subject, without which no objectivation could be performed. But the subject that diverges from the negative of the object also diverges from itself and only in so doing does it assert itself as such. Beckett tears to shreds the false subject that self-deceptively claims identity with itself, but he also savages the false absurd that claims to be the accepted "starting point." Adorno, as we have seen, credits Beckett only with an assumption of the absurd as a starting point, which is textually inexact since Beckett leads progressively to the absurd by way of the absurd, or rather to an objective absurd by way of an absurd struggle with the absurd. But this is also true in so far as there is no concrete difference between an absurd taken as a starting point and one taken as an end point. As often happens in Beckett, it is simply a question of upsetting contemporary commonplaces. The absurd is neither an *a quo* nor an *ad quem* term, nor is it a constant condition of man. All three hypotheses are abstract, while the absurd is man's historicity, not his eternity (neither hedonistic nor religious, in the modern sense of the term), and it is no adherence to concreteness either, unless this adherence asserts itself, time after time, historically well-determined, in opposition, in actual divergence, since it is an active attempt (of conscience or in practice) to diverge from the negative. And in actual fact Beckett, making the irony of history his own, relates the vain yet inevitable attempts of the divergent man-subject to fulfil himself.

It is by no means infrequent that, in the attempt to grasp Beckett's Word as a static fact (failing to recognize that such a fact is a function of motion) critics have hypostatized into an absolute some aspect or leitmotif of Beckett's narrative. This happens in particular with critics unresponsive to humour, but not only with them. Consider, for example, what Maurice Blanchot has written about Beckett in pages that anyone who has read *L'Espace Littéraire* could have predicted only too easily. After explaining that Beckett's monologizing voice hides behind a wide variety of masks, Blanchot cites the example of Molloy: "Molloy à son insu devient Moran, c'est-à-dire tout de même encore un autre personnage, métamorphose qui ne porte donc pas atteinte à l'élément de sécurité de l'histoire, tout en y introduisant un sens allegorique, peut-être décevant, car on ne le sent pas à la mesure de la profondeur qui se dissimule là". But the way in which the dynamic nature of Beckett's work functions cannot be ignored. Blanchot is so keen to get right to where "la parole ne parle pas, elle est, en elle rien ne commence", that he completely forgets the weighty, determining role played by the parodying and ironic element: that element which gives origin to memorable pages blending the evocative with the exorcising function of the word and tirelessly triggering off the mechanism of humorous inversion.

We have tried to explain that, if anything, it is Moran that turns into Molloy, not vice versa, and the character of Moran is particularly successful simply because he fights the absurd in the most contingent circumstances, not being vaccinated against it, like Camus' Sisyphus. Ignoring the "squalor" of contingent reality, Blanchot, writing completely in retrospect, brushes aside what is artistic in Beckett, as if this were dumb: it is in Blanchot, not in Beckett, that the lack of negation of the concrete, historical fact is all to the advantage of total negation, Nothingness. On the contrary, as we have pointed out early in the present essay, in art negation inevitably makes use of historic fact, no structure frees the work entirely from its mimetic function, and what counts is the way in which the original historic fact is instrumentalized. Beckett's work refuses to be downgraded to a mere illustration of a given fact pre-established by a philosophy, whereas in our opinion such downgrading is carried out both by Adorno and Blanchot, since instead of tackling the actual situation presented by Beckett as starting point, they are content to take the setting for granted, thus nullifying Beckett's cleverly subtle attempt to capture and involve the reader subjectively. The inter-subjectivity required by a reading of Beckett must be endorsed as such and not exploited to the whole advantage of *one* subject.

The fact that the objects evoked by Beckett are not just themselves but refer to something else by no means implies any lack of commitment towards the real: the identity of the object is not the object itself. Referring to something else in Beckett is referring away from the identity of the object to the object, that is to silence, since "to restore silence is the role of objects". The "pot" in *Watt* is "not a pot", not because the author invests it with a symbolical, allegorical or metaphorical hyper-identification, but because he restores it to its naked presence, unexorcised by the word. And if that obviously happens by means of words, it is necessary to define Beckett's word as exorcism in reverse. It tends not to render reality acceptable by rendering itself acceptable, not to conjure up, but to restore all the primordial sense of awe and amazement that reality stimulates, with its refusal to perform an act of abstract exorcism over it. In this way the objectuality of the "pot" in *Watt* is closely related to that of Sartre's "roots," and cannot be assimilated or measured. The naked presence of the object, unlike what happens in any metaphorical process, is in no way instrumentalized by Beckett in order to refer to the signified, but on the contrary in order to refer to the signifier, to the word that vainly tries to adhere to the object: "it was in vain that Watt said, Pot, pot. Well, perhaps not quite in vain but very nearly. For it was not a pot, the more he looked, the more he reflected, the more he felt sure of that, that it was not a pot at all. It resembled a pot, it was almost a pot, but it was not a pot of which one could say, Pot, pot, and be comforted." (*Watt*)

It may actually be that the image of the unexorcisable object is taken up by Beckett from the Freudian image of the unexorcisable "object" par excellence: "we approach the Id through comparisons, calling it . . . a pot bubbling over with drive" (*Introduction to Psycho-analysis*, lesson XXXI). Moreover, the very naming of this Freudian character is explicitly correlated by its discoverer to the inadequacy of names and the unspeakable character of what they try to designate. We in fact read in the same passage: "Don't expect me to tell you any more about the Id, apart from its new name. It is the dark, inaccessible part of our personality . . . and on the whole has a negative character, and does not allow itself to be described except as the antithesis of the Ego." The unnamability of the Id/pot, like Sartre's roots, is an effect of tension, indissolubly linked on one side with the attempt to give it a name, and on the other with the desire to be faithful to complete, lived reality, which are in fact divergent. The reassuring value of the word is bound to that particular brand of autism that makes up the original nucleus of Aristotelian mimesis, in which adherence to reality is replaced by a particular compromise, codified and accepted by a ritualistic intention. Albeit with different consequences, Sartre and Beckett both arrive at a negation of mimesis by attempting to adhere strictly to the real. Sartre's "roots", insufficiently exorcised, are unnamable, or only vaguely namable, just like Beckett's pot (shortly before the roots episode Sartre's character says: "Je suis au milieu des Choses, les innommables"). Mimesis is challenged as such, as soon as the privilege of the autistic content is broken, and reality is given as an entity in itself with which the word must seek perfect adherence, not compromise. It is therefore forced metacritically from within, falls into contradiction just when it reaches its most functional, its closest adherence, that is when adherence to something else becomes the very essence of mimetic coherence. The refusal of literature proclaimed by Sartre proceeds from this search for coherence. The incommensurability between hunger and the word "hunger", before assuming all its moral and political meanings, is incommensurability itself, the very emptiness that separates the object in itself (roots, pot) from the vain exorcism of the word. The word, whose exorcising-mimetic use is rejected (as unacceptable to the conscience), harks back to existential experience, to the definite and concrete subject that actually experiences. The exorcism that seems to be woven around Beckett's object is nothing but the annihilation of exorcisms, the crude contact with reality to which we are not accustomed. The overdetermination of the object named by Beckett, the fact that this named object seems to refer to something different from itself, is thus explained with this reflection: the named object refers to the object, but the object is by no means the same as the named object; it is in fact incommensurable to it. But restoring naked objectuality means restoring it to a concrete subject that senses it outside itself as such: the Unnamable is at the same time the real object and the real subject, both of them beyond representation: "every reality," as Sartre states, "contests literature." While in Sartre this liberated and anti-objectual subjectivity is called upon to transform the world through moral and political commitment and the "external" refusal of literature, with the risk of falling back into didacticism, in Beckett the technical aspects of the crisis of art lived from the "inside" are made explicit. Mimesis is always forced from inside of course, but Beckett's intention would seem to be to show how that happens by way of the word, choosing the word as a means to achieve human redemption. This particular metacritical use of historicity is reaffirmed by Beckett in the proud, human conviction of *not* belonging to eternity: "If I ever succeed in dying under my own steam, then they will be in a better position to decide if I am worthy to adorn another age, or to try the same one again, with the benefit of my experience" (*The Unnamable*).

Chronology

1906   Born Good Friday, April 13, at Foxrock, near Dublin, second son of William and Mary Beckett.

1927   Graduates Trinity College, Dublin, with degree in French and Italian.

1928   Begins two year fellowship at Ecole Normale Superieure in Paris. Friendship with Joyce begins, as does immersion in Descartes.

1929   Early writings in *Transition*.

1930   *Whoroscope; Proust*.

1931   *Le Kid*, parody of Corneille.

1932   Writes unpublished *Dream of Fair to Middling Women*.

1933   Death of William Beckett. Begins three years in London.

1934   *More Pricks Than Kicks*.

1936   Travels in Germany. *Echo's Bones*.

1937   Returns to Paris.

1938   Sustains serious stab wound from stranger. Begins relationship with Suzanne Dumesnil. *Murphy*.

1939   Returns to Paris after Irish sojourn.

1940   Is active in French Resistance movement.

1942   Flees to unoccupied France to escape Gestapo. Works as day laborer for two years in farming. Writes *Watt*.

1945   Goes to Ireland after German surrender. Returns to France for service with Irish Red Cross. Returns to Paris permanently.

1946–50   Productive period of writing in French, including the trilogy *Molloy*, *Malone meurt*, and *L'Innommable*, and the play, *En Attendant Godot*.

1947   *Murphy* published in French.

1950   Returns to Ireland for death of mother.

1951   *Molloy* published. *Malone meurt* published.

1952   *Godot* published.

1953   First performance of *Godot* in Paris. *Watt* published. *L'Innommable* published.

1954   Returns to Ireland for death of brother.

1955   *Waiting for Godot* opens in London.

1956   *Godot* opens in Miami, Florida for first American performance.
1957   *All That Fall* broadcast by BBC. *Fin de Partie* published. French first performance in London.
1958   *Krapp's Last Tape* and *Endgame* (in English) open in London.
1959   *Embers* broadcast by BBC. Honorary degree from Trinity College, Dublin.
1961   *Comment c'est* published. *Happy Days* opens in New York City. Shares, with Borges, International Publisher's Prize.
1962   Marries Suzanne Dumesnil, March 25. *Words and Music* broadcast by BBC.
1963   Play performed at Ulm. *Cascando* broadcast in Paris.
1964   Goes to New York City to help produce his *Film* (with Buster Keaton).
1969   Nobel Prize in Literature.
1972   *The Lost Ones.*
1973   *Not I.*
1976   *Ends and Odds; Fizzles; All Strange Away.*
1977   *. . . but the clouds . . .*
1978   *Mirlitonnades* (35 short poems).
1980   *Company; One Evening.*
1981   *Ill Seen Ill Said; Rockaby.*
1983   *Catastrophe.*

Contributors

HAROLD BLOOM, Sterling Professor of the Humanities at Yale University, is the author of *The Anxiety of Influence, Poetry and Repression* and many other volumes of literary criticism. His forthcoming study, *Freud: Transference and Authority*, attempts a full-scale reading of all of Freud's major writings. He is the general editor of *The Chelsea House Library of Literary Criticism*.

EDITH KERN, who was Professor of Literature at the University of Washington and at the New School for Social Research, has written on Sartre, Molière and Ionesco. She is the author of *The Absolute Comic* and *Existential Thought and Fictional Technique*.

NORTHROP FRYE, Professor Emeritus at the University of Toronto, is one of the major literary critics in the Western tradition. His major works are *Fearful Symmetry* (on William Blake), *Anatomy of Criticism* and *The Great Code: The Bible and Literature*.

HUGH KENNER, Professor of English at the Johns Hopkins University, is the leading critic of the High Modernists (Pound, Eliot, Joyce) and of Beckett. His books include *The Pound Era* and *The Stoic Comedians*.

THEODOR W. ADORNO was the central figure in the Frankfurt School of philosophy. His major works include *Negative Dialectics* and *The Philosophy of Modern Music*.

RUBY COHN teaches at San Francisco State College and has written extensively upon Beckett's work.

JACQUES GUICHARNAUD is Professor of French at Yale and the author of a major study of Molière.

WOLFGANG ISER, Professor of Literature at the University of Konstany, is a prominent theorist of reading and interpretation.

JOHN FLETCHER, who teaches at Durham University, has written frequently on Beckett.

FRED MILLER ROBINSON, Professor of English at the University of Massachusetts at Amherst, is the author of *Stumbling on a Smooth Road, Stevens' Trompe L'Oeil,*

An Art of Superior Tramps: Beckett and Giacometti and *Nonsense and Sadness in Donald Barthelme and Edward Lear*.

LINDA BEN-ZVI teaches at Colorado State University.

MARTHA FEHSENFELD has assisted Alan Schneider in several Beckett productions and co-edited *Beckett at Work*. She is editing a 3 volume collection of Samuel Beckett's letters.

S. E. GONTARSKI teaches at The Ohio State University in Lima and has written on Beckett's *Happy Days* and on Beckett's fiction.

ALDO TAGLIAFERRI is Editor of the Feltrinelli Publishing house in Milan, Italy. His books include a critical study of Beckett and a forthcoming analysis of narcissism in Western literature.

Bibliography

Alvarez, Alfred. *Beckett*. London: Fontana, 1973.

Baldwin, Helen Louise. *Samuel Beckett's Real Silence*. University Park: Pennsylvania State University Press, 1981.

Butler, Lance St. John. *Samuel Beckett and the Meaning of Being: A Study in Literature as Philosophy*. London: Macmillan Press, 1984.

Cavell, Stanley. "Ending the Waiting Game: A Reading of Beckett's *Endgame*." In *Must We Mean What We Say?* Cambridge: Cambridge University Press, 1976.

Coe, Richard N. *Samuel Beckett*. New York: Grove Press, 1970.

Cohn, Ruby. *Back to Beckett*. Princeton: Princeton University Press, 1973.

———. *Samuel Beckett, The Comic Gamut*. New Brunswick, N.J.: Rutgers University Press, 1962.

———, ed. *Samuel Beckett, A Collection of Criticism*. New York: McGraw-Hill, 1975.

———. *Just Play: Beckett's Theatre*. Princeton: Princeton University Press, 1980.

Copeland, Hannah Case. *Art and the Artist in the Works of Samuel Beckett*. The Hague: Mouton, 1975.

Dearlove, J.E. *Accomodating the Chaos: Samuel Beckett's Nonrelational Art*. Durham, N.C.: Duke University Press, 1982.

Doherty, Francis. *Samuel Beckett*. London: Hutchinson University Library, 1971.

Duckworth, Colin. *Angel of Darkness, The Dramatic Effect in Samuel Beckett with Special Reference to Eugene Ionesco*. London: George Allen and Unwin, 1972.

Easthope, Anthony. "Hamm, Clov, and Dramatic Method in *Endgame*." *Modern Drama* 4 (February 1968): 424–33.

Esslin, Martin. *Samuel Beckett, A Collection of Critical Essays*. Englewood Cliffs, N.J.: Prentice-Hall, 1965.

Federman, Raymond. *Journey to Chaos, Samuel Beckett's Early Fiction*. Berkeley: University of California Press, 1965.

Federman, Raymond, and Graver, Lawrence, eds. *Samuel Beckett, the Critical Heritage*. Boston: Routledge and Kegan Paul, 1979.

Finney, Brian. *Since "How It Is": A Study of Samuel Beckett's Later Fiction*. London: Covent Garden Press, 1972.

Fletcher, John. *Beckett, A Study of His Plays*. London: Eyre Methuen, 1972.

———. *The Novels of Samuel Beckett*. London: Chatto and Windus, 1964.

———. *Samuel Beckett's Art*. London: Chatto and Windus, 1964.

Friedman, Melvin J., ed. *Samuel Beckett Now, Critical Approaches to His Novels*. Chicago: The University of Chicago Press, 1970.

Gans, Eric. "Beckett and the Problem of Modern Culture." *Substance* 2 (1982):3–15.

Harvey, Lawrence E. *Samuel Beckett, Poet and Critic*. Princeton: Princeton University Press, 1970.

Hassan, Ihab Habib. *The Literature of Silence, Henry Miller and Samuel Beckett*. New York: Knopf, 1967.

Hayman, Ronald. *Samuel Beckett*. New York: Ungar, 1973.

Hesla, David H. *The Shape of Chaos, An Interpretation of the Art of Samuel Beckett*. Minneapolis: University of Minnesota Press, 1971.

Hoffman, Frederick John. *Samuel Beckett: The Language of Self*. Carbondale: Southern Illinois University Press, 1962.

Kenner, Hugh. *A Reader's Guide to Beckett*. New York: Farrar Straus and Giroux, 1973.

———. *Samuel Beckett, A Critical Study*. Berkeley: University of California Press, 1968.

Knowlson, James, and Pilling, John. *Frescoes of the Skull: The Later Prose and Drama of Samuel Beckett*. London: J. Calder, 1979.

Lyons, Charles R. *Samuel Beckett*. London: Macmillan Press, 1983.

Mooney, Michael E. "Presocratic Skepticism: Samuel Beckett's *Murphy* Reconsidered." *English Literary History* 1 (Spring 1982): 214–33.

Perlmutter, Ruth. "Beckett's *Film* and Beckett and Film." *Journal of Modern Literature* 1 (February 1977): 83–94.

Perloff, Marjorie. "Between Verse and Prose." *Critical Inquiry* 2 (December 1982): 415–33.

Pilling, John. *Samuel Beckett*. Boston: Routledge and Kegan Paul, 1976.

Porter, Abbott H. *The Fiction of Samuel Beckett: Form and Effect*. Berkeley: University of California Press, 1973.

Rabinovitz, Rubin. *The Development of Samuel Beckett's Fiction*. Urbana: University of Illinois Press, 1984.

Robinson, Michael. *The Long Sonata of the Dead: A Study of Samuel Beckett*. New York: Grove Press, 1970.

Rosen, Steven J. *Samuel Beckett and the Pessimistic Tradition*. New Brunswick, N.J.: Rutgers University Press, 1976.

Schulz, Hans-Joachim. *This Hell of Stories: A Hegelian Approach to the Novels of Samuel Beckett*. The Hague: Mouton and Co., 1973.

Scott, Nathan Alexander. *Samuel Beckett*. New York: Hillary House, 1969.

Simpson, Alan. *Beckett and Behan, and a Theatre in Dublin*. London: Routledge and Kegan Paul, 1962.

Webb, Eugene. *The Plays of Samuel Beckett*. Seattle: University of Washington Press, 1972.

———. *Samuel Beckett: A Study of His Novels*. Seattle: University of Washington Press, 1970.

Acknowledgments

"Moran-Molloy: The Hero as Author" by Edith Kern from *Perspective*, vol. 2 (Autumn 1959), copyright © 1959 by Perspective Inc. Reprinted by permission.

"The Nightmare Life in Death" by Northrop Frye from *The Hudson Review* 3, vol. 13 (Autumn 1960), copyright © 1960 by *The Hudson Review*. Reprinted by permission.

"Life in the Box" by Hugh Kenner from *Samuel Beckett: A Critical Study* by Hugh Kenner, copyright © 1961, 1968 by Hugh Kenner. Reprinted by permission.

"Trying to Understand *Endgame*" by Theodor W. Adorno, translated by Michael T. Jones, from *New German Critique* 26 (Summer 1982), copyright © 1982 by *New German Critique*. Reprinted by permission.

"*Comment c'est* par le bout" by Ruby Cohn from *Samuel Beckett: The Comic Gamut* by Ruby Cohn, copyright © 1962 by Rutgers University Press. Reprinted by permission.

"Existence Onstage" by Jacques Guicharnaud from *Modern French Theatre* by Jacques Guicharnaud, copyright © 1967 by Yale University Press. Reprinted by permission.

"The Pattern of Negativity in Beckett's Prose" by Wolfgang Iser from *The Georgia Review* 3, vol. 29 (Fall 1975), copyright © 1975 by The University of Georgia. Reprinted by permission.

"Beckett as Poet" by John Fletcher from *Samuel Beckett*, edited by Ruby Cohn, copyright © 1975 by John Fletcher. Reprinted by permission.

"Samuel Beckett: *Watt*" by Fred Miller Robinson from *The Comedy of Language: Studies in Modern Comic Literature*, copyright © 1980 by University of Massachusetts Press, Amherst. Reprinted by permission.

"Samuel Beckett, Fritz Mauthner, and the Limits of Language" by Linda Ben-Zvi from *PMLA* 2, vol. 95 (March 1980), copyright © 1980 by Modern Language Association of America. Reprinted by permission.

"Beckett's Late Works: An Appraisal" by Martha Fehsenfeld from *Modern Drama* 3, vol. 25 (September 1982), copyright © 1982 *Modern Drama*. Reprinted by permission.

"The Intent of Undoing in Samuel Beckett's Art" by S. E. Gontarski from *Modern Fiction Studies* 1, vol. 29 (Spring 1983), copyright © 1983 by Purdue Research Foundation. Reprinted by permission.

"Beckett and Joyce" by Aldo Tagliaferri, translated by Aldo Tagliaferri and Daphne Hughes, from *Beckett e l'iperdeterminazione letteraria* by Aldo Tagliaferri, Giangiacomo Feltrinelli, Milan. Translation copyright © 1985 by Aldo Tagliaferri. Reprinted by permission.

Index

A

Abbot, H. Porter, 238
absurdity, 51, 257,
    see also comedy
Act without Words (*Acte sans paroles*), 119,
    120, 122
Adorno, Theodor W., 51–81, 253,
    255–59
"Alba," 138, 141, 142
All That Fall (*Tous ceux qui tombent*), 20,
    106, 113, 114, 120, 122, 128,
    214
allegory, 103, 116
aporetical style, 149–52
Arikha, Avigdor, 219, 226
Artaud, Antonin, 242, 243
auto-eroticism, 19, 21

B

Bair, Deirdre, 197
Balzac, Honoré de, 198, 237, 238
Barthes, Roland, 241
Beckett, Samuel
    characters of, 7–16, 19, 91, 94, 197,
        210, 214
    and comedy, *see* comedy
    and existentialism, 51–81, 109
    late works of, 219–26
    life of, 197–99, 228, 232
    paradoxes of, 152–60, 190
    poetry of, 137–46
    relation to Proust, Joyce, and other
        writers, 18, 251,
    representational form, unwillingness
        to wholly abandon, 227–45
    stature of, 5, 137, 219
    vision of, 6, 36, 118–19, 239, 242
Ben-Zvi, Linda, 193–218
Blanchot, Maurice, 259
Borges, Jorge Luis, 196
Brecht, Bertolt, 57, 80, 228, 229,
    242–44

Burke, Kenneth, 125
. . . but the clouds . . ., 222–24

C

Campbell, Joseph, 11, 14
Camus, Albert, 256, 258, 259
Carroll, Lewis, 164, 174
Cartesian dualism, 1, 62, 95, 123, 212,
    see also Descartes
"Cascando" (poem), 141–142, 146, 202
Cascando (radio play), 122
Cavell, Stanley, 132, 135
Cendres (*Embers*), 19, 122
Chadwick, C., 115
Chaplin, Charlie, 106, 108, 115, 120–21,
    160
characters, 7–16, 19, 91, 94, 197, 210,
    214
Cluchey, Rick, 231
Coe, Richard, 152, 155, 171
Cohn, Ruby, 83–101, 197, 223
Come and Go, 224
comedy, 1, 4, 18, 151, 155, 158–59
    absurdity, 51, 257
    of language, 88–89, 147–49
    as raw material, 66, 106, 107, 123
    in *Watt*, 160, 174–75
Comment c'est, 83–101
Company (*Compagnie*), 220
Corneille, Pierre, 237
Critique (*Beiträge zu einer Kritik der
    Sprache*, by Fritz Mauthner),
    193–201, 216–18
Curtius, Ernst Robert, 62

D

"Da Tagte Es," 144
Dante, 18, 21–24, 137, 139, 141,
    146, 226, 244
"Dante and the Lobster," 101, 141
"Dante . . . Bruno. Vico . . . Joyce"

(Beckett's essay on Joyce), 155,
170, 198, 234, 240, 247
darkness and light,
imagery of, 152–60
death, life in, 17–25
Derrida, Jacques, 229, 238
Descartes, 2, 23, 194, 199, 209,
see also Cartesian dualism
Devlin, Denis, 214
"Dieppe," 145
Dis Joe (Eh Joe), 117, 123, 138, 211, 221,
222, 224, 228, 231, 240–41
Don Quixote, 66
"Dortmunder," 142
Dostoievski, Fyodor, 13, 237, 238
dramatic conventions, 27–28, 42, 43, 52,
222–24
Eleutheria, 31–36
Endgame, 42–49
suitability of for Beckett's vision,
118–19
Waiting for Godot, 28–31, 36–42, 46,
103–23, 151
Dream of Fair to Middling Women, 198–99,
203, 232–36, 241
Durrell, Lawrence, 19
Duthuit, Georges, 155

E
Echo's Bones, 139, 140, 144
Eco, Umberto, 247
ego, 2, 18, 19, 208, 210
Eh Joe (Dis Joe), 117, 123, 138, 211, 221,
222, 224, 228, 231
Eleutheria, 31–36, 238
Eliot, T.S., 51, 122, 137, 139–42,
146
Ellmann, Richard, 193
Embers (Cendres), 19, 122
Emerson, Ralph Waldo, 4
En Attendant Godot, see Waiting for Godot
"End, The," 36
Endgame (Fin de partie), 3, 4, 86, 128,
131, 135, 145, 205, 210, 228,
230, 231
discussion of, 42–49, 51–81, 253, 255
and Murphy, 19
standing of, 49
and Waiting for Godot, 20, 46, 76,
114, 116–22

Ends and Odds, 196
"Enueg I," 138, 139
"Enueg II," 139
existentialism, 51–81, 109
"Expelled, The," 153

F
Faulkner, William, 147, 155, 176
Fehsenfeld, Martha, 219–26
Feuillerat, Albert, 235
fiction
indictment of traditional novel,
198–99
pattern of negativity in, 125–36
see also names of specific works
Film, 117, 221, 222, 224, 228, 230, 231,
244
Fin de partie, see Endgame
Finnegans Wake, 1, 2, 21, 31, 69, 236,
242, 250, 251
Fizzles, 203, 211
Fletcher, Angus, 5
Fletcher, John, 137–46
Footfalls, 221–25
form, 227–45
Four Poems, 143, 145
Four Quartets, 145
"From an Abandoned Work," 32
Fry, William, 158
Frye, Northrop, 17–25, 156

G
Gargantua, 66
Gessner, Nicholas, 215
Ghost Trio, 222–24, 231
Gide, André, 237
gnosticism, 3, 4
Goethe, Johann Wolfgang von, 9, 14
Gontarski, S.E., 227–45
Gourmont, Rémy de, 104–5
Gruen, John, 233
Guicharnaud, Jacques, 103–23

H
Haeckel, Ernst Heinrich, 100
Happy Days (Oh! Les Beaux Jours),
117–22, 128, 214, 221, 222, 230,
239, 244
Hardy, Thomas, 1, 238
Hartley, Anthony, 8

Harvey, Lawrence, 139, 144, 145
Heidegger, Martin, 61
Helsa, David, 193
Hobson, Harold, 243
Hoefer, Jacqueline, 161
Hollander, John, 5
"Home Olga," 232, 234
How It Is, 1, 4, 5, 208
Huxley, T.H., 47, 71

I
Ibsen, Henrik, 68, 69
Imagination Dead Imagine, 126
Iser, Wolfgang, 125–36

J
J. M. Mime, 224
Jaspers, Karl, 58, 61, 257
Joyce, James, 3, 138
  Beckett's essay on ("Dante . . . Bruno.
    Vico . . . Joyce"), 155, 170,
    198, 234, 240, 247
  relationship to Beckett, 1, 2, 18, 22,
    51, 61, 147, 227–28, 232–36,
    239, 243, 247–61

K
Kafka, Franz, 5, 17, 20, 51, 67–68, 70,
    73, 115, 137, 173, 194–95, 240,
    249
Kandinsky, Wassily, 233
Kaun, Axel, 203
Keaton, Buster, 150–52, 160, 174
Kenner, Hugh, 2, 27–49, 157, 158, 174
Kern, Edith, 7–16, 106, 108, 133, 115,
    193
Kierkegaard, Søren, 55, 58, 182
Kleist, Heinrich von, 223
Klopstock, Friedrich Gottlieb, 100
Knowlson, James, 194, 223
Krapp's Last Tape (La Dernière Bande), 3,
    4, 19, 116, 118, 120, 122, 138,
    221
Kühn, Joachim, 196, 216

L
La Dernière Band (Krapp's Last Tape), 3,
    4, 19, 116, 118, 120, 122, 138,
    221
Lacan, Jacques, 254, 255
Laing, R.D., 127

language, 72, 83–84, 90, 123, 126, 132,
    166, 254
  aporetical style, 149–52
  comedy of, 88–89, 147–49
  imagery of light and darkness, 152–60
  limits of, 193–218
late works, 219–26
Laurel, Stan, 160
"Le Calmant," 35–36
"Lessness," 239
Leventhal, A.J., 109
Lewis, Jim, 224
"L'Expulsé," 32, 34–35
life in death, 17–25
light and darkness,
  imagery of, 152–60
Luce, Arthur Aston, 199
Lukács, Georg, 126, 257

M
"Malacoda," 141
Malebranche, Nicolas, 95
Malone Dies, 1, 2, 23, 33, 36, 145, 202,
    204, 207, 208, 215, 249, 252,
    255
Mann, Thomas, 1, 53
Mauthner, Fritz,
  influence on Beckett, 193–218
Mélèze, Pierre, 123
Mercier et Camier, 36–39
Merleau-Ponty, Maurice, 127, 129, 134
mime, 224–25
Molière, 66, 106
Molloy, 2, 4, 18, 33, 36, 129, 131, 159,
    210, 249, 256
  discussion of, 7–16, 20–23
Monegal, Emir Rodriguez, 196
Mood, John, 184
More Pricks Than Kicks, 99, 139, 141, 207,
    234
Murphy, 1, 2, 3, 4, 21, 24, 27, 43, 86,
    99, 129, 142, 153, 166, 207,
    215, 221, 231, 234
  discussion of, 18–19
myth, 16, 227

N
Nabokov, Vladimir, 137
negativity,
  pattern of in fiction, 125–36
Nietzsche, Friedrich, 1, 9, 14–16
Nizan, Henriette, 150, 152

Not I, 221, 228, 229, 240, 244
Nouvelles, 31, 32, 34–36

O
O'Hara, John., 150
Oh! Les Beaux Jours (*Happy Days*),
    117–22, 128, 214, 221, 222, 230,
    239, 244
Ohio Impromptu, 221, 222
Omer, Mordechai, 226

P
paradoxes, 152–60, 190
Paroles et musique (*Words and Music*), 122
Pascal, Blaise, 109, 110
"Peintres de l'empêchement," 83
Piece of Monologue, A, 220, 221
Pilling, John, 194, 223
Plato, 17
Play, 117–22, 222, 244
plays, *see* dramatic conventions; names of
    specific plays
Poems in English, 143
poetry, 137–46,
    see also names of specific
    poems
"Premier Amour," 35
prose works,
    pattern of negativity in,
    125–36
Proust, Marcel, 1, 9, 11–13, 16, 18, 21,
    22, 61–63, 235, 240, 243
Proust, 3, 18, 24, 81, 140, 154, 168, 171,
    198, 204–5, 209, 231, 234, 236,
    240, 242–43
Putnam, Samuel, 233

Q
Quad, 224–25

R
Racine, Jean Baptiste, 237, 238
Radio II, 196, 197, 211
representational form,
    unwillingness to wholly abandon,
    227–45
Rickert, Heinrich, 62
Rilke, Rainer Maria, 3
Rimbaud, Arthur, 139, 237
Robbe-Grillet, Alain, 28
Robinson, Fred Miller, 147–92
Robinson, Michael, 181, 190
Rockaby, 221

romanticism, 116, 243

S
"Saint Lô," 144
"Sanies I," 140
"Sanies II," 140
Sartre, Jean-Paul, 51, 58, 104, 109, 115,
    125, 155, 233, 260, 261
Schiller, Johann von, 53
Schneider, Alan, 49, 219, 221, 222, 231
Schönberg, Arnold, 67, 75, 233
Schopenhauer, Arthur, 1–3, 76, 194, 236,
    245
Seddon, Peter, 222
"Serena," 138
"Serena II," 140
Shenker, Israel, 232, 237
Sontag, Susan, 241, 243
Stendhal, 62, 236
Sterne, Laurence, 197
Stevens, Wallace, 147, 148, 167
Stravinsky, Igor, 75
structuralism, 254
subconscious, 16, 242
Sublime mode, 5
surrealism,
    distrust of, 242, 243
Swift, Jonathan, 1
symbolist drama, 103, 104–5

T
Tagliaferri, Aldo, 247–61
Texts for Nothing (*Texts pour rien*), 148,
    149, 211, 238
That Time, 211, 221, 228, 240
Theatre II, 211
theatrical conventions, *see* dramatic
    conventions
"Three Dialogues," 155, 156, 200, 203,
    205
Tous ceux qui tombent (*All That Fall*), 20,
    106, 113, 114, 120, 122, 128,
    214
trilogy, (Beckett), 2, 3, 4, 16, 36, 156,
    180, 238, 249, 251,
    see also Malone Dies; Molloy;
    Unnamable, The

U
Ulysses, 1, 21, 236, 251
Unnamable, The, 1, 20, 129, 131, 202–3,
    207, 217, 250, 252, 261
    discussion of, 23–25

V

Vinteuil, 13, 15, 18
"Vulture, The," 144

W

Waiting for Godot (En Attendant Godot), 3,
    4, 120, 128, 145, 151, 222, 223,
    234, 238–39, 244
  and *Comment c'est*, 86, 98, 99
  discussion of, 20–21, 28–31, 36–42,
    103–23
  and *Eleutheria*, 32, 33
  and *Endgame*, 20, 46, 76, 114,
    116–22
  language in, 207, 214, 215, 218
  standing of, 17

Warrilow, David, 220
Waste Land, The, 23, 139, 140
Watt, 1, 2, 3, 4, 201, 203, 234, 238,
    260
  discussion of, 19–20, 147–92
  structure of, 190–92
Weiler, Gershon, 194, 215
Whitelaw, Billie, 221, 225
Whoroscope, 197–98
Wiesengrund, 257
Williams, Tennessee, 73
Wittgenstein, Ludwig, 1, 161
Words and Music (Paroles et musique), 122

Y

Yeats, William Butler, 24, 42, 223

DATE DUE

Bloom, Harold, editor
Modern critical views: Samuel Beckett

DEMCO